Russian Research Center Studies, 44

POLITICAL CONTROL OF LITERATURE IN THE USSR, 1946–1959

42862

POLITICAL CONTROL

of LITERATURE

in the USSR, 1946–1959

HAROLD SWAYZE

HARVARD UNIVERSITY PRESS

Cambridge, Massachusetts

1962

Distributed in Great Britain by Oxford University Press, London

The Russian Research Center of Harvard University is supported by grants from the Carnegie Corporation, the Ford Foundation, and the Rockefeller Foundation. The Center carries out interdisciplinary study of Russian institutions and behavior and related subjects.

Library of Congress Catalog Card Number: 62-9432

Printed in the United States of America

For my Mother and Father

Preface

◇◇

> The relations that exist between the social and political
> condition of a people and the genius of its authors are
> always numerous; whoever knows the one is never com-
> pletely ignorant of the other.
>
> Alexis de Tocqueville

Any study of the politics of a contemporary society, however limited the immediate purpose of the inquiry, contributes in
some measure to an awareness of the values which that society
respects and the condition of human life to which it aspires. Perhaps this is necessarily so in an age of highly organized, regulated
societies, when it becomes increasingly difficult to use the word
politics only in its narrower meaning. As Lionel Trilling has remarked, "it is no longer possible to think of politics except as the
politics of culture, the organization of human life toward some
end or other, toward the modification of sentiments, which is to
say the quality of human life." This statement has special force
when applied to the Soviet Union, where politics takes on a meaning so broad that it embraces virtually every facet of human activity and experience.

The attitude which any nation displays toward its artistic talent,
the treatment it accords writers and artists, and the views it holds
on the proper role of art and literature in the life of the society
afford revealing insights into the nation's aims and aspirations. The
Soviet Union is no exception. Soviet theories about the social role
of belles-lettres disclose much about the values at least of the ruling
group, the leadership of the Communist Party, and about the
quality of human life which its policies are fostering. Even more

is revealed by the Soviet regime's treatment of the "genius" of its authors, when genius is taken to mean, as J. E. Spingarn put it, "the creative faculty, the power of self-expression, which we all share in varying degrees."

The following pages represent an effort to analyze the methods by which imaginative writing is controlled in the USSR. The analysis includes an outline of the basic assumptions and aims of Soviet literary policies, a discussion of the problems with which the Soviet regime has had to cope in belles-lettres, and a description of the main features of the structure of literary controls. My specific purpose is to elucidate the process whereby an equilibrium is maintained between the pressure of controls and the resistance of those subjected to control; hence, most of the study is devoted to an examination of the forces which give rise to periodic oscillations in the party's policies in the realm of belles-lettres.

The study concentrates on the period from August 1946, when the Central Committee of the party issued an important decree on literature, to the Third All-Union Congress of Soviet Writers in May 1959. The opening chapter is concerned with the theoretical premises of political controls in belles-lettres. An analysis of the course of literary politics from 1946 to 1959 occupies the following four chapters. Chapter Six is a survey of the principal instruments of control in literature; it deals with the administrative organization of Soviet literary life, some special devices of control, and the problems that these create.

A word must be said about the limitations, with respect both to sources and to scope, imposed by focusing on official policies and the conflicts that they engender. The study is based largely on nonbelletristic materials — party and governmental decrees and proclamations, official and semiofficial speeches, reports of the proceedings of writers' congresses and conferences, and articles and essays dealing with various aspects of Soviet literature and literary life. But Soviet literary politics cannot be made intelligible without reference to what Soviet authors are actually writing, and, although it was not feasible to attempt to couple an extensive survey of literature from 1946 to 1959 with a detailed account of the literary politics of the period, several novels, stories, plays, and poems are discussed in the following pages. They are for the most part works which provoked disputes in the USSR; they were selected for discussion primarily for what they, or the controversies centering about them, reveal about the nature and processes of Soviet literary politics. They cannot, therefore, be regarded as typical of the whole body of recent Soviet literature, though they do point to significant currents in Soviet writing. In addition, I have attempted to characterize broad trends in Soviet writing, by citing wherever possible the words of Soviet authors, critics, and scholars who, in the opinion of this writer, describe the trends accurately. Treatment of various topics which are related but not central to the purposes of this study — regional literary developments, policies governing the publication of Western literature in the USSR, and the like — has been omitted so that the main themes might be delineated more sharply and explored more thoroughly.

This volume owes much to a large number of people, only a few of whom can be mentioned by name. It is hardly conceivable that the study would have been undertaken and completed without the encouragement, advice, and helpful criticism of Professor Merle Fainsod, to whom I am indebted in more ways than I know. It was my good fortune to be able to discuss various facets of Soviet literature and literary politics with Professors George Gibian, Sidney Monas, and Walter Vickery, and I am grateful to them for reading my manuscript in one or another of its variant forms. Most of the research for this study was completed while I held a Foreign Area Training Fellowship granted by the Ford Foundation. Support provided by the Inter-University Committee on Travel Grants enabled me to study at Moscow University during the academic year 1958–1959. Responsibility for the views expressed in the book is, of course, my own.

Ann Arbor, Michigan
September 1961

H. S.

CONTENTS

CONTENTS

POLITICAL CONTROL OF LITERATURE
IN THE USSR, 1946–1959

I ◇◇◇◇◇

The Theoretical Foundations
of Literary Controls

◇◇◇

Underlying Soviet control of belles-lettres is an elaborate theory which justifies the existence of the control system and the demands made on writers. Precisely because the Soviet regime endeavors to furnish a theoretical rationale for the practical tasks involved in regulating artistic activity, an examination of the premises of the theory affords insight into the character and problems of Soviet literary politics. For the contradictions and incoherencies within the theory are reflected in the party's program for literature, and they enter the realm of practical literary politics as contributories to the forces which induce periodic modifications of the party's literary "line." Moreover, an examination of these premises reveals the contours of the area within which creative activity is confined, temporary and fluctuating restrictions established, and specific exactions made.

In analyzing the theoretical foundations of literary controls, it is necessary to touch upon matters which are in one way or another related to problems of aesthetics. But the intricacies of Soviet aesthetic theory are beyond the scope of the present discussion. The purpose here is to characterize Soviet aesthetic theory in a general manner and to indicate its relationship both to the Marxist theory of social change and to principles of practical politics in the sphere of Soviet literature. With respect to aesthetic theory, the crucial question is whether or in what terms Soviet aesthetics recognizes and accounts for the distinctive qualities of artistic creation, the qualities that distinguish artistic endeavor from other kinds of human activity (with emphasis here on the exemplification of such qualities in imaginative writing). Attention in this book is centered on the theoretical principles of the control system established during the Stalinist period. These principles, however, must be seen in their larger setting; hence reference is made to their Marxist antecedents as well as to some of the alternatives to them which arose within the context of Russian Marxism. This approach is not an outgrowth of the belief that in the writings of Marx and Engels are to be found the causes that led unavoidably to Stalinist solutions. But even in Soviet aesthetics, attitudes and practices are ultimately justified in terms of Marxist theories or elaborations of Marxist theories, and they can often be best understood in conjunction with an examination of their alleged source. Moreover, Marxism, in spite of its inconsistencies and ambiguities, cannot be quite all things to all men, and even in the realm of aesthetics, which it leaves largely unexplored, Marxism does not provide unlimited scope for theorizing: it at least prejudices reflection on such crucial matters as the nature of the social functions of art and the relationship between art and politics. The following discussion includes a brief treatment of Plekhanov's writings on art because the tensions within Plekhanov's aesthetic theory and the manner in which they tend to find a resolution point to the bias inherent in Marxism and the confines within which any effort to develop a Marxist aesthetics must take place. In addition, Plekhanov's views afford revealing contrasts to Lenin's views on art and to later interpretations of Lenin's contribution to aesthetic theory. The discussion of the antecedents of Stalinist aesthetics is abbreviated and schematic, and no effort is made to analyze the various theories of "proletarian" aesthetics that contended for recognition during the 1920s, fascinating as the debates of those years sometimes were; thus the developments of the postwar years may be better brought into focus.

Marx and Engels devoted little attention to questions of aesthetics as such. Most of their writings on art and belles-lettres are actually concerned with social and ethical problems treated in particular works rather than with broader problems of art. But some key concepts of their science of history claim attention because they have become fundamentals in a theory of art. Central to the

Soviet rationalization of controls over the arts is the view that history is, among other things, a process whereby men, as members of social classes, gradually shed their illusions and adopt ideas which ever more closely approximate an ultimate truth that can be known. The view embraces the postulates that a material reality exists apart from mind, that mind is dependent upon it, and that truth is essentially a reproduction of that reality. In conjunction with the thesis that history is the history of class conflicts, this view provides the basis for a doctrine of "ideologies." Just as changes in productive relationships determine the supersession of one class by another, so do they condition the mutation of the sets of ideas which arise from the economic substructure. These sets of ideas — political, philosophical, religious ideologies — reflect and serve the interests of the social classes which adhere to them; they are at worst gross distortions and at best defective approximations of the truth about various aspects of reality. But as successively more "advanced" classes achieve domination, truth is apprehended more adequately. Dialectical materialism, the scientific theory which makes it possible for man to view the world objectively, is associated with the proletarian consciousness and appears in history with the rise of the proletariat, "the class which no longer counts as a class," [1] the class which has been relieved of false world views and can see existing ideological superstructures for what they are — "just so many bourgeois prejudices, behind which lurk in ambush just as many bourgeois interests." [2]

It is evident that there is a strong pragmatic strain in Marxist thought despite its absolutist stand on the question of the status of truth. Ideas not only reflect but serve the interests of their adherents, and Marxism itself is more than an explanation of the past and present and a scientific prediction of the advent of socialism: it is an instrument for guiding the forces of history toward the realization of the inevitable, a first step in the process of reshaping history and human society. Indeed, this is precisely why it is "scientific" and true, for control over events is, for Marx and Engels, the proof of true thinking. Engels once wrote in a particularly revealing passage that "the most telling refutation" of skepticism about the possibility of knowledge of the real world and other such philosophical fancies is practice, viz., experiment and industry. If we are able to prove the correctness of our conception of a natural process by making it ourselves, bringing it into being out of its conditions and using it for our own purposes in the bargain, then there is an end of the Kantian incomprehensible "thing-in-itself." [3]

These are among the ideas that lie behind the doctrine of the unity of theory and practice, and they account in part for the Soviet preoccupation with the intimacy of the relationship between thought and action.

Marxian scientific historicism is permeated by a crusading spirit which implies a set of ethical values. Some indication of the character of these values is to be found in Marx's prophetic utterances about the role of art in the ideal society, utterances which Lenin sometimes echoed when expounding his own visions. When man has grasped the working of economic laws and is no longer their slave, thought Marx, when the detested capitalist order has disintegrated and freedom is actualized, man will be able to develop his capacities fully, to become a complete human being. This "objectivization of human existence," Marx once wrote emphatically, means "making man's *senses human* as well as creating *senses* corresponding to the vast richness of human and natural life"; it will bring "the complete *emancipation* of all human senses and aptitudes." [4] And in *The German Ideology* Marx and Engels looked forward to the reintegration of art in the life of the individual and the community. In a society based on communism, they asserted, "the exclusive concentration of artistic talent in a few individuals and its consequent suppression in the large masses" disappears with the elimination of the division of labor: "there are no painters; at most there are people who, among other things, also paint." [5] Since the reign of positive science will eliminate the grounds for the various forms of false consciousness — including artistic "ideologies," presumably — these forecasts taken together appear to be a curious inversion of Hegel's dirge on the arts in his *Lectures on Aesthetics*, where he declared: "Thought and reflection have superseded fine art," and "Art in its highest form is and for us must remain a thing of the past." [6] If tendencies leading toward the realization of these dismal assertions can be discerned in Soviet society, they are the product of yet another inversion and of factors very different from those which either Hegel or Marx had in mind.

G. V. Plekhanov's views on art were widely influential in Russia through the twenties, and their repudiation in the early thirties was an event of considerable significance, as a comparison of them with the theories of "Leninist aesthetics" will indicate.[7] The emphasis which Plekhanov placed on economic determinism in social change was reflected in his demand for objectivity in aesthetics and art criticism. "There is no force on earth," Plekhanov once wrote, "which could say to art: You must take this and not another direction." [8] And elsewhere he said:

Scientific criticism does not give art any kind of prescriptions; it does not say to it: You must hold to such and such rules and methods. It limits itself to observing how the various rules and methods which reign in various historical epochs *arise*. It does not proclaim *the eternal laws of art;* it attempts to study *those eternal laws whose operation conditions* its historical development. . . . For it everything is good in its time; it does not have any predilections just for this, and not for another school of art. . . .[9]

Such statements taken by themselves appear to be vigorous arguments for relativism in art criticism, although Plekhanov believed, as he indicated in the essay from which the longer quotation is taken, that objective or "scientific" criticism contributes to historical progress much in the manner that scientific Marxism does.[10] Plekhanov in principle rejected claims on art which fail to take the peculiar nature of art into account. For, even though he regarded art principally as a means of knowing reality, he made an important distinction between artistic and discursive modes of expression. Art represents reality in concrete images and its language is the language of images, whereas science represents reality by means of abstract concepts and employs the language of logic. And Plekhanov repeatedly insisted that the writer cannot use the language and devices of argumentation and remain true to his art: "if the writer employs logical deductions instead of images, or if he invents images to prove a certain theme, then he is not an artist but a journalist, even though he writes not essays or articles but novels, stories, or plays." [11] Significant also is Plekhanov's analysis of the process of criticism into two acts, the first of which is to translate the idea of a given work "from the language of art into the language of sociology" — to find for a work its "sociological equivalent," by which Plekhanov meant revealing the class consciousness expressed in a work and the social factors that entered into its creation.[12] The first act is incomplete without the second, which is to determine the aesthetic merits of a work. This viewpoint was elaborated in various ways during the twenties. Trotsky's statement of it reveals its significance more fully:

> It is very true that one cannot always go by the principles of Marxism in deciding whether to reject or to accept a work of art. A work of art should, in the first place, be judged by its own law, that is, by the law of art. But Marxism alone can explain why and how a given tendency in art has originated in a given period of history; in other words, who it was who made a demand for such an artistic form and not for another, and why.[13]

Although Plekhanov deplored the use of art as an instrument to achieve specific goals, he nonetheless attempted to reconcile his view with certain kinds of utilitarian claims. Thus, in his essay on French drama and poetry he concluded that only what is useful can seem beautiful to man, though he qualified this conclusion in a way which seems to make utility irrelevant to aesthetic pleasure. For Plekhanov denied that the utilitarian and aesthetic viewpoints are identical: "Utility is perceived by *reason*, beauty by *intuition*. The province of the first is *calculation*, that of the second is *instinct*." [14] He added that man is almost never actually aware of the utility of what seems beautiful — indeed, that utility can normally be discerned only through scientific analysis. This, then, adds another dimension to the distinction between artistic and scientific expression, and it suggests that utility lies far beneath the immediate causes of aesthetic enjoyment.

The manner in which such inconsistencies are likely to be resolved within the context of Marxist historicism is indicated by Plekhanov's more elaborate sociological interpretation of art history, "Art and Society." [15] In his analysis of the differing social conditions which gave rise to "pure art" theories, on the one hand, and "utilitarian" theories, on the other, Plekhanov goes beyond objective analysis to indicate the direction that art should take, though it will be observed that in Marxist terms this is identical with the direction that art *must* take. It is significant that Plekhanov here takes the utilitarian attitude toward art to mean the inclination to regard works of art as "a judgment on the phenomena of life and the joyful readiness that always accompanies it to participate in social struggles." [16] Plekhanov demonstrates that there has never been an "art for art's sake" and that those who professed such theories really served the cause of the bourgeoisie, though at first unconsciously. He now asserts explicitly that "the merit of a work of art is, in the final analysis, determined by the 'specific gravity' of its content." [17] It is apparent that truth, which means essentially the truth of social relations, becomes for Plekhanov the principal criterion of aesthetic evaluation. Plekhanov approves the view that the value of a work of art is determined by the loftiness of its idea, that art "is one of the means of spiritual intercourse among men, and the loftier the sentiment expressed by a given work of art, the better will the work fulfill its role as a means of intercourse, other conditions being equal." [18] To foresee the conclusions to which this leads, it is only necessary to place it against the Marxist view that history is the gradual advance toward truth through class conflict and that the ultimate good is the victory of the proletariat. Because Plekhanov regards art as an aspect of the economically determined superstructure, he is able to claim: "The ideologies of the ruling class lose their intrinsic value in the same measure as that class ripens for destruction; the art created in the spirit of that class declines with it." [19] The implication is that a vigorous art, one whose ideals are "lofty," can only be an art which is associated with the proletarian cause and that truthfulness in depicting society can best be attained by those who adopt the Marxist viewpoint. It is noteworthy that, in an earlier manuscript which provided the basis for this essay, Plekhanov said explicitly that some bourgeois writers during the decline of their class will go over to the side of the proletariat and that both their world view and their creative work will gain considerably from this.[20] Thus, Plekhanov linked the possibility of high artistic achievement to a definite world view and a particular cause, and he tended to regard the liberation of the proletariat as the value of values, the ultimate criterion for evaluating everything. Nonetheless, there remain in his writings, somewhat inconsistently, a demand for objectivity and a defense of relativism in aesthetics and art criticism. Plekhanov's emphasis on the distinctive character of aesthetic experience, on the non-rational and nondiscursive character of artistic expression, and his insistence on aesthetic as well as sociological evaluation of art were incompatible with the crude intellectualist reductions of theories which regard art solely as an instrument of political action. The apotheosis of "Leninist aesthetics" in the thirties marked a more emphatic effort to resolve the tensions apparent in Plekhanov's thinking on problems of art and belles-lettres.

Lenin's contribution to the Soviet theory of art and literature lay primarily in his applying to those realms, however unsystematically, ideas which were among his major innovations in Social Democratic revolutionary theory — his emphasis on conscious action as a factor in social change, his insistence on the final authority of a disciplined revolutionary party, and his borrowing from the narodnik heritage (to the degree that the last is reflected in the importance Lenin attributed to the popular character of art). Lenin, in fact, added nothing to aesthetic theory as such. His remarks on various writers and even his articles on Tolstoy are concerned with social questions rather than with problems of art. But the importance of his article of 1905, "Party Organization and Party Literature," can hardly be exaggerated, if only because of the use made of it in later years. Lenin declared in the article that literature "must become party literature" and said that *partiinost* in literature means that literary affairs "must become a *part* of the general proletarian cause . . . a part of organized, systematic, united Social Democratic party work." [21] And he seemed to outline a general program for party supervision of literary activities, asserting that writers "must without fail enter party organizations," that newspapers must become attached to such organizations, and that publishing houses, libraries, and such, must be accountable to the party.[22] On the other hand, Lenin was mainly concerned with the question of party discipline at a time when socialist parties and their press had been legalized; and he emphasized that he was speaking only of party literature and the party's right to expel writers who would not subject themselves to control. Furthermore, Lenin observed that in the realm of literature "it is absolutely necessary to provide a broad scope for individual initiative, individual inclinations, scope for thought and imagination, form and content," and he warned that literary affairs "must not be mechanically identified with the other parts of the party affairs of the proletariat." [23] If there is an apparent inconsistency between the advocacy of freedom for the writer and the principle of party control, it is resolved by Lenin's view that the freedom of the bourgeois writer is really "only disguised dependence on the moneybag" and by his assertion that a truly free and diverse literature can only be one that is "*openly* bound to the proletariat." [24] It is this identification of freedom with party control that makes Lenin's writings such a fertile source for citations justifying divergent viewpoints and that permits such breathtaking transitions as the following one, recorded by Klara Zetkin:

Every artist . . . has the right to create freely, according to his ideal and independently of anything else.

But we are Communists, of course. We must not stand with folded arms and let chaos develop as it will. We must guide this process according to a systematic plan and mold its results.[25]

If Lenin's writings leave any doubt about his views on the question of subjecting literature to party control, the policies he pursued after the revolution go far to dispel them. In 1920, the Proletkult — a cultural organization, headed by A. A. Bogdanov, which endeavored to remain free of party and government control — was placed under the Commissariat of Education upon Lenin's insistence. The Central Committee published a letter giving the reasons for this, the core of which is contained in the following passage:

The Proletkult remained "independent" [after the revolution], but this was now independence from the Soviet government. Because of this and for a number of other reasons, socially alien elements rushed into the Proletkult, petty-bourgeois elements which sometimes actually took the guidance of the Proletkult into their own hands. Futurists, decadents, adherents to an idealist philosophy inimical to Marxism, and, finally, simply ne'er-do-wells from the ranks of bourgeois journalists and philosophers began here and there to direct all the activities of the Proletkult.[26]

Lunacharsky's remarks at a meeting of the Central Committee's Press Section in May 1924 cast an interesting light on Lenin's attitude and motivations:

He [Lenin] feared Bogdanovism, feared that the Proletkult might give rise to all sorts of philosophical, scientific, and ultimately political deviations. He did not want the establishment of rival workers' organizations alongside the party. . . . For this reason, he personally directed me to draw the Proletkult closer to the government, to subject it to control.[27]

Thus, the principles were established that cultural organizations could not be independent of government, and ultimately party, supervision and that there could be no place in such organizations for artists whose views differed from those of the party or, it would seem, whose practices in art suggested divergent views. It may be observed that the Central Committee's attitude toward "futurists, decadents," and the like, was not incompatible with Lenin's own tastes in art, which were conservative, as he himself admitted.[28]

Lenin's writings also furnish authoritative support for requiring a popular art, for insisting on the principle of *narodnost* in the arts. Lenin was, of course, acutely aware of Russia's cultural backwardness, and many of his remarks on cultural matters focus on the need to increase literacy and to make the achievements of the past widely accessible in order to provide a basis for cultural advance. And he was certainly alert to the emotional impact of art and its inherent educative potentialities. Such concerns are apparent in utterances of his which have been used to justify practices of which he might not have approved:

Art belongs to the people. It must penetrate with its deepest roots into the very midst of the laboring masses. It must be intelligible to these masses and be loved by them. It must unite the feeling, thought, and will of these masses; it must elevate them.[29]

This hints as well at the utopian vision which was the ultimate justification of Lenin's politics, the vision of a society in which man might develop his capabilities freely, a society whose culture and art, nourished by the wealth of humanity's past attainments, would contribute to the growth and enrichment of the human spirit.

The foregoing sketch may help to elucidate the specific significance for belles-lettres of the triad of concepts — *partiinost, idei-*

nost, narodnost — which Soviet ideologists regard as the basis of literary policies. It must be observed at the outset, however, that the partiinost of Soviet literature "is identified with ideinost and narodnost," [30] as one critic said in a typical statement indicating that the latter two terms tend to dissolve in an all-embracing partiinost; for the party is, after all, the guardian of the ideology and the embodiment of the people's will. Obviously the principles overlap and, though each may represent a unique idea or set of ideas, the task here is not to analyze each to its irreducible core of meaning, but rather to determine how together they form a theoretical framework and justification for controls.

It has been pointed out that Marxist theory posits an evolutionary scheme which, combined with a sociology of knowledge, leads to the conclusion that an absolute truth is more closely approached as successively more advanced classes achieve a dominant position in society. This truth is the truth of Marxism, which demonstrates that history is a gradual advance toward a classless society. The proletariat is at once the objective embodiment of this truth and the class that is best able to perceive the meaning of history and to hasten the realization of history's purposes. Or, more precisely, these are the attributes of the most advanced segment of this class, the Communist Party. Thus the program of the party is both a projection of historical laws and an instrument for achieving the inevitable and ethically desirable outcome of the processes of history. What is true, as well as what is ethically good, must be what corresponds to party policy and, on the basis of the pragmatic principle inherent in Marxism, to what serves the party's aims. The circular argument thus justifies authoritarian truth determination and at the same time leaves great scope for variations of program, since the party is the single source of truth. If representing the truth is conceived to be literature's main function and truth to be the ultimate aesthetic standard, it is evident that the more tenaciously a writer cleaves to the party line and the more scrupulously he reproduces the party viewpoint in his work, the greater will be the aesthetic merit of what he creates. The doctrine of partiinost in literature renders Plekhanov's second act of criticism, the aesthetic judgment, theoretically irrelevant. And the doctrine removes the obstacles which Plekhanov's theory, to the extent that it took account of extrapolitical standards for evaluating art, placed in the way of transforming art into a tool for advancing specific political purposes.

Soviet thinking on art and belles-lettres does not on its surface appear so crude as this, of course. Although scientific knowledge and aesthetic knowledge are considered to have essentially the same content, and although sometimes the distinction between aesthetic and scientific cognition has been explicitly rejected, a difference between art and science is more often recognized and even stressed; for art is frequently characterized not merely as the representation of reality in images but as imagistic cognition of reality — as "thinking in images." Thus it is of central importance to determine the character and profundity of the distinction, a necessity, indeed, that became apparent in the preceding discussion of Plekhanov's views. The crucial question is whether art as aesthetic cognition is considered to be an autonomous mode of cognition, independent of intellectual cognition and conceptual knowledge, or whether it is considered to be inadequate and incomplete in itself, in need of guidance and verification from some other source. If aesthetic cognition is understood to be dependent upon or derivative from conceptual knowledge, it tends to become indistinguishable from the latter, or at most to be treated as an accessory to it. If the primary function of belles-lettres is the cognition and truthful representation of reality — which can only be reality as it is defined by the party ideology — the content of belles-lettres must be the content of that ideology in disguise; it must be the knowledge of conceptual cognition and not that of independent aesthetic cognition. Pious declarations that art is a "special means of cognizing reality" are by themselves insufficient to maintain the distinctions necessary for accounting for the peculiarities of aesthetic experience. Proclaiming the need to ascertain the "defining characteristics" of art, Soviet ideologists are unable, if not unwilling, to preserve the requisite distinctions because their formulations must be fit into the Procrustean bed of Leninist-Stalinist aesthetics, whose form is determined by partiinost. And within this framework of ideas, the theoretical basis for the existence of art is at best uncertain. The force of the doctrine is to reduce art to a subsidiary mode of describing a reality that may be more truly and adequately described by the use of the conceptual tools at the disposal of the party; it is to treat art as a means of illustrating truths attained in some way other than through aesthetic cognition. Eloquent testimony to this is provided by Soviet ideologists' obsession with the question of "typicalness," which often seems to imply a metaphysics of essences, and their insistence that belles-lettres should be concerned with "types," which are concepts produced by analysis and abstraction; thus literature is presented with the task of clothing intellectual constructs in sensible forms. The problems created by this viewpoint have been discussed in the Soviet Union for the past twenty-five years or more. It is some indication of their seriousness that, despite the backlog of theorizing, a participant in a conference on aesthetics in 1956 found it necessary to object to the "widely promulgated view that art is distinguished from science only by its forms and methods of reflecting life" and that he queried: "If art and science are distinguished only by the methods of representation, then what has given rise to two forms of social consciousness which are actually identical in terms of their tasks and aims? If the artist does the same thing as the scientist, then why is there a division of labor and in what lies the advantage of one over the other?" [31]

Although the exaltation of partiinost appears in principle to close the gap between political and aesthetic criteria, it cannot remove the need for taking account of aesthetic values in actual practice; nor can it eliminate the tensions that arise between a theory which in its essence denies aesthetic values as such and a program which places considerable reliance on art as an instrument of political action. For even if works of art are regarded only as instruments of indoctrination, they must possess a modicum of artistic merit if they are to be effective as such; and to admit this is already to point to distinctions which apparently have been rendered meaningless. The interplay between these incompatibilities and the concern about it displayed by writers and party officials are among the forces which mold the course of Soviet literary politics. It is the existence of such tensions that is acknowledged by halfhearted, ill-defined references to the differences between art and science, between "thinking in images" and "thinking in concepts," and the like. The existence of two orders of values is symbolized by the fact that socialist realism rather than dialectical materialism has been canonized as the basic method of Soviet literature. But it is not easy to say exactly what socialist realism means beyond "fulfilling the party's program for belles-lettres," or "partiinost." [32] A sampling of writings on socialist realism indicates that the vast quantity of material devoted to this subject consists largely of terminological hairsplitting, efforts to manipulate previous formulations into conformity with a shifting party line, and consciously or unconsciously misleading and confused attempts to reconcile the irreconcilable. Penetrating analysis of aesthetic problems and methodologically significant discussion of literary criticism have long since vanished from the pages of philosophical and literary publications, and if debates arise whose significance extends beyond some immediate political development or policy trend, their deeper implications are obscured by the garb of conformity. For these reasons, the following pages contain no specific discussion of socialist realism, though the ostensible importance of the doctrine as the basis of Soviet literature might seem to require it. But this study as a whole is an exploration of at least some of the meanings of the term.

The Soviet approach to aesthetics results in what is not only an intellectualist but also a pedagogic and moralistic theory of art: art is not merely a subsidiary to the intellectual cognition of reality. As with all intellectual endeavor, from a Marxist point of view, art serves some specifiable end external to art itself. Art is instrumental to the realization of the inevitable and desirable outcome of the historical process, which is the victory of the proletarian cause. Thus, a justification is already provided for requiring art to disseminate certain kinds of knowledge and to inculcate ideas and modes of behavior that are adapted to proletarian purposes. The recognition that art conveys information and has a moral impact is transformed into the theory that these are virtually the only purposes of art, and even in principle the possibilities for discussing aesthetic problems as such, or investigating something that may be called aesthetic enjoyment, are narrowly circumscribed.

A series of corollaries is drawn from the basic formulations of Soviet art theory to make unmistakably explicit what the theory entails with respect to the tasks of depicting reality and inculcating moral and political values. Correct representation of reality is dependent upon adherence to a specific world view: "Knowledge of Marxism-Leninism," goes a typical statement of the point, "makes it possible for the artist to see the true social essence of the profound processes of reality in development. . . . The truth of life and Communist ideinost are inseparable from one another." [33] To affirm the need to adopt a definite ideological position is, of course, to affirm the principle of partiinost, since that is regarded as the highest form of ideinost, just as it is said to be the highest expression of narodnost. And the meaning of partiinost has become even broader than that which Lenin seemed to intend in his famous essay, for it now applies to party and nonparty writers alike. As Fadeyev generously declared at the Second Writers' Congress:

The partiinost of Soviet literature is not an exclusive thing, the peculiar property of writers who are party members and in general of the few. It is the historical property of our Soviet literature. . . . when we speak of the partiinost of Soviet literature, we have in mind the historical fact that Soviet writers, both party and nonparty, recognize the correctness of the Communist Party's ideas and defend them in their work, and therefore naturally acknowledge the guiding role of the party in literary affairs.[34]

The rationale for this was provided, historically, by the determination that, classes having been eliminated, Soviet society had become homogeneous in composition and uniform in viewpoint. Furthermore, the doctrine of the unity of theory and practice leads logically to the conclusion, "any deviation from the principle of partiinost produces an unwitting distortion of reality," [35] or "whoever is not armed with Marxist-Leninist ideas loses perspective in his daily work and inevitably makes mistakes." [36] But more than distortion and error is involved, for ideas, according to the theory of ideologies, reflect and serve class interests, and ideas that diverge from proletarian ideology represent hostile class interests. As Karl Radek stated the point at the First Writers' Congress: "When it seems to a person that he is defending only some individual shade of opinion against it [the party], it will always become apparent on the basis of a political test that he is defending interests alien to the proletariat." [37] It was because Lenin shared this viewpoint that he so frequently devoted his energies to discrediting ideas by revealing their origin rather than by demonstrating their falsity. Because art is a part of the ideological superstructure, it has been possible to employ the same technique in discrediting unorthodox schools of art. Such reasoning was implicit in the Central Committee's letter on the Proletkult, and it has since been employed many times in many ways. The argument was stated quite bluntly in 1922 by the Marxist critic P. S. Kogan: "behind the struggle between styles, forms, and artistic schools," said Kogan, "lies hidden the struggle between ideologies, and still further back, the struggle between classes." [38] Like all elements of the superstructure, art inevitably participates in the class struggle, and even ostensibly neutral, escapist, "pure" art actually serves bourgeois interests, as Plekhanov demonstrated so forcefully. Such arguments buttress the claim that only a single method is possible in Soviet art:

Socialist realism is the only method of our art. . . . Any other method, any other "direction," is a concession to bourgeois ideology. . . . In our country, where socialism has been victorious, where there has arisen a moral and political unity of the people unprecedented in the history of mankind, there is no social basis for different directions in art.[39]

Against the elaborate rationale underlying such statements, the metaphor that normally accompanies them—that within the limits of a single "direction" there can exist diverse "tendencies" — is not very reassuring.

From the basic formulations that give rise to a moralistic-pedogogic theory of art are derived certain propositions that justify specific didactic claims. The "socialist" of socialist realism in a sense points to this facet of the system of exactions. For if "realism" means artistic cognition of an external reality, "socialist" connotes the "dialectics" of dialectical materialism and signifies the artistic representation of reality in its "revolutionary development" — or discerning the rose of the future in the cross of the present. This view finds expression in the conviction that a principal task of literature is showing "advanced" types of Soviet man, or Soviet man as he ought to be, or creating "valid examples for emulation," as Konstantin Simonov once put it.[40] Indeed, the phrase which Stalin is supposed to have uttered in conversation with Maxim Gorky and which has been quoted relentlessly ever since — that writers are "engineers of human souls" — only casts into terms presumably more suitable to the spirit of this century an old thesis about the function of literature, one which Aristophanes characterized in the line: "As the teacher instructs little children, so do the poets speak to those of maturer age." [41] The moralistic-pedagogic viewpoint gives rise to the theory of "the necessary unity of aesthetic and ethical evaluations in Soviet art," [42] and it manifests itself in the widespread belief that "it is necessary to judge the value of a book by the educative effect it has on the human soul." [43]

If literature is to be socially effective as a device for instruction and edification, it must create an impact that is not only intensive but extensive. For this reason, the principle of narodnost is invoked and another criterion applied — the one designated by Simonov's rhetorical question:

when a book addresses itself to our whole society and in principle, ideally, can be read by the whole society, is not the very popular character [obshchedostupnost] of this book one of its artistic criteria? Is not the creation of literary works . . . which will in equal measure stir a citizen with a higher education, a university professor, and one who has only completed a seven-year school, a machinist in a factory — is not . . . the ability to create such a book not only a political and an ideological achievement, but an aesthetic achievement as well? [44]

The same interest is among the factors that lie behind the Soviet opposition to experimentalism in literature and the bias in favor of exploiting traditional forms of folk literature and familiar devices of nineteenth-century realism. "In the province of form," goes the usual rationalization of this, "socialist narodnost signifies high perfection of artistic expression combined with simplicity and intelligibility, with accessibility to the masses. Lenin said that art must be intelligible to the masses." [45]

Thus, there are fundamentally three standards for estimating the merit of a literary work: the truthfulness, or party-minded spirit, of the work's portrayal of reality, the work's pedagogic potentiality, and its intelligibility to the broad masses — all prerequisites for transforming literature into a serviceable social tool. In terms of Soviet doctrine, belles-lettres become an adjunct to politics and pedagogy, a sugar coating on the pill of knowledge and morality. Insistent demands that Soviet literature meet high artistic standards suggest that significant aesthetic criteria are officially acknowledged; but public discussion reveals little about the special properties of these criteria and even less about the theoretical grounds for recognizing the claims of such criteria. This is hardly surprising, for the logical outcome of the Soviet position is the attitude reflected by Simonov when he remarked that "the recognition of self-contained artistic values is foreign to us." "For us," said Simonov, "the first and main criterion for evaluating literature is the contribution it makes to our Communist cause." [46] This in turn points to the basic Soviet premise about the nature of all literature, a premise stated in a revealing context by Kornely Zelinsky when he announced his belated insight into the nature of lyric poetry. Under pressure from the party press, Zelinsky repudiated his earlier view that the essence of lyric poetry is self-revelation and prepared the way to a new conclusion by observing that the question *"to what purpose* does the lyric poet 'reveal himself'?" must be placed foremost:

Without an answer to this question, the thesis of "revelation" becomes agitation for *bespartiinost* [nonpartyness] in art. . . . Outside Bolshevik ideinost . . . there is no lyric poetry as the expression of the "soul" of Soviet man. . . . Politics is not a genre of Soviet poetry. It is its essence, its nature. That is the crux of the matter.[47]

The theory that politics has a profound impact on literature has become the thesis that politics is the essence of literature.

The basic principles and corollaries of the Soviet theory of art form the larger structure within which specific exactions and restrictions are imposed. Many problems that have arisen since the war — some of which will be discussed on later pages — are direct outgrowths of the contradictions of the structure. A word must be said at this point about the sources of the problems, for the tensions they create in the literary community, the discontent they provoke among writers, and the wider dissatisfaction engendered by their impact on literature itself are among the basic ingredients of Soviet literary politics.

The "truthfulness" so often referred to in Soviet writing on belles-lettres may be taken to denote two concepts, rather different, though perhaps not wholly unrelated. The truthfulness of a literary work may signify the correspondence of the work's content to an external reality — its customary meaning in Soviet literary parlance — or it may signify the internal coherence of a work — a standard

employed, however it is denoted, in practical Soviet literary criticism. But the party's views on literary questions place formidable obstacles in the path of those who would adhere to such standards.

To begin with the second point, a work's internal coherence is, in the final analysis, a matter of successful expression, and it is at least in part a function of the unity of a writer's conception or understanding in a given instance — of his successful assimilation of diverse elements of experience — as it is also a matter of the mastery of technical skills. The coherence standard is implied by a phrase that recurs frequently in Soviet criticism, though it has become virtually meaningless through arbitrary usage: "the unity of form and content." And the idea is implied on those occasions when works are criticized for disjunction of journalistic and artistic elements, for artistically unconvincing treatment of socially "useful" themes, for intellectualizing or abstract moralizing. Soviet criticism cannot elaborate this standard on a theoretical level or apply it rigorously because of the threats it contains: it might foster a preoccupation with modes of expression and technical questions to the exclusion of a concern for political purpose, or it might give rise to an emphasis on self-expression and individual insight that would cast doubt on the universality of the party's truth. To avoid such dangers it has been necessary to stigmatize as "sincerity abstractly understood, truthfulness abstractly understood," or worse, the view that "every artist who views life from his own vantage point, who sees in it what it is given him to see and writes about it sincerely, is in his own way right." [48] Writers are caught in a vicious circle whereby works which express their own feelings and special insights may be branded "subjectivistic," "pessimistic," "retreats from reality," and works produced as an effort to meet official requirements may be declared "abstract" or "schematic." [49] But the assumption made at least formally is that the writer's approach to the world about him does not diverge from that necessitated by the party ideology. A fairly common formulation of the view, which typically seems to have one term missing, is that a prerequisite for stirring readers is "the poet's own excitement, his sincere, organic belief in what he says. In other words, poetic realization of a theme requires lofty ideinost." [50] Behind this lies the perhaps not

unreasonable belief that sincere acceptance of the party's world view will not impede creative activity but will be beneficial to it. Leaving to one side the question of the restrictions of the world view itself, it must be observed that something which may make greater demands on conviction than belief in a fixed philosophy is required of writers: they are expected to adhere to a shifting program and to cultivate a blind faith in the rightness of the party, whose determinations of truth, like its evaluations of literature, may change radically from time to time. What seems an arbitrary identification of writers' subjective dispositions with the party ideology becomes, ironically, an additional rationalization for insisting that works be written to reflect the party's views and revised to keep pace with its fluctuating line. That the subordination of the claims of self-expression to those of orthodoxy has impaired the quality of Soviet literature is abundantly demonstrated by Soviet literary criticism itself. The conflict between these claims is a main current in Soviet literary politics.

Another fundamental contradiction in the official theory of art lies in the claim that reality must be portrayed truthfully but also in its "revolutionary development," that is, in a didactically purposeful manner. How to reconcile these demands is a question that continually plagues Soviet writers. The problem is revealed clearly enough in one of Fadeyev's efforts to demonstrate that its solution lies within the realm of possibility:

> One may ask: Is it possible to portray truthfully a living human character "as he is" and at the same time "as he ought to be"? Of course. This not only does not diminish the strength of realism, but it is what genuine realism is. Life must be shown in its revolutionary development. I shall take an example from the realm of nature. An apple as it is in nature is a rather bitter wild fruit. An apple grown in a garden (particularly in such a garden as Michurin's) is an apple "as it is" and at the same time "as it ought to be." This apple reveals more truly the essence of an apple than does the wild fruit.[51]

This may be realism, but it suggests realism of a Platonic variety rather than what is usually meant when the term is applied to literature and art. Soviet theorists have never pretended to subscribe to a naturalistic literary theory of the sort represented by Stendhal's definition of the novel as a "mirror walking down a roadway," which as an ideal of objectivity toward which literature should

strive is undoubtedly unattainable, if not undesirable. But in Soviet usage, "realism" and "truthfulness" are mainly honorific terms meaning representation of that aspect of reality in which the party happens to be interested and representation of it in a manner approved by the party. And writers must steer a difficult course between a "crude naturalism" that portrays reality in undesirably somber tones and an "embellishment of reality" that portrays it in unbelievably bright ones. The real question is not so much whether Soviet theory prevents literature from approaching photographic objectivity as it is one of whether the political and moral didacticism required by the theory is compatible with depicting the myriad facts of human life and expressing complex imaginative intuitions in literary works. Soviet writers are continually reminded that, while they must reveal life in all its diversity, their principal aim must be "to expose relics of the past, to aid the development and victory of the new, to affirm that victory, to create an image of the positive hero." [52] If "positive" characters are to be created that they may be imitated, "negative" characters must be portrayed to be condemned. The enemy, Alexei Surkov once said, "must not only be shown but also exposed with the whole power of the work of art. He must be morally vanquished, as actually happens in our life, and the persons who triumph over this enemy must not be left in the shade." [53] Soviet literary pundits sometimes sound remarkably like Dr. Johnson who, similarly unable to differentiate between the functions of belles-lettres and those of a moral tract, could not "discover why there should not be exhibited the most perfect idea of virtue; of virtue not angelical, nor above probability, for what we cannot credit, we shall never imitate, but the highest and purest humanity can reach. . . . Vice, for vice is necessary to be shewn, should always disgust." [54] A striking example of the extent to which such attitudes have entered into Soviet thinking is to be found in an article by Ilya Ehrenburg which is notable for its generous views on various problems of creative writing. In support of his position, however, Ehrenburg suggests at one point that showing "angelical virtue" may be incompatible with literature's pedagogic purposes:

The critics claim that only irreproachable heroes can set the reader an example. Is this so? . . . Some readers genuinely try to imitate the ideal hero. To others these heroes seem remote and unattainable; they learn from the example of people who are not lacking in weaknesses, they learn from such characters' mistakes and successes. They want to learn not how to be born a hero but how to become one.[55]

That they may fulfill their pedagogic tasks, Soviet writers are expected to develop clearly defined attitudes and to display their views without perplexing ambiguities in their treatment of fictional characters and situations. This viewpoint was affirmed with customary forthrightness at a writers' conference early in 1957, where the main speaker said, after approving the representation of man "in all his manysidedness, complexity, and fullness":

But socialist realism, like all realism, all truthful and progressive art, demands precision in evaluating people, in revealing their main, defining features. This is why we are not preparing to shelve the terms "positive" and "negative."

We have a criterion for evaluating a person, however complex and contradictory he may be. It is his social activity and labor.[56]

Yet such views themselves ultimately lead to that "vulgar simplification, schematism, and 'poster-painting'" in literature which the same speaker disparaged, and they serve as rationalizations for limiting the writer's choice of colors to black and white. The rigidity of outlook and the political and moral purposefulness officially required of Soviet writers leaves little scope for the exercise of what Keats called "negative capability" (the willingness to remain "in uncertainties, mysteries, doubts"[57]), a concept which points to the difference between the aesthetic and the didactic and signifies the creative writer's ability to stand before his subject matter in full awareness of its complexity and wealth. This is hardly permitted by an ideology that makes it possible, as Ehrenburg once put it,[58] for writers to "ascertain the direction in which human relations are evolving" and to "know which feelings will develop and which are doomed to extinction," by an ideology that makes it possible not only to foresee the course of human events but to know how to measure good and evil, by a doctrine that creates the conviction that praise and blame are central in art. The official viewpoint hardly takes into account the imaginative experience which is an exploration of variety and possibility and which no more offers simple, pat solutions than does life itself. Ultimately these tensions between the claims of the doctrine and the needs of the artistic temperament for expression also find their way into practical literary politics. They do so necessarily through conflicts over particular problems in various literary genres — problems that center on such issues as the distinction between "positive satire" and "slander" or, in lyric poetry, between self-analysis and decadent subjectivism; in comedy, problems created by the bias against "laughter for laughter's sake" and "unprincipled entertainment"; in tragedy, by the doctrine of the inevitable victory of the "advanced" and the theory of "optimistic tragedy." These and related problems, which illustrate the impact of the larger theory on particular aspects of literary practice, are beyond the scope of this study, though they will be discussed to the extent that they enter into the literary-political controversies treated in the following pages.

In terms of the broad structure of Soviet society and politics, the significance of literary controls is in many ways identical with that of controls over other spheres of human endeavor. The official ideology, which claims to be a complete program for remolding the present in the image of the future, requires that all pursuits be directed toward and evaluated in terms of that end. Activities that tend to become autonomous, to set up their own goals and standards, must be politicized and integrated into the broader scheme of things. Any activity (to paraphrase Hitler's remark on ideas) may be a source of danger if it is looked upon as an end in itself. But there are additional considerations which give controls over art a special meaning and urgency. True creativeness implicitly threatens a doctrine which, in spite of its dynamic appearance, is deeply conservative and inflexible in its hostility toward the undetermined, the uncertain, the inexplicable, toward whatever fails to fit into existing categories of thought and analysis, in short, toward whatever is profoundly original. Moreover, the Soviet regime has displayed an acute awareness of the vast influence that works of art may exert precisely because of their appeal to the imagination, their power of suggestion, their claim on the emotions. And the regime has far outdone other authoritarian systems in striving to guide these potentialities into desired channels, to foster a literature of a certain kind and a certain content, one that will play an active role in indoctrinating the masses and integrating the individual into the social whole. Having understood that literary values are political values, when "politics" is understood in its broadest sense, and that literature has a formative effect on human character whether that is intended or not, the Communist Party has set out to harness literary forces to the service of specific political tasks while limiting and controlling the range of influences, usually not readily predictable, that literary works may have. For it is precisely the qualities which render literature useful to the regime as an instrument that make it a potential danger as well. Left with a modicum of autonomy, literature — and not only good literature — may readily manifest its propensity to become "subversive," in one sense or another, with respect to existing standards and values. Herbert Read's provocative "Art *is* revolution" [59] suggests several rather simple notions whose relevance to belles-lettres has been well grasped in the Soviet Union. One of the services a writer performs for his fellow men is to express what he has lived, his peculiar insights into human experience and the world about him, in the form of art; and this itself may threaten to undermine belief in a single defined truth. Not even Soviet history has provided evidence to substantiate the view that a writer's experience will necessarily fall into, be compatible with, or be in any way relevant to the categories of the party ideology — and pluralism rears its ugly head. In the case of literary works consciously concerned with social problems, the point is obvious. But even though a work may set out not to criticize from a certain point of view but only to portray reality objectively, to "remove the coverings" which prevent phenomena from being perceived clearly, a "subversive" element is present because illusion is shattered and hypocrisy exposed:

If society sees itself and, in particular, sees itself as *seen* [Sartre has written], there is, by virtue of this very fact, a contesting of the established values of the regime. The writer presents it with its image; he calls upon it to assume it or to change itself. . . . thus, the writer gives society *a guilty conscience;* he is thereby in a state of perpetual antagonism toward the conservative forces which are maintaining the balance he tends to upset.[60]

But there is another, less direct but perhaps more profound, manner in which the "subversive" character of literature manifests itself, one that derives from the fact that a literary work, as a product of imagination, is not limited to a concern with actuality in any narrow sense. Because its purview extends outward, beyond the immediate, it inevitably provides a perspective for viewing and evaluating present realities. Patently "escapist" literature provides an illustration of this, however limited; for, in spite of its apparent disregard of the conditions of actual life, escapist literature has implicit in it a criticism of reality and a set of values for making such judgments. And Soviet ideologists are quite properly suspicious of works which tend in that direction. It is perhaps not unreasonable to suggest that a work which, instead of providing a surrogate for life, leads to a re-entering of life through experience of an imaginative interpretation of it, an interpretation which cannot be reduced to simple maxims and precepts, may have even greater "subversive" potential. To apply to the whole of belles-lettres what John Dewey said about poetry, literary works may be a criticism of life

not directly, but by disclosure, through imaginative vision addressed to imaginative experience (not to set judgment) of possibilities that contrast with actual conditions. A sense of possibilities that are unrealized and that might be realized are when they are put in contrast with actual conditions, the most penetrating "criticism" of the latter that can be made. It is by a sense of possibilities opening before us that we become aware of constrictions that hem us in and of burdens that oppress.[61]

It is to avoid such dangers that the Soviet regime has elaborated a literary doctrine and developed practical devices to confine imagination and creativeness within specified compartments. But this activates forces which tend to weaken the affective powers of literature and to reduce its usefulness as an instrument of social control. Maintaining a balance between these contrary tendencies is a central problem of Soviet literary politics.

II ◈◈◈◈◈

The Heyday of Zhdanovism, 1946–1952

◇◈◇

The problem of discerning reasons for the fluctuation of policies in various areas of Soviet life and, even more, of establishing the significance of broader fluctuations in the pattern of Soviet politics is a continuing challenge to analysts of Soviet affairs. Several years ago, before Stalin's death, the author of a brilliant and penetrating article in *Foreign Affairs* argued that waverings in Soviet policies are largely the outgrowth of shrewd and cynical manipulative efforts on the part of party leaders, in particular, of Stalin himself.[1] Attempting to steer a course between the dangers of extremism and apathy — "between the Scylla of self-destructive Jacobin fanaticism, and the Charybdis of post-revolutionary weariness and cynicism" — Stalin, according to this view, "created an artificial dialectic, whose results the experimenter himself could to a large degree control and predict. Instead of allowing history to originate the oscillation of the dialectical spiral, he placed this task in human hands." [2] In a footnote, however, the necessary qualification is made that the "artificial dialectic" did not "arise in a void" but out of "urgent practical needs." [3] In the Soviet Union, the author further suggests, officially inspired views and trends tend to develop to absurd extremes because they are not modified as they would be in a freer society by forces of habit, tradition, and uncontrolled thought; therefore, the party must periodically step in to check trends that are reaching a danger point and to set them moving in a new direction.

This thesis, perceptive as it is, tends to overemphasize the element of conscious, manipulative control and to oversimplify the conditions in which the "dialectic" operates, at least so far as it applies to the dialectics of Soviet literary politics; but with qualifications it becomes a useful tool for analyzing the policies of Stalin and his successors. Conscious decision to set a new course or add a new theme has always played a leading role in determining literary policies. But such calculation does not occur in a vacuum, is not arbitrary or unrestricted in its choices, nor do its results simply represent the imposition of a willful scheme on an existential situation. Party policies are, of course, developed for the purpose of resolving particular, urgent problems, very often in an effort to break or weaken forces of resistance or opposition. Nonetheless, not all impulses which give birth to such policies, or the ingredients which constitute them, have their origin in the top political ranks of Soviet society, among party and government leaders. Recalcitrant elements in the Soviet literary world leave an undeniable trace on the unfolding of any particular policy, deflecting the policy in unforeseen directions, carrying it to undesired lengths, exploiting its hidden loopholes, clothing it with unintended meanings. Ultimately the party leadership may react to this by attempting to redefine the policy or to turn the forces it has set in motion back to the original, or at least to some officially approved, channel. These forces, together with the contradictions, incoherencies, and tensions in the control system as a whole — in both the theoretical formulation of the social role of literature and the institutionalization of the resulting demands — produce a kind of dialectic within the system, a self-perpetuating process whose oscillating movement cannot be explained as the outcome of a single person's, or even a single set of persons', intentions. It must be recognized that a number of other influences affect the evolution of Soviet literary policies, among which are the international situation, the regime's internal policy in other areas, and personal ambition and rivalries within the Soviet literary world itself.

This chapter and the three following ones are primarily concerned with major trends in Soviet literary politics in the postwar years. Attention is centered on those events which heralded a new tack or emphasis in the regime's program, and an effort is made to distinguish the forces which led to such modifications and to place their significance in the larger pattern of literary politics.

THE BACKGROUND OF ZHDANOVISM: THE WAR YEARS

An immediate purpose of the party's postwar decrees on cultural matters was to reverse certain attitudes and trends that had emerged during the war years, particularly during the period just after the German invasion. Especially remarkable among these trends were the intensified manifestations of Russian nationalist sentiment, as distinguished from Soviet patriotism, and the increased attention paid to old Russian forms and traditions at the cost of slighting Stalinist contributions and specifically socialist elements in Soviet life. Undoubtedly the upsurge of national feeling among the Soviet population was a spontaneous reaction to the Nazi invasion of the homeland; but the Soviet regime expended considerable energy to strengthen these feelings as a means of bolstering public morale during the difficult war years. Stalin may have startled the Soviet citizenry when, in a speech in 1941, he added the old Russian mode of address, "Brothers and Sisters," to his customary "Comrades." [4] But this merely presaged further measures which would be taken to reinforce such a spirit. The government established, for example, military orders named after Suvarov, Kutuzov, and Nevsky and commissioned the writing of a national anthem. Another indication of the mood of these years was the more tolerant attitude toward religious practices and the improved position of the Russian Orthodox Church. And there was a notable slackening of political and ideological controls in most realms of Soviet life. These changes, together with expanded contacts with the West and propaganda underscoring the common Allied war effort, created an atmosphere within the Soviet Union very different from that which had prevailed during the thirties.

The new spirit manifested itself in the literary world partly in the form of diminished ideological supervision and external pressure. It did not, however, give rise to a revision of official theory regarding the social and political functions of the Soviet writer. If anything, that theory which regards the writer's pen as a weapon to be used in service of the state gained strength; only now the writer's purpose was to contribute to military success rather than to socialist construction. The attention devoted to the writer during those years of struggle is a measure of the importance which the regime attributes to belles-lettres and a vivid illustration of its deep-rooted utilitarian approach to the art of writing. But at a time when the war was everyone's major preoccupation, it would have been surprising had Soviet literature not been voluntarily enlisted in the war effort. Even though there were no revisions of official doctrine, there were striking changes in Soviet literary practice. The impact of the war, the sacrifice it demanded, the deprivation and suffering that it brought opened new realms of experience to thousands, and Soviet writers, in the freer atmosphere of the early war years, often represented this experience and expressed their moods and sentiments in terms that would not have been tolerated a few years before. A trend away from the schematism and stereotypes of the thirties was noticeable, particularly during the tense period of retreat before the Nazi onslaught. Rather than expending their energy in glorifying the party leader or stakhanovite worker, writers tended to concern themselves more with ordinary people, with their capacity for suffering, their heroism, and their elemental patriotism. Another indication of the mood of the time was the quiet rehabilitation of poets formerly regarded with disfavor. Anna Akhmatova, whose work had not been published for nearly two decades, reappeared on the literary scene, and Boris Pasternak, always regarded with suspicion and in 1937 once again found guilty of formalism, received the cautious approval of some literary critics and was listed, along with Akhmatova and others, as a writer contributing to the war effort.[5]

With the improvement of Soviet military fortunes after the battle of Stalingrad, shifts in the wartime mood of the country could be detected. In the literary world this was already noticeable in 1943, and it was marked more clearly at the Ninth Plenum of the Writers' Union in February 1944, when the new president of the union, Nikolai Tikhonov, trumpeted the old refrain about Soviet writers' civic responsibilities. More than an "engineer of souls," the writer, said Tikhonov, is a "statesman" and among his basic tasks is "consolidating the ideas of our state system." [6] The plenum itself was significant as an effort to revitalize the work of the union, which had grown lax in recent years. Thus, with the second stage of the Soviet military campaign, the tide of affairs began to change in the realm of literature as well, though it finally required forceful and dramatic action by the party to divert wartime literary currents to their original channel.

During the latter part of the war, criticism of various writers for deviation from orthodoxy pointed to the new ideological cross-currents. The sensational attacks on Mikhail Zoshchenko and Konstantin Fedin were particularly significant as indications of the limits beyond which a writer could not safely go. Zoshchenko opened his condemned work *Before Sunrise* with the statement, "I am unhappy and I don't know why," and proceeded to sort through the events of his past to find the traumatic experience that would explain his present discontent.[7] Evidence of such unabashed preoccupation with oneself would have appeared odd in the pages of a Soviet journal at any time, and its publication during the war years was particularly startling. An outburst of public criticism occurred not long after the final installment of the memoirs had been suppressed. Zoshchenko was accused of occupying himself with philistine emotions and interests, selecting the ugliest facts of his biography for public discussion, and ignoring social forces and the great events of the time. The journal *Bolshevik* published a letter, ostensibly from rank-and-file Leningrad workers, which complained about Zoshchenko's exclusive interest in himself, his melancholy and apathy, and his cynical and vulgar attitude toward women.[8] The work was discussed by the presidium of the Writers' Union and again criticized at the Ninth Plenum.[9] Beyond its rather frank documentation, which violated Soviet critics' Victorian convictions, it was the manifestation of extreme individualism, Zoshchenko's concern with his inner world of experience, and his apparent isolation from events going on about him that incensed the party critics. Individualism was one of the diseases which the regime vigorously set out to cure once the war had ended.

Even more revealing in some ways was the attack on Fedin's *Gorky Amongst Us*, a projected three-volume memoir. Criticism was initially directed at the second volume, which appeared in 1944. The final installment was not published. *Pravda* opened the onslaught in an article which described Fedin's work as "a deeply apolitical book, in which events of the literary world are shown torn from life, closed off in a sphere of narrow professional interests and relations," a book of "highly questionable ethics and distorted perspective." [10] Another critic referred to the book as "a stubborn, deliberate defense of . . . apolitical art" and accused Fedin of "taking up a position that contradicts the precepts of Gorky." [11] These charges were echoed at a meeting of the presidium of the Writers' Union, where Fedin was charged with neglecting the historical-political setting of the period he described and with being "objective," "dispassionate," and "tolerant" toward reactionary writers. At the same meeting Tikhonov accused Fedin of misrepresenting Gorky's views on art and asserted that "an artist who tries to restore individualism in general has nothing in common with the development of socialist individuality." [12] In fact, Fedin had given a fairly accurate representation of Gorky's breadth of interest and tolerance in literature, his apolitical orientation during the twenties, and his role in encouraging the Serapion Brothers, a group now viewed with disfavor in the Soviet Union. But this did not correspond to the official attitude toward Gorky as the creator of the Writers' Union and proponent of the doctrine of socialist realism, an attitude based partly on Gorky's activities after his return from Italy, when he allowed himself to be used as a tool in the process of imposing Stalinist controls over literature.

Thus Fedin manifested the same malaise as did Zoshchenko: lack of political consciousness and incipient individualism. But Fedin went a step further, for he raised the whole question of the nature of literature and the function of the writer, and in doing so he called into question certain hallowed tenets of Soviet literary theory. Moreover, he approached historical truth closely enough to threaten to reveal the false tones in which the official ikon of Gorky had been painted. In the second volume of his memoirs, Fedin presented the view, which he linked with Gorky's name, that although literature may be tendentious, the writer himself is not consciously so, that this tendentiousness is not purposeful on the part of the writer. This the critics found particularly objectionable. The author of the *Pravda* article accused Fedin of rebelling against that tendentiousness and partiinost "which have been verified by life, by the whole development of literature," and another critic asserted in opposition to Fedin that "ideinost and tendentiousness . . . do not contradict the laws of art but, on the contrary, constitute its basic law." [13] Furthermore, Fedin committed an error of which others, such as Alexander Fadeyev and Valentin Katayev, were later to be judged guilty: that of minimizing the role of the party. The original *Pravda* article complained that Fedin's book did not show how the party had "wisely and patiently rallied, strengthened, and cultivated the powers of Soviet literature, directing its growth, inspiring it in serving the people." These criticisms are forceful illustrations of the persistence of the party's basic policy even during years when certain deviations in practice were tolerated. The incident also indicated that the party was once again intent upon shortening the reins of control.

There were further signs of an increasing concern with ideological orthodoxy as the regime turned its attention to problems of reconstruction at the end of the war. In the face of natural inclinations on the part of Soviet citizens to relax, the regime called upon its people to make new sacrifices in order to restore a damaged economy and ultimately to achieve the Communist utopia. The impression created by developments from 1944 onward, that the postwar period might produce something similar to the internal political climate of the thirties, was reinforced by events of the early months of 1946. Stalin's speech of February 9 was an indication of the shifting current. His remarks on the capitalist West suggested a return to the old theory of two irreconcilably hostile worlds and pointed to renewed anti-Western agitation. His representation of the war as a test of Soviet institutions that proved their worth and their superiority to those of Western societies presaged a return to unrestrained glorification of party and state. Both themes would play an important role in postwar literary politics.

The changing line was quickly reflected in some parts of the literary community. In April 1946, *Literaturnaya gazeta* ran an editorial which closely paralleled Stalin's speech of February, though it made more crudely explicit what Stalin's words had implied.[14] The editorial asserted that the war had been a test which "Soviet culture sustained with honor" but which that of England and the United States had failed. *Literaturnaya gazeta* went on to specify certain tasks of Soviet literature, indicating some basic purposes of the assault on the arts that broke out several months later. The article declared that it is the duty of Soviet literature to counteract the false ideals and prejudices of the "capitalist reaction," that Soviet literature "must convince the reader of the advantages of the Soviet social order, to counterbalance the lies and slander of our enemies." In addition, the editorial complained about Soviet writers' "superficial" descriptions of foreign countries, and it held up in distinction the example of Mayakovsky, whose poems about foreign countries "are permeated with a sense of the fundamental distance between the two worlds." Other articles and editorials stressed the role of literature in the First Five-Year Plan, recalling pointedly the contribution of belles-lettres toward fulfilling the plan in 1928–1932.

The party's reaction to an article written by Fyodor Panfyorov in 1945 was particularly revealing with regard to the revision in official attitude that began quietly in 1943 and developed into rigid dogma after the end of the war.[15] The episode indicated how much realism the postwar application of socialist realism would permit in works of literature. The article, broadly concerned with hindrances to a thriving literature, scattered critical barbs in many directions. Panfyorov devoted much space to the question of truthfulness in literature, particularly truthfulness in describing and analyzing the course of the war and the situation behind the front lines. Urging study of the question of the Red Army's retreat to Stalingrad and what had made possible its advance to the Elbe and victory, Panfyorov continued: "It is necessary to study all this: to study, to seek life's truth, hence artistic truth as well. And the truth of life says that heroism is not a continuous triumphal procession. Heroism is the surmounting of the most terrible difficulties. . . ." But, asked Panfyorov, what do those who are obstructing the development of literature say to this? He presented the following illustrative dialogue:

"Retreat? There was no retreat. This was a planned departure to exhaust the enemy."

"If you please," objects the writer, "what kind of planned retreat was it when at one time the fate of our country was hanging by a hair. Why, Comrade Stalin and his colleagues told us of this."

"Forget it. One must forget about this. . . ."[16]

Both *Literaturnaya gazeta* and *Pravda* published articles vigorously objecting to Panfyorov's essay. The *Pravda* article scolded him for "mechanically separating the periods of defense and offense" and added, "F. Panfyorov completely fails to understand the significance of the period of our active defense . . . and is inclined to see in it only its dark sides." [17] This made even clearer what had been becoming apparent for a long time — that it would no longer be possible to write the truth about the war, to write about the experience and suffering of ordinary people. Instead, only party leaders, army officers, and the "most advanced elements" of the fighting force would be portrayed wearing the nimbus of heroism and the laurels of victory. This was one of the lessons underscored by the later attack on Fadeyev's *Young Guard*.

The strengthening currents of criticism exposed ever more starkly what the regime regarded as basic defects within the literary community. The more orthodox critics began to denounce with greater insistence the tendency toward "individualism" among writers, an individualism that was accompanied by lack of educative purposefulness and political awareness in their works — basically the faults of Zoshchenko and Fedin. The lyrical outpouring which wartime experience had evoked from many poets, and which made their work popular, now came under attack as a manifestation of excessive preoccupation with the self and its private experience. One critic, for example, now scolded Konstantin Simonov, and other poets as well, for expressing only melancholy and longing for his beloved and his homeland while he had been abroad, thus neglecting the political significance of events in foreign lands.[18] Yet it was probably such personal themes that made works like Simonov's "With You and Without You" so popular during the war, an indication that the disease had spread beyond the intelligentsia. It is significant in this respect that a volume of Sergei Yesenin's verse was published in 1946, a selection that included many of his despondent poems. Yesenin had been popular, particularly among the younger generation, during the late twenties and early thirties, partly because of his "hooligan" poetry, whose self-castigation and limitless despair are impressive, partly because of his quiet, melancholy descriptions of rural Russia. At one time this aroused official concern, and "Yeseninism" came to be regarded as a force undermining the body politic, a sign of degenerate individualism and pessimism. It is some indication of the postwar mood of Soviet society that his work should have been published at all. The weaknesses which the regime discerned were probably outgrowths of war weariness and a desire merely to enjoy living for a while — a mood which even the ultraorthodox Alexei Surkov expressed succinctly in his poem "Evening," composed in 1944:

> And after victory we will make a halt,
> Drink a cup, and rest to our heart's content.[19]

Furthermore, criticisms of the activities of the Writers' Union and writers' clubs seemed to indicate a certain apathy on the part of writers toward the political and social functions entrusted to them by the party.

Another problem was the emphasis that had been given to Russian nationalism at the expense of specifically Soviet patriotism. The press began to scold artists for "placing an equal sign between the old patriotism and Soviet patriotism," and efforts were made to eliminate this error.[20] Confusing the two types of patriotism, it was said, obscured the new qualities of Soviet man and society. In addition, writers' interest in the past distracted attention from current problems and tasks. To clear the path for glorifying Soviet life, the regime also had to cope with the problem of admiration of things Western, particularly of the higher living standards, that had developed among some elements of the population during the war. Isolated efforts in this direction had already been made. In 1945, for example, the journal *Oktyabr* published two of Sergei Mikhalkov's fables satirizing those whose approval of Western products and culture reflected unfavorably on Soviet life.[21]

Though there was ample forewarning of changes to come, many writers appeared slow to catch the new mood. Perhaps a coldly realistic analysis of trends was obstructed by persisting expectations of a brighter postwar life — expectations such as those recalled by Olga Berggolts when she wrote, toward the end of 1945: "About three months ago it seemed to us at times that the war would hardly have ended when immediately, on the very next day, our whole mode of existence, all our daily life, would change suddenly, unrecognizably." [22] During the course of the war, many writers had expressed similar hopefulness and optimism about the postwar development of Soviet literature. Or it may have been that the writers' apparent sluggishness was part of an effort to resist the trend. There is some support for the latter suggestion in remarks made at the Tenth Plenum of the Writers' Union by one or two writers who seemed to warn against interference in the processes of creative activity when they questioned whether success in belles-lettres can be organized.[23] Although the speeches of the leaders of the Writers' Union at the Tenth Plenum reflected doctrinaire attitudes, the plenum itself did not mark the beginning of stricter enforcement of the emerging literary line. Perhaps such tendencies were momentarily smothered by the exhilarating effect of final military victory. In any case, there were many different cross-currents during this period, and the situation was more fluid than it would become later on. It is significant in this regard that Zoshchenko, in spite of the harsh criticism directed against him, was again active in the literary life of Leningrad by 1944. He was serving as a member of the Leningrad branch of the Writers' Union, and later he worked on the journal *Zvezda* and assumed duties as an editor of children's books. A collection of his stories was scheduled to appear, and other of his works were printed in the journal *Leningrad*. In April 1946, Zoshchenko was listed among those awarded medals for "valiant work in the Great Fatherland War." [24]

THE ONSLAUGHT

The party opened the campaign to correct these lapses in a dramatic way. On August 14, 1946, the Central Committee issued a decree on literature, "Resolution on the Journals *Zvezda* and *Leningrad*." This decree, together with its elaboration in two speeches by Andrei Zhdanov, set forth the policies that were to prevail during the first fifteen years of the postwar era.[25] The decree on literature was followed on August 26 by the resolution, "On the Repertoire of the Dramatic Theaters and Measures for Its Improvement," and on September 4 by another pertaining to the cinema, "On the Moving Picture *Bolshaya Zhizn*." While the latter two decrees contained matter of particular significance for their respective fields, they added little to the basic principles stated in the first decree.

The main task of the resolution on literature and of Zhdanov's speeches was to emphasize the educative function of literature, the duties of the writer to the people, party, and state, and, above all, the necessary political orientation of art. The core of the resolution is contained in the following passage:

our journals are a mighty instrument of the Soviet state in the cause of the education of the Soviet people, and Soviet youth in particular. They must therefore be controlled by the vital foundation of the Soviet order — its politics. The Soviet order cannot tolerate the education of the young in the spirit of indifference to Soviet politics, in the spirit of a devil-may-care attitude and ideological neutrality.

The power of Soviet literature, the most advanced literature in the world, consists in the fact that it is a literature which has not and cannot have interests other than the interests of the people, the interests of the state. The task of Soviet literature is to aid the state to educate the youth correctly and to meet their demands, to rear a new generation strong and vigorous, believing in their cause, fearing no obstacles and ready to overcome all obstacles.

Consequently any preaching of ideological neutrality, of political neutrality, of "art for art's sake" is alien to Soviet literature and harmful to the interests of the Soviet people and the Soviet state. Such preaching has no place in our journals.[26]

This was a rather vigorous reassertion of the principles of ideinost and partiinost in literature, and Zhdanov's task was to draw out the meaning of this in greater detail.

As it might have been expected, Zhdanov, in defining the role of literature and the writer in the Soviet state, cited Lenin's article, "Party Organization and Party Literature," and pointed out that in it "are laid all the foundations on which the development of our Soviet literature is based."[27] The point was, of course, that all literature must in effect be party literature and serve party purposes. Zhdanov succinctly formulated the regime's conception of the immediate tasks of literature when he remarked, "The Soviet people expect from Soviet writers genuine ideological armament, spiritual nourishment that will aid in fulfilling the plans for great socialist construction, for the restoration and further development of our country's national economy."[28] Since primary emphasis was to be given to current problems of reconstruction, Zhdanov castigated "a one-sided infatuation with historical themes" and the "attempt to utilize only vacuous subjects of a purely diverting nature." [29] The party's pronouncements on literature once again made it abundantly clear that the aesthetic significance of literary works occupies a very subordinate position in the official Soviet hierarchy of values. "Not personal tastes and old aesthetic attachments, but Bolshevist ideinost" was again sounded as the slogan of the day.[30] Zhdanov's concluding characterization of the party's interest in literature hardly requires additional comment: "Bolsheviks value literature highly. They see clearly its great historical mission and role in strengthening the moral and political unity of the people, in welding and educating the people." [31]

Another aspect of the party's attitude toward the writer's role in society was revealed by the condemnation of passivity or "neutrality" — ideological, political, or artistic — as scarcely distinguishable from anti-Soviet activity. Simonov was only rephrasing the literary decree on this point when, for the edification of Moscow writers, he said: "The ideological struggle in the whole world has acquired a bitter character. And if among us are found people inclined to say 'but I will lie down and rest a little' or 'but I will go gather flowers,' we must condemn them as deserters." [32] The decree cited unfavorably works by several Soviet authors, but it concentrated on Zoshchenko and Akhmatova, whom it read out of Soviet literature. Although the charges against the two writers were many and sweeping, they reduced finally to those of "neutrality" and "apolitical" orientation. In addition to these charges, the decree insisted, after presenting a somewhat distorted interpretation of Zoshchenko's "Adventures of a Monkey," that the writer had produced a "vulgar parody" of Soviet life, a "hooliganistic portrayal of our society." Here the party was again pulling at that thorn in its side, the problem of literary satire, and the immediate import of its charges was to indicate that the limits of tolerable criticism had been severely curtailed. But Zhdanov in his speeches made the ultimate purpose of the attack on Zoshchenko clear. Zhdanov directed attention to certain unfavorable aspects of the writer's past, recalling Zoshchenko's lighthearted attitude in 1922 toward ideology and emphasizing his connection with the Serapion Brothers, whose manifesto had defended individual freedom in art and whom Zhdanov now characterized as preachers of "art for art's sake" and of "rotten lack of political principle." The criticism of Akhmatova, too, was directed at a specific evil of Soviet literary life, for she was guilty, said the decree, of creating verses "saturated with a spirit of pessimism and melancholy," which is another way of referring to such phenomena as contemplation, soul searching, and absence of political messages.

In defining the duties and responsibilities of literature, the party decree indicated the general nature of the content that should be found in literary works. Soviet writers must concern themselves largely with current themes, and their writings must inculcate loyalty to party and state. In comedy and satire, writers would be held within the approved limits of "self-criticism." Above all, Soviet belles-lettres must show the best aspirations of Soviet man, must be positive and optimistic. In Yegolin's later formulation, "Socialist realism is a style that says "yes" to life." [33] Zhdanov gave considerable attention to this point. Emphasizing the achievements of Soviet society and culture and the magnificent new qualities of Soviet man, he asserted:

To show these new high qualities of the Soviet people, to show our people not only as they are today, but also to give a glimpse of their tomorrow, to help illumine, with a searchlight the road ahead — such is the task of every conscientious Soviet writer. . . . While selecting the best feelings and qualities of the Soviet man and revealing his tomorrow, we must at the same time show our people what they must not be, we must castigate the remnants of yesterday, remnants that hinder the Soviet people in their forward march. Soviet writers must help the people, the state, and the party to educate our youth to be cheerful and confident in their own strength, unafraid of any difficulties.[34]

Unadulterated admiration for the Soviet system was a basic ingredient in Zhdanov's speeches, and the glorification of Soviet life that Zhdanov advocated was coupled with anti-Westernism. The Soviet social order, Zhdanov declared, is "a hundred times higher and better than any bourgeois social order" and "has the right to teach others a new universal morality." [35] The decree on literature specified "servility before contemporary bourgeois culture" as a major cause for the unsatisfactory situation in belles-lettres, and writers were called upon to correct this error. Zhdanov asserted more bluntly that Soviet literature must "boldly lash and attack bourgeois culture, which is in a state of marasmus and corruption." [36] Literature was also being asked to play its part in the developing "cold war."

The assault on the arts provided the party with an opportunity for bringing under fire the several organizations that supervised activities in the arts. The decree on literature initiated an attack on the Writers' Union, criticized the work of editorial boards, raised some questions about the operation of the Central Committee's own Agitation and Propaganda Department, and cleared the ground for attacks on the various party organs responsible for checking on these bodies. The decrees on drama and the cinema extended the attack to the Committee on Affairs of the Arts, the Ministry of Cinematography, and related agencies. Other than general laxity, the party found a major weakness to be what it termed "friendship relations" — the sacrifice of "principled" criticism to the interests of private friendships. Apparently mutual-protection groups, which plague the regime in agriculture and industry, had developed in the cultural bureaucracy as well. Under the conditions created by these friendship relations, complained the literary decree, "writers cease to perfect themselves and lose their sense of responsibility to the people, to the state, and to the Party." [37] The decrees opened the door to a shake-up within the responsible organizations which would serve the purpose of making each man acutely aware of his obligations to, and dependence upon, the party and the state.

If the party's purpose was to drive home the decree's points by throwing the literary world into a turmoil, the events of the next few months indicate that the goal had largely been accomplished. The concluding passages of the decree provided the initial impetus by requiring the Writers' Union to take measures to overcome shortcomings revealed by the party. It set the example by discontinuing the publication of *Leningrad* and by appointing A. M. Yegolin, acting director of the Central Committee's Agitation and Propaganda Department, as the editor-in-chief of *Zvezda*. In its resolution of September 4, 1946, the presidium of the Writers' Union took further steps.[38] It relieved Tikhonov of his post as president of the union, though he became a deputy secretary on the union's reorganized secretariat, now composed of a secretary-general, four deputy secretaries, and eight members. Alexander Fadeyev became secretary-general and, as such, the leading functionary of the union, for the office of president, re-established at the Ninth

Plenum, was discontinued. The resolution also expelled Akhmatova and Zoshchenko from the union. It announced a meeting of the plenum of the union's board, recommended that its republic and oblast divisions meet to discuss the party decree, and ordered a discussion of journal editors' plans for fulfilling the requirements of the decree. It promised, in addition, a radical reconstruction of the system of training young writers. During the course of the year, several changes were made on the editorial boards of the various literary publications. The meeting of the presidium and a gathering of Leningrad writers which followed the publication of the decree on literature set examples which were imitated many times throughout the Soviet Union during the following months. Meetings of writers and other artists provided opportunities for recanting and for criticizing local evils. The atmosphere of these gatherings is suggested by the report of the presidium's meeting in September.[39] The speakers unanimously approved the party decree and admitted their own errors. Aseyev found Tikhonov's confession unsatisfactory, and Fadeyev in turn, though agreeing on this point, adopted a rather bullying tone and reminded Aseyev of his mistake in approving the work of Pasternak. It seemed a favorite device to deprive some writers even of those meager laurels that they had won during the war. Fadeyev now claimed that Pasternak had contributed nothing to the war "except a few poems which no one could regard as Pasternak's best," and later on Pasternak's work was judged "alien to the Soviet people." [40] This was in line with the example set by the decree, which asserted that Zoshchenko "gave no aid to the Soviet people in their struggle against the German robbers" — this in face of the fact that the writer had been awarded a medal for his part in the war effort. In light of the new state of affairs, it would not have been surprising had some writers decided "to crawl into crevices" and to "stop writing for, say, about half a year," as V. Vishnevsky declared at the meeting that some had. This shows some underestimation of the longevity of Zhdanovism.

ZHDANOVISM: APPLICATIONS

The Eleventh Plenum, held in the summer of 1947, more than compensated for whatever political and ideological shortcomings the leaders of the Writers' Union had tolerated at the Tenth Plenum. The principal theme at these meetings was Soviet patriotism, a theme that was coupled with assertions of Russian superiority to the West and attacks on "servility before the West"; the secondary theme concerned manifestations of "bourgeois nationalism" among the various republics of the USSR. It became apparent later that the major event of the plenum was Fadeyev's report, which traced the errors of I. Nusinov's *Pushkin and World Literature* to their source in the work of Alexander Veselovsky. Nusinov's work had been condemned for overemphasizing Pushkin's ties with the West and for neglecting the peculiarly Russian elements of the great poet's genius. Now Fadeyev proclaimed the "school" of Veselovsky the "main forefather of servility before the West in a certain part of past and present Russian literary scholarship." [41] In his remarks closing the discussion of the report, Fadeyev indirectly urged a campaign against the heritage of Veselovsky. The upshot of this was a genuine controversy among literary scholars, a controversy whose outcome was determined by an editorial in *Kultura i zhizn* which declared the whole discussion unnecessary and a mistake.[42] For the newspaper, the correct conclusion was evident: Veselovsky's influence was a pernicious one. Though the details of the conflict are beyond the scope of this study, the episode is significant as an indication of the regime's determination to root out of literature all ideologically alien elements and to insist upon the distinctiveness of Russian culture.[43]

Of more significance for the creative writer were the party's attacks on Fadeyev's *Young Guard*,[44] published in 1945, and Simonov's novelette, *Smoke of the Fatherland*,[45] attacks which were intended as concrete illustrations of certain aspects of the new literary policy. The episodes were designed as exercises in the problem of content and the treatment of particular themes in works of literature. But they were even more significant as lessons in literary politics and as reaffirmations of the principle of institutionalized insecurity.

Because both works had been approved by authoritative sources, the onslaught was certain to have a forceful impact on the literary community. From the tribune of the Eleventh Plenum, Fadeyev praised Simonov's novelette even before its completion, and the work received favorable reviews upon the instant of its publication. Fadeyev's novel, awarded a First-Class Stalin Prize in 1946, had been received with almost unanimous rejoicing. Of the few critics who found minor faults in the novel, only one even approached the grounds upon which the party later built its case, and for this he was reproached.[46] For the most part, the response to the novel was enthusiastic, even ecstatic. What is more significant, many critics lauded the work for the very things in which it was later found wanting. For example, V. Yermilov, who has exhibited a remarkable capacity for survival in the Soviet literary world, wrote that in Fadeyev's novel "the elevated ideological and moral countenance of Soviet people, of Soviet youth, and the *leading role of the party* of the people is revealed with a depth as yet unsurpassed in our literature," and he characterized the two central party figures in the novel as superb representations of "the Leninist-Stalinist type of statesman." [47] Such remarks continued to appear in Soviet literary publications until the moment of the party's outburst against the novel, which indicates that the re-evaluation came as a surprise. Several different dramatizations of *Young Guard* had been staged in theaters throughout the Soviet Union, and, although the party press attacked the novel through criticism of these, the earlier reviews of the stage versions reveal a remarkable lack of awareness on the part of critics of the essential weakness of the novel itself. Some of the dramatizations were criticized, of course, but usually for technical and dramatic weaknesses or for unfaithful transposition of the novel's contents. In addition to this, a Ukrainian composer, Yu. Meitus, based an opera on the novel, and Sergei Gerasimov composed a scenario for a film version. Thus the attack could hardly fail to cause a stir, the more so because of Fadeyev's authoritative position in the literary bureaucracy.

The editorial in *Kultura i zhizn* which opened the attack on *Young Guard* in 1947 was followed by a similar editorial in *Pravda* and a more detailed elaboration in *Literaturnaya gazeta*.[48] Fadeyev's fundamental error, as it emerged from these criticisms, was leaving the party organization out of his work. *Kultura i zhizn* complained that Fadeyev had not given "a correct presentation of the activities of Bolsheviks behind enemy lines, of the people's real leaders, who did not drop the reins of leadership and who knew how to organize the masses." Particularly galling was the Nazis' capture of the principal party leaders in the novel, Valko and Shulga, because of the incautious behavior of the two men. Remarking that Valko and Shulga appeared "incapable, inexperienced, and even foolish," *Pravda* asserted: "Perhaps the event described in the novel was not invented, but it is absolutely atypical, uncharacteristic." This tends to raise doubts about the party in the minds of youth, *Pravda* went on, and the novel implies that party members should learn from Komsomols, rather than the other way about, since the Komsomols were shown to be bold and effective in their underground work. In addition to this, Fadeyev's critics objected to the scenes depicting evacuation before the enemy's approach, scenes which disclosed a considerable amount of panic and chaos. *Pravda* denied that there had been any disorganization or panic, and *Literaturnaya gazeta* waxed even more eloquent on this point:

The evacuation of people, factories, and equipment was one of the great deeds accomplished by our people in the terrible years of the Fatherland war; it was an example of the iron will and organization of the party and Soviet state mechanism. And to substitute scenes of panic for artistic disclosure of this victory of the heroic Soviet home front is to distort reality and history in the crudest fashion.

The editors of *Literaturnaya gazeta* had apparently adopted in all seriousness Panfyorov's parody of the obstructors of truthful artistic representation of the war.

Fadeyev accepted this criticism in the officially approved manner, thus setting an example for his brethren, and during the next four years he rewrote the lengthy novel. In doing this he did not have to plow virgin soil, however. He might have consulted Gerasimov's new film scenario or the revised operatic version, whose creator received "valuable assistance" in his labors from Ukrainian party organizations, according to one report.[49] In the second version of the novel, which appeared in 1951, Fadeyev carefully eliminated anything tending to create an impression of chaos, confusion, or panic during the period of evacuation, and he added sections showing how the party organized the whole movement. He attached many new passages describing the widespread and carefully planned operations of the party underground. In particular, he reprieved one of the lesser figures of the first version,

Lyutikov, from an early death and expanded his role, making him into the party guide for the Komsomols. Fadeyev now credited Lyutikov with words, plans, and ideas formerly attributed to the youths, and the author disclosed that in all important matters the party, through Lyutikov, took the initiative or granted approval. Fadeyev made numerous other changes, corresponding to the lesser criticisms of the work.

As far as thematic material is concerned, this incident was merely a culmination of trends that had been developing since 1943 or 1944, trends which made impossible anything approaching objective description of the war. P. Vershigora, author of the war memoirs *People With a Clear Conscience*, objected to these developments in no uncertain terms when he entered into a controversy over Olga Dzhigurda's memoirs, *The Ship "Kakhemia."* Vershigora insisted that Dzhigurda's work was a sincere account of many people's war experience and that her critics were those who "shun living truth and prefer oleographs to fearless, truthful stories about the complex and sometimes contradictory events of wartime reality." His comment on writing about the defense of Leningrad is particularly relevant to the Fadeyev case:

At a highly responsible conference devoted to the fortunes of literature about the war, a certain well-known writer who stayed in besieged Leningrad during the whole blockade complained, and not without foundation, that it had been impossible for him to write the truth about the days of the blockade since about 1944, that is, from the time when the canals of literature and criticism filled up with people who did not experience the blockade. They interpret every attempt to portray the blockade realistically as slander on the inhabitants of Leningrad.[50]

The postwar insistence on glorifying all things Soviet, the party in particular, rendered such honesty impossible. It was necessary to portray the party as omniscient, omnipresent, and infallible and to represent the people's spontaneous and courageous resistance of the invader as a manifestation of party planning and organization. Lest anyone miss the point, Lev Subotsky made one lesson of the Fadeyev episode clear in an admirably simple formulation: "In light of the criticism of *Young Guard* it has become especially clear that the enormous historical content of the epoch cannot be fully expressed in a work of art if the work does not reveal the great

role of the Bolshevik Party in the whole life of the people and if
it does not create vivid images of the avant-garde of the people,
the Bolsheviks." [51]

Fadeyev's novel had come to be regarded as an outstanding example of a work written according to the precepts of socialist
realism, and, in view of the criticism of the novel, the story of its
origin is of no little significance. In an article published shortly
after Fadeyev received a Stalin Prize — an article whose title, "In
the Study of Life Is the Guarantee of Success," now has an ironic
ring — Fadeyev remarked that he had been commissioned to write
the novel, and he emphasized the point that he had based the work
on documentary evidence, had gone to the Donets Basin to talk
with those who actually knew the persons portrayed in the novel,
and so on.[52] Kornely Zelinsky in his biographical essay on Fadeyev
provides some additional details.[53] After the liberation of Krasnodon, in 1943, the Central Committee of the Komsomol organization, having learned of traces of underground work by a youth
organization there, sent a commission to the area to study the
matter. The result was a three-volume collection of documents
about the youth group. Apparently the Komsomol organization re-
quested that Fadeyev write a novel on the basis of this material,
and Fadeyev, according to Zelinsky, spent nearly a month in
Krasnodon. It is interesting that in discussing the question of artistic
method Zelinsky remarks that Fadeyev was "bound by the documents and exact in everything that touches upon the factual side
of the matter," but that as an artist he was "free in everything that
relates to the portrayal of the spiritual life and ideological world
of the 'young guards.' " [54] But party critics, accusing Fadeyev
of distorting reality and history "in the crudest fashion," had concerned themselves largely with the area in which Fadeyev had
been "bound by documents" rather than that in which he had been
artistically "free." This is some indication of the nature of "reality"
in postwar Soviet literature. It is difficult to regard even the first
version of the novel, with its cheap sentimentality, two-dimensional
characters, and youths who proclaim their dedication to Stalin,
Party, and Fatherland in the style of *Pravda* editorials, as a
genuinely realistic account of Soviet people and life under the German occupation. Even so, the two forms of the novel stand, in some

sense, for the two different phases of official policy toward literary representation of wartime experience. Fadeyev's first version was found wanting by the standards of the second phase. This, too, is evidence of the growing extremism of Zhdanovism. The party now demanded not only a varnish on reality but a high gloss on the varnish. The Fadeyev incident provides more insight into the meaning of socialist realism than the hundreds of articles written on the subject during the last twenty years. As far as the "realism" part of it is concerned, that is something manifestly determined by the party definition of reality, a definition that changes abruptly from time to time. But in view of the social energies that went into the writing of *Young Guard*, it at least has a strong claim to be considered the outstanding example of socialist realism as practiced during the Stalinist era.

The issue of *Kultura i zhizn* that criticized *Young Guard* also contained an article by N. Maslin attacking Simonov's *Smoke of the Fatherland*.[55] Maslin noted that Simonov had tried to show what true Soviet patriotism is by contrasting it with a so-called instinctive patriotism, but unsuccessfully, for the latter concept was confused and the former remained, in the work, an empty abstraction. The main character, Barsagin, through whom Simonov revealed his main themes, Soviet patriotism and anti-Americanism, was merely a "moralizing *intelligent*" who did not express his thoughts in action, said Maslin. "Short-order writing" was a major target of this and of later reviews. The basic idea of the work, wrote Maslin, "is realized not in artistic images, but some place alongside, in declaratory judgments pronounced by the author." Maslin hastened to add that socialist realism does not exclude journalistic elements from literature, that artistic and journalistic principles can be organically united in a literary work. But Simonov did not succeed in doing this, and "on the whole work lies the mark of haste." Maslin was standing on solid ground when he wrote this, for Simonov's novelette is distinctly a propaganda tract, and in parts it bears the aspect of an unconscious parody on Soviet "topical" literature. But the question that arises is why Simonov was singled out for criticism when so many such works had been approved or passed unnoticed. It may have been that the attack was stimulated by a particularly obvious difference between official evaluation of the work and unofficial, unpublished judgments of it. A report of one writer's remarks, made at the Thirteenth Plenum, on the character of critical work in the Writers' Union tends to support this suggestion:

G. Nikolayeva mentioned, as an example of unprincipled conduct, those writers who in private conversations sharply criticize this or that work, but when they step on a platform begin to "burn incense," out of friendship considerations. This happened, for instance, at the discussion of Simonov's novelette *Smoke of the Fatherland*.[56]

There was a more important reason for the attack on Simonov, however, one related to the fundamental reason for the assault on Fadeyev.

The nature of party criticism of Fadeyev and Simonov, as well as later comment upon it in literary publications, indicated that the main lesson to be drawn from the event was that no one, not even the most favored authors, could be secure from attack. Here the party was attempting to cope with an evil inherent in a system where policy decisions are imposed from above and initiative, should it come from below, is in danger of being cut short ruthlessly. The result in the literary world is that certain persons come to be regarded as "authorities" and spokesmen of the party — persons whose word must be weighed with special care and whose example, even in creative work, tends to be imitated by everyone else because it is thought to be proper and "safe." The editors of *Literaturnaya gazeta* were getting at this when they observed: "But we still not infrequently encounter the operation of an unwritten 'law,' established by we know not whom, according to which a writer who has achieved authority by one or more literary successes is virtually declared infallible." [57] Such a phenomenon inevitably leads toward stagnation and a stifling of creative initiative. But the effect of removing such authorities — and, it may be suggested, the underlying purpose in doing so — is to put writers on guard and, at the same time, heighten their awareness of the standards to be met. For with no unassailable authorities to imitate, each writer must assiduously verse himself in the party's current demands on literature, keep abreast of political-literary developments, and refine his sensitivity to shifts in the political wind. In addition, the Fadeyev affair provided instruction in the proper Bolshevik manner of reacting to party criticism. The "success" of Fadeyev's revision was represented as a justification of the party's criticism and a proof that heeding party commands is artistically beneficial.[58] The whole affair had about it the atmosphere of a carefully prepared morality play, though commentary that appeared in the Soviet press several years later suggested that the event had not been staged with Fadeyev's foreknowledge.[59] Nonetheless, the critical articles were unusually restrained in tone, and deprecatory references of a personal nature, not uncommon in such cases, were absent. Fadeyev had to pay the price of rewriting his novel, but he retained his post as first secretary of the Writers' Union and continued to act as the regime's leading spokesman in literary matters at home and abroad.

Another noteworthy occurrence of 1947 was the controversy that arose over a cycle of poems by Margarita Aliger. The controversy was not initiated by the party press and was not nearly so sensational as the attack on Fadeyev's novel. But it was an event of considerable significance, for it centered on the crucial question of the writer's right to self-expression, and it furnished revealing examples of the manner in which insistence on scrupulous adherence to orthodoxy impinges on the process of literary expression. The Aliger incident was an outgrowth of the postwar effort to eradicate what was regarded as harmful individualism in literature, and it was only one of many similar cases that were soon to follow. But not until several years later, after the baneful effects of these policies had aroused more widespread concern, would the issues again be presented so clearly as they were during the discussion of lyric poetry in 1947. The significance of the Aliger affair was increased by another incident, involving an article on lyric poetry by Kornely Zelinsky, which occurred at the same time. Both the poems and the article appeared in an issue of *Znamya* which went to press shortly before the party issued its decree on literature.[60]

A main theme of Aliger's poems is that the war, with the privation and suffering that it entailed, left a scar that can never be effaced, that the future can never be quite like the past, that life, though at times it may seem a burden, will and must go on. The verses were evidently inspired by a sense of personal loss and a melancholy which were not in keeping with the spirit of the party's bright vision of the postwar world. Some weeks after the party had established its postwar literary line, Semyon Tregub attacked the poems, declaring them to be excessively egocentric and pessimistic:

The whole cycle amazes the reader with its poverty of ideas and poetical feebleness. The verses are full of a diseased, despondent egoism — of oneself, for oneself, with oneself, with one's own "how I feel," without perspective, without inspiration. . . . The great expectations of youth which give "small fruit," life which promises much and gives little — this is the theme of her new verse.[61]

But Konstantin Simonov, who had been on the editorial board of *Znamya* when the poems were published and had since become chief editor of *Novy mir*, published a vigorous defense of Aliger. Asserting that he was not amazed by the alleged poverty and feebleness of the poems, he continued:

I cannot and do not wish to consider a sober, sensible viewpoint as poverty of ideas. Life is difficult, full of struggles and trials. These struggles and trials stand before us in the future. And a poet is right when he reminds me, the reader, of this.[62]

The new editor of *Literaturnaya gazeta*, V. Yermilov, supported Tregub against Simonov,[63] and the matter seemed to close uncertainly when *Novy mir* published another interchange between Tregub and Simonov in which each reasserted his previous views.[64] But the incident gained in interest with the appearance of a collection of Aliger's verse in 1955. For the collection contained most of the controversial poems, now included in a group entitled "Victory," and it disclosed that Aliger had revised some of the poems to comply with criticisms made of them. It is worthwhile to note a few of the changes as concrete illustrations of the meaning of another facet of Zhdanovism.

In her revisions, Aliger attempted to produce a more positive impression by placing greater emphasis on "courage" and "will" and by modifying or omitting a number of passages which referred to feelings of disturbance, uncertainty, and anguish. Moreover, the 1955 edition omitted a poem which had sounded a note of deep despair,[65] a poem which Tregub understood to mean that "all effort to change things is foolish and vain." [66] The detailed scrutiny to which the critics subjected the poems in 1947 was striking, but equally impressive was Aliger's care in clarifying possible ambiguities and correcting comparatively minor ideological defects. For example, one of Tregub's complaints was that a poem entitled "Great Expectations" advanced the gloomy and erroneous view that reality is always wanting in comparison with a person's dreams. The lines in question read as follows in the original version:

> And in a time of cruel sufferings
> There always appears to people
> The star, known from childhood,
> Of great expectations.
>
> Struggle and privation are gratifying
> When they are dedicated to it.
> And even great achievements
> Are poorer than great expectations.[67]

Rejecting Tregub's interpretation, Simonov wrote that these are "beautiful, courageous lines," and he insisted that he saw behind them "a seeker, a person who is not inclined to rest content, a person who, having achieved something, does not remain satisfied with it but thinks of the future struggle, of the great expectations of the future." [68] Nonetheless, the poetess changed the final stanza to read as follows:

> And the young soul gets strength
> For struggle and privations
> In the name of the great achievements
> Foretold by this star.[69]

A poem entitled "August" was subjected to more substantial revision. In its original version, the closing stanzas of the poem were:

> Companions, uncertainty does not threaten us.
> The time we longed for has come.
> But beyond the mountain the terrain changes.
> We have just descended from the mountain.
>
> We still live in a strange light.
> We still breathe out of rhythm with the plain.
> On the heights the vision sharpens,
> There we see both forward and back.
>
> And on familiar faces and objects,
> On the windless August day,
> The relentless shadow of the arduous mountain
> Lies quiet and inevitable.

Now the dawns are not so rosy,
The blue heaven not so bright——
The untroubled spark in the gaze is rarer,
Words are quieter, more guarded, and needed more.

We shall grow accustomed to this and love it.
We have, after all, only one life, a brief one.
—— A somber summer this year.
Among the small firs, a log house.[70]

Tregub disliked the poem and criticized it in the following terms:

There is depravity in the poetical allegory itself. Our path to communism, torn by the war, does not pass along a plain. It is also a path along mountain heights! Our ordinary days are glorious days in the calendar of history. The false central allegory gave birth to false colors, suggestions, intonations. Thus the light in which we live seems "strange" to the poetess. And we still breathe "out of rhythm" with the plain. Our postwar August day is quiet, windless. For whom? For whom have the dawn and the sky's blue paled? . . .[71]

And Tregub added that the first two lines of the final stanza "humiliate us." But Simonov defended the poem, claiming that Aliger had only meant to say that, although the war had ended, the feelings which it aroused remain: "They lie on our surroundings like the shadow of a great mountain. . . . This is a valid feeling. It exists in the soul of many of us who lived through the war. In a moment of terrible strain, the sight and feelings of many of us were sharpened, and for some they have remained so. And this is natural." [72] For the 1955 edition, Aliger modified the poem in various ways and omitted the two offending lines of the final stanza:

Companions, uncertainty does not threaten us.
The time we longed for has come.
Steeper is the road and wider the space.
We are high up, on the summit of the mountain.

We live in unceasing light,
We breathe deeply, not in rhythm with the plain.
On the height the vision sharpens,
The gaze is more intent and more exact.

And on familiar faces and objects,
On the windless August day,
The relentless shadow of the arduous mountain
Lies inevitable and stern.

Well, comrades, we shall pass through this as well,
Dispersing the shadow with persistent labor,

With a song sung by no one before,
With belief in the future, with a word of greeting ——

—— A somber summer this year.
Among small firs, a log house.[73]

Underlying the dispute over Aliger's poem was a certain disagreement as to how to understand the social and pedagogic tasks of poetry. Simonov touched upon the matter in his first reply to Tregub when he said: "You are wrong in saying these verses humiliate us. They do not humiliate me. They simply compel me to reflect on life. And perhaps in this lies one of the purposes of lyric poetry?" [74] Neither Simonov nor Zelinsky denied that poetry has an educative function, but both displayed a somewhat more generous understanding of what this should entail than did their critics. The main theme of Zelinsky's article was that self-revelation is the essence of lyric poetry, and his principal criticism of recent Soviet poetry was that it took its materials too much from the external world, rather than from the inner world of experience. After asserting that poetry is an "instrument which illuminates 'the secret of secrets' of the human soul," Zelinsky wrote:

Chekhov said that "sincerity is talent." This is even more true with respect to lyric poetry. To be a lyric poet, it is necessary to be exceedingly sincere before one's self . . . in order to be able, as Yesenin said, "to caress the souls of others with the blood of one's feelings," that people may, as Blok said, "find in the pale glow of art the destructive fire of life." This is talent.

There is realism and there is realism. The realism of lyric poetry is the most terrible realism, one which bares a person's innermost recesses and catches the soul in its contradictions and processes of becoming. This is, therefore, the most powerful realism. . . .[75]

But as if to ward off anticipated criticism, Zelinsky justified his views in terms of the official utilitarian attitude toward belles-lettres:

I by no means wish to say, in raising the slogan "freedom for one's own song," that the task of struggling with capitalist survivals does not exist for literature today. . . . Not at all. What I say does not take from literature its educative function. . . . But lyric poetry will fulfill its educative task only if it enriches, not impoverishes, the world of thoughts and feelings of the young Soviet reader.[76]

Because of the views expressed in this article, *Kultura i zhizn* called Zelinsky a "preacher of formalism," [77] and Fadeyev, writing in *Pravda*, characterized the article as "barely disguised agitation for nonpartyness in the worst sense of the word." [78] Another critic, V. Pertsov, asserted that Zelinsky's thesis was wrong because "it does not place before the poet any kind of social ideals," and he added, "What the party needs is a lyric poetry of struggle and great deeds, for our poetry, like all our literature, is party poetry." [79] As a consequence of the widespread criticism of his position, Zelinsky acknowledged his errors and revised his opinions. [80]

ZHDANOVISM: A SUMMING UP

Toward the end of 1947 and in 1948 there was evidence of growing dissatisfaction with the scant harvest that Zhdanovism had thus far produced. Discontent was manifested most strongly and openly with regard to the situation in dramaturgy. The Central Committee's decree of February 10, 1948, on Muradeli's opera *The Great Friendship* stimulated wider discussion of dramatic productions, and a flurry of criticism arose following the Council of Ministers' decision of March 4 to curtail state grants to theaters in an effort to make them economically self-sufficient. [81] The discussions, surveys, and articles that appeared after this event demonstrated that the council's decision was an outgrowth of concern about decreasing theater attendance and, ultimately, about the substandard repertory that had induced it. Writing in *Kultura i zhizn* a few days after the decision, Vladimir Prokofyev presented the themes basic to numerous other articles written during the spring and summer of 1948 on problems of the theater. [82] Prokofyev declared that the quantitative growth of Soviet dramaturgy had not been accompanied by a corresponding qualitative growth, and he complained that instead of meeting life in its complexity and fullness, "the spectator finds on the stage a scheme; instead of profound artistic thought, didactic discourse; instead of living Soviet people, conventionalized impersonations of virtues and vices." Prokofyev's analysis led to the conclusion: "The poor quality and monotony of repertory are among the serious reasons for the sharp decline in attendance and the fall of box-office returns in many theaters." A number of temporary retirements from dramaturgy, another negative result of postwar literary policies, aggravated the situation. At the Twelfth Plenum, A. Sofronov pointed out that many authors who had previously written for the stage had ceased doing so, and another speaker added that only fifty of the one hundred twenty Moscow dramatists were currently active.[83]

There was little improvement in the situation during the next few months. Theater managers and directors apparently took advantage of the relaxed control over repertory and the increased emphasis on attracting spectators to produce works of low ideological content. The editors of *Teatr* complained now that "the more significant" works of Soviet playwrights, those plays concerned with "vital contemporary problems," were being included in theaters' repertories far less frequently.[84] And some reviews of current productions indicated that, even when these ideologically significant plays were produced, speeches and dialogues carrying the burden of the "message" were occasionally cut. In its editorial, *Teatr* went on to say that the leading positions in repertory plans were now occupied "solely by light, undemanding comedies, melodrama, and the so-called 'semi-classic.' "[85] Later on objections were raised about the reappearance of plays by "Western bourgeois-liberal authors," plays which "have no ideological or artistic value for a Soviet audience."[86] Toward the end of November 1948, the Committee on Affairs of the Arts, the Commission on Dramaturgy of the Writers' Union, and the All-Union Theatrical Society (VTO) organized a conference on problems of the Soviet theater, and at the same time the drama critics of the VTO held a meeting. It appears that these conferences, at which opinions were expressed with a frankness not to be found in the ordinary journal article, were the immediate cause of the campaign initiated at the Twelfth Plenum. At any rate, Fadeyev based his initial charges against drama critics on stenographic reports of these meetings. In his speech at the Twelfth Plenum, Sofronov remarked candidly that the Writers' Union had raised the "special question" of dramaturgy because "the state of dramaturgy at the present time raises serious apprehensions."[87] The situation had become acute enough to stimulate drastic action, and the effects were to be felt far beyond the realm of the theater.

Sofronov's report on dramaturgy and Fadeyev's remarks on the same subject injected a sensational note into the proceedings of the mid-December meeting of the Twelfth Plenum with their sharply worded attacks on prominent drama critics guilty of promulgating "apolitical, provincial-aesthetic" literary theories. Reports of the plenum suggest that these accusations came as a surprise and did not meet with taciturn acceptance; but the accounts are too abbreviated to make clear the precise nature of the reaction. Later developments may explain the self-assured, blustering tone adopted by the accusers, particularly by Fadeyev. For in January 1949, both *Pravda* and *Kultura i zhizn* published editorials making basically the same points, and other newspapers and journals quickly followed their example. The consequence was a campaign in literature against "rootless cosmopolitans," a campaign replete with recantations, reprisals, and purges. Thus it may have been that Sofronov and Fadeyev spoke with the foreknowledge of higher party authorities, although there is some evidence that a decision was later taken to make the most of the charges which the two speakers had raised on their own initiative. The *Pravda* editorial of January 28 called the drama critics "antipatriotic" and "rootless cosmopolitans," terms which Fadeyev and Sofronov had not used, even though they had prepared the way for such charges. And several years later Fadeyev remarked about the campaign: "Although we still had not fully made out the true features of this opponent, we dealt him a blow at the Twelfth Plenum of the Writers' Union in 1948. Our party press taught us to understand this trend correctly as antipatriotic, and it exposed the connection of these people with the ideologists of cosmopolitanism in the West." [88]

It is an indication of the seriousness of the problem that every effort was made not merely to ferret out error but to prove the existence of a vicious plot among drama critics. In its editorial of January, *Pravda* accused certain drama critics of trying to create a "literary underground" to defame all the best in Soviet drama,[89] and before a month had passed this charge was substantiated. Reporting a Moscow meeting of playwrights and critics in February, *Literaturnaya gazeta* disclosed that the five alleged ringleaders at first denied that they constituted a "group," but, "Driven to the wall, they were forced to admit, though reluctantly and withholding things, the existence of a group, of collusion, of premeditated and coordinated action. In a statement handed to the presidium, Yu. Yuzovsky frankly admitted that the purpose was 'to inflict damage on Soviet dramaturgy from a lateral position.' " [90] Yuzovsky's "confession" is all the more remarkable because of his stubborn refusal to recant at the Twelfth Plenum.[91] This is only one of several indications that writers did not at first recognize the seriousness of Sofronov's and Fadeyev's outbursts at the plenum. At a Leningrad conference that preceded the Moscow meeting, the existence of an "antipatriotic" group in that city had been established,[92] and now I. Lukovsky announced that there had been organizational ties between the Leningrad and Moscow groups. "All this permitted A. Sofronov to state with complete justification," said the *Literaturnaya gazeta* report, "that the antipatriotic group of critics utilized the experience of the anti-Soviet underground." Presumably the editors of *Pravda*, among others, were now satisfied But more than one responsible editor or writer must have found himself in the curious position of V. Vishnevsky, who remarked at the Moscow meeting: "I edited the journal *Znamya* for four years and permitted the publication of articles by Borshchagovsky, Altman, Danin, and other cosmopolitans. I regret that I did not recognize their methods, the more so since they have aimed fire at my plays for two decades." [93] It had been a belated awakening for everyone.

The more specific charges and some of the supporting evidence marshaled against the critics are revealing in reasons for the discontent and resistance that were making themselves felt in the Soviet literary world. In addition, the charges brought against critics point to the party's real purposes, obscured somewhat by the surrounding tissue of lurid accusations, in pursuing the anticosmopolitan campaign in literature.

The Twelfth Plenum and the events immediately following it disclosed that the fundamental complaint, shared by those who were attacked with many who were not, was that values of art were being sacrificed to ideological and political demands. This was indicated at the plenum by various speakers in different ways, perhaps most concisely by A. Perventsev when he observed:

"There have taken root strange and preposterous theories to the effect that a political play of high ideological content cannot at the same time be artistic." [94] Party spokesmen were really pointing to the same basic discontent when they raised the cry, as it was later repeated by *Pravda*, that the cosmopolitan critics had tried "to discredit the outstanding products of our literature and art, fiercely pouncing upon patriotic, politically purposeful plays on the pretext of their alleged artistic imperfection." [95] The examples selected by party spokesmen to clinch the charges of antipatriotic sentiment and "aestheticism" only illustrate more fully the existing dissatisfaction with the regime's insistence on idealizing reality and reveal a widespread concern with the stifling effect this was having on literature. Some drama critics objected in particular to the excessive glorification of Soviet man, to the practice of portraying "positive" characters only in heroic dimensions, concentrating solely on their social awareness, devotion to duty, and inevitable success. Thus Fadeyev, quoting from an unpublished stenograph of a recent conference on drama, found it necessary to rebuke L. Malyugin for his assertion that the trouble with Soviet drama was that playwrights, while correctly attending to themes of work and social activity, "have stopped concerning themselves with a character's personal life," as if trying to conceal this aspect of a man's life.[96] The critic Yuzovsky had written in 1943 that the "philosophy" which asserts that because a figure is Soviet "he must without fail achieve victory" has nothing in common "with the dialectics of our life"; *Pravda* now used this against Yuzovsky, remarking that this attitude was "particularly outrageous" for having been written "after the great victory of the Soviet Army at Stalingrad." [97] Several leading literary bureaucrats were especially scandalized by a monograph on the Soviet actor Nikolai Khmelyov, written by Malyugin in 1948. One passage is particularly striking, for it reflects on more than postwar literary developments:

Khmelyov greedily reached out for an image of contemporary man; but the eternally cheerful, never-despairing heroes of many contemporary Soviet plays were alien to him, heroes to whom everything came easily — without struggle, without set-back, without suffering. . . . Khmelyov thus did not receive a role which would have demanded from him the art of *disclosure* and not only the art of *embellishment*.[98]

These were only some of the indications that "the style that says 'yes' to life" had led to an intolerable dullness in literature. Sofronov expressed his own realization that the postwar policy had reached extremes when, as he turned his attention to the defects of Soviet dramaturgy, he remarked: "There has even arisen a theory that conflict in our time can appear only in a clash of the excellent with the good." [99] This was a foreshadowing of the "no-conflict" campaign, which was one consequence of the stream of criticism unleashed at this time. Other writers and critics who turned their attention to poetry found that the situation there was little better than in drama or prose writing in general. Among them was the critic D. Danin, who in 1947 described Soviet poetry as "featureless" because of its cold and abstract character, its failure to show individuals in their fullness and depth.[100] For this and other articles discussing weaknesses of Soviet literature, Danin was later labeled an "antipatriotic cosmopolitan." The behavior at the Twelfth Plenum of Nikolai Pogodin, an experienced and respected playwright, is some indication of the depth of discontent and the strength of the reaction against current literary policies. *Literaturnaya gazeta* gives the following account:

> The majority of speakers at the plenum of the Writers' Union were imbued with the same thought: our writers must continually turn to life, study it, elaborate in their works the cardinal problems of contemporary life. Therefore the participants of the plenum censured the speech of N. Pogodin, who said that these appeals have already become obsolete, that it is worthless to offer such "recipes" to qualified writers. . . .[101]

The refusal of Pogodin, Yuzovsky, and others to recant at the Twelfth Plenum and the rebellious spirit which the sketchy newspaper accounts suggest may explain why *Pravda* and *Kultura i zhizn* jumped into the fray the next month.

Thus certain discontented writers pointed quite boldly to symptoms of a decline in Soviet letters, and their criticism implied that official prescriptions on content and method in literary works were a cause of the unsatisfactory state of affairs. Some writers even went beyond this, and in doing so they threatened to raise the whole question of the nature of the control system. Fadeyev's quotations from unpublished records of conferences held in November 1948 are revealing in this respect. Pogodin was ap-

parently among the most outspoken, and some of his remarks are
worth quoting at length. It is not too difficult, perhaps, to understand why the following observation incensed Fadeyev:

For some time, in my opinion, . . . anemia developed in the theaters. It
seems to me that it appeared after the war. The causes, as I see them, . . .
at least so far as the theater and the playwright were concerned . . . lay
in the constraints and commands that arose with respect to this or that
work for the theater, phenomena which had a pernicious effect on theatrical
art and the growth of dramaturgy.[102]

Moreover, Pogodin's illustration regarding the Moscow Art Theater and its director, Surov, pointed to rather unpleasant aspects
of the impingement of politics and bureaucracy on the theatrical
world. Pogodin queried about the people of the Art Theater:

  How do they reason? . . . "Surov is in the thick of things now; Surov
. . . he's a party man, he obviously knows what's what, and that means this
is a sure thing. Let's produce it." This is how things actually happen. And
you ask: What are you producing? . . . "We don't know ourselves."
  Plays are written to order for us, but in general they are difficult to
produce. This is the result of irresponsibility, of a cynical indifference that
has already established itself.[103]

Fadeyev also disclosed that Pogodin had lamented the "leveling
down" that had occurred in the theatrical world, complained that
all theaters had become alike, and looked back with some nostalgia
to the twenties, when there was much greater variety in Moscow's
theatrical life. This attitude, in one form or another, appears to
have been rather widespread. It was enough in evidence, at least,
to draw from Perventsev the comment, "the hucksters of dramaturgy began to raise a fuss and announced the birth of a kind of
'theatrical NEP.' "[104] Probably the March decree of the Council
of Ministers, the increasing concern with box-office returns, and
the relaxation of controls over repertory selection had raised hopes
of greater freedom for the theaters.
  The effort to prove the existence of a plot could not have been
very convincing to anyone who had followed the work of the
accused men. The conspiracy charges were in part an effort to find
scapegoats for an admittedly unsatisfactory situation, and the
"cosmopolitan" label linked the difficulty to international politics
and the theme of capitalist hostility. Thus Simonov reminded the

Soviet public that cosmopolitanism in art is "the effort to demolish national roots and national pride, for it is easier to move rootless people from their place and sell them in servitude to American imperialism." [105] The practice of citing questionable passages from works written as much as twenty years earlier hardly demonstrated the persistence of a conspiracy. These citations were often misinterpreted, and in some instances critics were censured for views which, at the time of writing, were quite orthodox. On the contrary, these efforts revealed something quite different — a continuing and genuine concern on the part of the accused with the fate of Soviet letters and, as perusal of their earlier articles indicates, an expressed sympathy with the ultimate purposes of the regime both in literature and politics. It is true that the events of 1948 uncovered a degree of discontent that may have looked like opposition to the party. But if there was a kind of literary opposition, it certainly was not an anti-Soviet plot, and it does not even appear to have been a self-conscious opposition. It was much more likely the consequence of a real interest in aesthetic values and a miscalculation about the existing limits of "criticism and self-criticism." One of the charges against the critics was that they found fault with officially approved plays — plays "approved by the Soviet people," as the press normally phrases it — and praised lesser-known plays. For this they were accused of slandering Soviet dramaturgy from a standpoint of "aestheticism." Their articles, it is true, were signals of discontent with the prevailing type of Soviet play, and their interest in plays of lesser ideological content suggests greater devotion to the theater than to politics. But it will be noted that the charge was a stark contradiction of the lesson of the Fadeyev incident — that any work, no matter who its author or what its value, could and should be criticized. Taking all into account, the "cosmopolitans" had ample cause to reflect ruefully, in the manner of Daniil Granin's Krivitsky, that "it is better to keep silent than to speak, and better to speak than to write." [106]

The actual motivation of the party's attack on the "cosmopolitan critics" was not that the critics had been mistaken in their analysis of the situation in literature (the party press had already pointed to this), or that they should not have expressed at least some of their views. It was, rather, that they had carried their analysis beyond the limits which the party regarded as proper. Objections that literary representations of Soviet people were not true to life and complaints about stereotypes and dullness threatened to become attacks on the content of the postwar literary line, on the interpretation of reality and application of socialist realism, through the implication that current political and ideological demands were incompatible with high artistic standards. More than that, some writers pointed to the method of enforcing the line, to bureaucratic controls as such, as a basic fault. Together, these tendencies suggested the heresy of antipartiinost in literature. The point is strengthened by the fact that the party, as it set out to cope with the situation in belles-lettres, itself adopted many of the cosmopolitan critics' views, only with a difference. This became clearer later on, though more than a hint of it was made at the Twelfth Plenum. For Sofronov in his report repeated many of the criticisms that the cosmopolitans had already raised, although he tried to place on their shoulders responsibility for the defects he described, and his fundamental points were embodied in the resolution of the Twelfth Plenum.[107] The difference was that the party's literary spokesmen would, after certain refinements of party policy, find the cause of remaining defects not in the policies themselves or in the existence of a control system, but rather in the failure of writers to adhere to the standards set by the party and in the shortcomings of those responsible for making the system work. But the cosmopolitan critics had been the first to direct attention to weaknesses in belles-lettres that would increasingly concern the party during the coming years, and in doing so they added to the growing evidence that Zhdanovism set in motion forces that were defeating its own purposes. For this reason, if nothing more, the discontent articulated by the much-abused critics and by other elements of the literary community was among the factors which led to a readjustment in the party's literary line.

Another factor, anti-Semitism, played a role in the anticosmopolitan campaign. Though little was said about this openly, it was indicated by the unusual practice of printing in parentheses the real names of critics who had adopted pseudonyms, thus disclosing the Jewish origins of some of those under attack. Only in the case of Pavel Antokolsky does there appear to have been any sort of open reference to the matter: in a report to a gathering of Moscow poets, M. Lukonin claimed that a cycle of Antokolsky's poems was "permeated with sentiments of Zionism, of bourgeois nationalism." [108] Because the anticosmopolitan campaign coincided with a severe attack on Jewish cultural institutions generally, Western writers have sometimes tended to identify the two and regard the whole anticosmopolitan campaign as a manifestation of anti-Semitism. In literature, anti-Semitism played a secondary role in a campaign whose ultimate significance is quite different. Not all writers and critics brought under fire were Jewish, after all, though in individual cases Jewish background may have been more significant as a cause for attack than anything the writer had said or written. But in general the regime played on anti-Jewish feeling to drum up support for its accusations, and it may have been that the suggestion of Zionism helped to strengthen the absurd charges of a literary underground linked to international political forces.

The immediate consequences of the campaign, if familiar in form, were unusually severe for a number of writers. Many Jewish writers — the victims of the campaign against the Jewish community as a whole rather more than of the anti-cosmopolitan drive in literature — were imprisoned, and some were executed.[109] Other writers disappeared for years from the literary scene, and only after Stalin's death did their names reappear on the pages of Soviet publications. Yet, as noted earlier, there were many indications that the importance of the charges initially raised at the Twelfth Plenum was underestimated by many of the participants. It is somewhat curious that A. Kron, whose work as head of the drama commission was severely criticized at the plenum, and Ye. Kholodov and I. Altman, both alleged members of the antipatriotic group, were appointed to the new drama commission, though Sofronov replaced Kron as chairman.[110] But they served unusually short terms, for a March listing of the members of the commission showed that they had been dropped.[111] There were several references in the press, following the Twelfth Plenum, to critics' self-defenses and refusals to confess. Before long, however, reports of recantations began to appear. It was noted above, for whatever it is worth, that Yuzovsky was said to have confessed his own sins as well as those of his colleagues, Malyugin, Boyadzhiyev, Varshav-

sky, and Shtain. In the February issue of *Znamya*, Sofronov, recalling that Pogodin's reaction to criticism at the Twelfth Plenum
left something to be desired, noted with satisfaction that participants in the first session of the new drama commission "heard a
fervent, deeply felt speech of Pogodin, in which he honorably
acknowledged the error of his views and condemned his mistakes." [112] Various penalties were imposed on those who bore the
main brunt of attack. Brovman, Levin, and Antokolsky, for example, lost their positions at the Literary Institute of the Writers'
Union, and Lev Subotsky was relieved of his post as a secretary of
the union. Altman and Levin were expelled from the party, and
Danin was deprived of his standing as a candidate member of the
party.[113] The list might be extended considerably to demonstrate
that the immediate consequence of the tempest unleashed at the
Twelfth Plenum was a veritable purge in the literary world.

ZHDANOVISM REVISITED

During the latter part of 1949 and early in 1950 there was
mounting evidence of an effort to soften certain aspects of the
postwar literary line, and at times it even appeared that a significant revision of the policies enunciated by Zhdanov might ensue.
The first strong hint of this came with attacks on two plays that
had received favorable recognition. The attacks were in accordance
with the custom in Soviet literary politics of consecrating a symbolic offering to a new policy trend in order to dramatize the
emergence of the trend and to give writers direction. The two
sacrifices in this case were A. Sofronov's *Beketov's Career* and
V. Kozhevnikov's *River of Fire*, both topical plays on industrial
themes.[114] Sofronov's play had received first prize in a union contest for the best comedy of the year, and Kozhevnikov's work had
been reviewed favorably by *Literaturnaya gazeta* and *Komsomolskaya pravda*. The Committee on Affairs of the Arts had recommended both for production. In each case, *Kultura i zhizn* initiated
the attack and *Pravda* added its support within several days.[115]
Other publications thereupon revised their previous opinions, and
the editors of *Novy mir* acknowledged their error in publishing the
works. The party criticism of the plays' contents revealed com-

mon complaints: both plays failed to portray the party organization properly, and both neglected to represent the high moral and social consciousness of Soviet people, the cohesiveness and awareness of the factory collective which makes inevitable the exposure and defeat of "negative elements." But what was remarkable about the attacks — and this was their real significance — was the emphasis they gave to dramatic and literary considerations. In addition to the usual charge of "ignorance of life," the *Pravda* article on Kozhevnikov's play, for example, paid considerable attention to evidence of "haste," "negligence in work on the material," and disregard for "the laws of the genre of drama." Both plays were built on the same pattern as a whole series of other "industrial plays," and in issuing these charges the party was really raising a question about all of these.

It became increasingly clear during the following weeks that a primary purpose of the attacks on the two plays was to draw greater attention to artistic considerations in literary works. Party leaders had become more sensitive to the adverse effects of Zhdanovism's exaggerated emphasis on political elements, effects that countered the regime's pragmatic interest in literature. Nikolai Gribachev put his finger on the party's problem when, after complaining that Soviet critics had reduced evaluation of a literary work to "eulogies of its content, completely ignoring questions of artistic form," he added that "without artistic form there cannot be profound ideological content." [116] In a manner somewhat reminiscent of Stalin's partial adoption of the program of the Left Opposition after its elimination, the literary bureaucrats hoisted standards captured from "antipatriotic cosmopolitans," although the cosmopolitan purge continued. When Fadeyev addressed a party meeting at the Writers' Union, a meeting devoted to the *Kultura i zhizn* and *Pravda* articles on the plays of Sofronov and Kozhevnikov, he gave indirect support to this interpretation while endeavoring to deny it:

Some writers and critics are now expressing the opinion that questions of raising the artistic quality of works of literature seemed to arise after the exposure of the antipatriotic group of drama critics and the rout of groups of rootless cosmopolitans in our literary environment. Such a view implies an assumption to the effect that in the past the privilege of raising such questions belonged to the rootless cosmopolitans.[117]

And party members of the union heard Fadeyev urge editors not to publish critical articles which "throw out general phrases about the content of a work but do not say a word about how this content was embodied in artistic form." [118] Literary critics were being warned that the interpretation of the postwar literary line had been one-sided, the tenets applied too rigorously.

The Thirteenth Plenum represented a continuation of the effort to deal with some of the less desirable consequences of Zhdanovism. Although some sharp words were exchanged at the sessions, this plenum was remarkable for its restraint, as compared with the twelfth, and even more by the sober concern of some speakers about the current situation in literature. Fadeyev in particular showed an awareness of the need to breathe new life into literary activities and to eliminate the paralysis that had developed among critics during the vigorous anticosmopolitan campaign. He noted in his report that the campaign "bore a rather fierce character" and, it is true, added that "the homeless cosmopolitans must not assume that this was just a passing campaign." [119] But when Fadeyev turned to the question of literary critics' neglect of aesthetic problems, he asserted: "We need not fear, now that we have inflicted such a crushing blow on the formalist school — we need not fear that we Marxists will not be able to solve the problem of form or that a critic who works in these problems will be accused of formalism." It is hardly surprising that Soviet literary critics, with the fate of the cosmopolitans fresh in their minds, displayed great care in their writings, particularly when they touched on problems of artistic quality and form. But it was precisely the problem of quality to which the party was now devoting increased attention, and Fadeyev was saying, in effect, that the extremes of the anticosmopolitan drive had come to an end and that the crime of aestheticism, as an aspect of antipatriotic activity, would no longer be so quickly raised or easily proved. Later in the year, *Literaturnaya gazeta*, editorializing on problems of dramaturgy, touched upon one aspect of the problem that Fadeyev was dealing with at the Thirteenth Plenum: "Some critics even now feel an unworthy fear before authorities; they are afraid that someone (who?!) might accuse them of making 'attacks' on leading Soviet playwrights." [120] This very accusation had, of course, been one of the major counts against the cosmopolitans.

Fadeyev's concluding speech at the plenum was an impressive plea for hard and serious work on the part of writers, particularly young writers, and a warning against complacency and self-satisfaction. As such, it revealed perhaps more clearly than anything else the widespread concern with the quality of current literary production. Fadeyev complained that young writers "have no enthusiasm for study," and he repeated several times that it is necessary "to study and to study," that it is not enough just to "know life" but that writers must also make themselves familiar with the achievements and traditions of the past.[121] Actually, his remarks were an assault on what was once widely known as *komchvanstvo*, or "Communist conceit." When the critic A. Belik expressed his views, later developed in an article in *Oktyabr*, Fadeyev cautioned the audience against accepting certain of his remarks, though Fadeyev's rebuke was far more restrained than *Pravda*'s later criticism of Belik. Fadeyev observed that Belik was correct in saying that socialist realism is the most revolutionary method in literature and that it had "created a revolution in art." But he asserted that Belik was wrong in slighting the classics, adding, "Comrade Belik forgets that one may write badly with the most revolutionary method, if one does not study and does not work hard at one's task." In their dual purpose of breaking through the heightened sense of constraint that resulted from the cosmopolitan drive and of directing greater attention to problems of literary quality, speakers at the plenum stressed another theme — the harmfulness of merely destructive, "blackjack" criticism. Fadeyev's comment on Yermilov's methods was typical. When Yermilov criticizes, Fadeyev asserted, it is his aim "not to correct the mistakes of a writer, but to annihilate him as an 'opponent.'" The same point was involved in the later attack on Belik.

Pravda's criticism of Belik pointed even more unmistakably to a new tendency in literary policies, and its significance was enhanced by Stalin's letter on linguistics, which appeared three months later. The violence of the attack on this relatively unknown critic can be properly explained only against the background of the

Thirteenth Plenum. Belik's article, published in February 1950, was a long and dogmatic presentation of ultraorthodox views, based largely on Zhdanov's criticisms of G. Aleksandrov's book on Western philosophy.[122] Belik's theory of partiinost in literature, his views on the distinctiveness of Russian culture from that of the West, and his remarks on the uniqueness of Soviet literature as contrasted with classical Russian literature are an indication of the extremes to which Zhdanovism had progressed by 1950, at least among some segments of the literary world. Belik was actually attacked for being *plus royaliste que le roi même*. Belik committed his basic error when, in criticizing A. Tarasenkov's *Ideas and Images of Soviet Literature*, he presented his own definition of socialist realism. Belik rebuked Tarasenkov for viewing partiinost as only one condition rather than as "the basic law" of socialist realism, and he went on to say that socialist realism is "the party method of creativity, i.e., a specific form of the cognition and transformation of reality." [123] Furthermore, Belik objected to Tarasenkov's broad understanding of socialist realism, one that admits of diverse literary styles within the larger method. Quite reasonably, it would seem, Belik argued that if socialist realism is "the only correct and the ruling method of socialist literature, then there must necessarily exist manners and means of expression, laws of composition, of plot, of creating images, etc., which correspond to this method." [124] Because of these assertions, *Pravda* accused Belik of supplanting the "correct and profound definition" of socialist realism contained in the statutes of the Writers' Union "with confused and contrived judgments, with his own home-made definitions, while ignoring the basic requirement of socialist realism: that it be true to life." [125] *Literaturnaya gazeta* revealed the source of irritation more directly when it noted that Belik had replaced the "broad concept" of socialist realism with the notion of a "party method," which Belik had, according to the newspaper, fabricated himself.[126] Belik had based part of his argument on the rarely quoted phrase from Lenin's "Party Organization and Party Literature": "writers must without fail join party organizations." Now, for the first time, attention was directed to the historical context of Lenin's article. *Pravda* referred to the "moral and political unity of Soviet society" that socialism had produced, remarked that it is "unjustifiable and harmful to contrast party writers to nonparty writers," and accused Belik of trying to revive "the sectarian views of the RAPP-ists" which the party had long ago condemned. Other objections raised against the Belik article were significant in terms of current developments in literature and criticism. For example, it had not been enough for Belik that Tarasenkov declared Soviet literature "a step forward in the artistic development of mankind"; Belik wrote that Tarasenkov does not understand that it is "not a step and not a stage, but a new epoch." *Pravda* showered scorn on him for that remark and condemned the general tone of the article. "One cannot create a socialist art," warned *Pravda*, "by outcries and blackjack criticism." Due notice was taken of Belik's tendentious quoting out of context and his calculated omissions and distortions, all of which have been standard practice in Soviet criticism.

It is evident that one reason for the sharp rebuke that Belik received was that in his theoretical formulations Belik touched on aspects of the party's literary policies which party leaders did not wish to have discussed quite so frankly. Indeed, Gleb Struve has written that Belik's real crime "consisted in revealing, wittingly or unwittingly, the fact that the king was naked, by openly equating Socialist Realism with the current Party line." [127] Though correct so far as it goes, this interpretation does not elucidate the broader significance of the episode. For in these terms, it is curious that two earlier articles which Belik wrote in collaboration with others and which express essentially the same views passed virtually unnoticed.[128] Further, what Belik had to say on the question of socialist realism and partiinost was essentially the same as what almost everyone else had been saying since the end of the war. Belik, however, had presented an extreme, if logical, formulation of the theory of partiinost, and his blustering tone made the article a particularly suitable target. It should be observed as well that Belik's speech at the Thirteenth Plenum, according to a later report, contained exactly the same assertions as did his article; yet it called forth no response from the plenum's participants, save for Fadeyev's comparatively mild reproach.[129] It seems reasonable to assume that participants in the plenum's proceedings regarded Belik's remarks as an orthodox interpretation of the party line. If one of his errors had been to expose the real meaning, or essential meaninglessness, of socialist realism, another had been to affirm unashamedly the existence of rigid party control over all writers. As the *Pravda* article put it: "The neo-RAPP-ist Belik mechanically applies innerparty conceptions to the field of literature." One of the fundamentals of Stalinist totalitarianism is that the distinction between those belonging to the party and those who do not has lost meaning and that there has developed a solid Communist and nonparty "bloc." The dissolution of independent literary groups in 1932 and the creation of the Writers' Union was officially declared to be an expression of that. What the event represented in fact was precisely the extension of "innerparty" concepts, demands, and controls to include all writers and the entire field of literature. To say this openly would have been risky at any time. But it was particularly undesirable during a period when the party was coping with manifestations of discontent within the ranks of literature. While the party's spokesmen were attempting to mitigate the dissatisfaction, Belik's formulations would only put writers, particularly nonparty writers, even more on guard. More generally, Belik's whole article was attuned to the pitch that prevailed during the height of the anticosmopolitan campaign, and the party was now attempting to reduce somewhat the tension that threatened to produce paralysis and stagnation in literary affairs.

Certain passages from Stalin's first letter on linguistics and their consequent interpretation reinforce the view that it was not so much what Belik said as when he said it that explains the outburst. In one section of his essay, Stalin made an appeal for freer discussion in the sciences that at once seemed to extend to other realms of intellectual endeavor and to be something more than a reiteration of the demand for more "criticism and self-criticism." At least his description of the situation in linguistics as an "Arakcheyev-like regime," his strictures on a "self-contained group of infallible leaders . . . which has begun to ride rough-shod and behave in a most arbitrary manner," and his assertion that "no science can develop and flourish without a struggle of opinions" could be interpreted as the signal for a change of climate in the realm of Soviet culture.[130] References during following months to the Belik incident and to Stalin's efforts in linguistics revealed that writers, critics, and scholars had understood both events in this way. It became customary to cite appropriate passages from Stalin's essay when approaching sensitive areas of literary theory and practice or when directing criticism toward persons holding seemingly secure positions in the literary hierarchy.

The period extending from the linguistics pronouncements to Stalin's death witnessed a certain moderation of the stringency in cultural affairs that had reached a peak of intensity in 1949. At the same time, there was abundant evidence that the basic principles of Zhdanovism had undergone no significant revision. The tendencies that had suggested a possible relaxation or even a meaningful change found their ultimate embodiment in the campaign against "no-conflict" drama in 1952. This campaign, together with leading articles in party publications and the documents of the Nineteenth Party Congress, indicated the extent of the "change" that had occurred in the party's literary policies.

During this period, writers and critics, including the party's spokesmen in literary affairs, appeared almost eager to discuss the shortcomings of Soviet literature. It is perhaps not surprising that the complaints raised were strikingly reminiscent of those voiced earlier by the cosmopolitan critics. The phrase "dullness and dreary imitativeness prevail" flowed easily from the pens of those who turned their attention to the darker aspects of the situation in the arts. Schematism, repetition of one and the same theme, overemphasis on social and political problems to the exclusion of human relationships, exaggerated didacticism, and low literary standards were cited among the main faults of current writing. No less a journal than *Bolshevik* provided space for A. Surkov to criticize writers who remove from their characters' sphere of interests "everything or almost everything that does not relate directly to productive activities." [131] Others were more outspoken than Surkov in complaining that dullness frequently stemmed from overemphasis on labor and technology and neglect of human emotions. V. Komissarzhevsky noted that many playwrights were bashful about showing love on the stage — that when it comes to a love scene, playwrights and actors consider it good form to be "restrained" and "inarticulate" to the point of incomprehensibility; but when it comes to technology, "all the heroes become unbelievably loquacious and eagerly deliver whole scientific-technical lectures to each other." [132] Yet at the Twelfth Plenum Fadeyev had rebuked the antipatriotic critic Malyugin for making a similar point.

There was great concern over the situation in dramaturgy, where a basic fault was repeatedly said to be "the use of stale, boring conflicts, familiar to the audience from beginning to end." [133] In various articles on the theater, Soviet actors, too, revealed a discontent very similar to that which Malyugin had ascribed to Khmelyov, for they complained that roles in contemporary plays did not provide material adequate to their talents. The campaign against the no-conflict theory in drama was in part an effort to remedy the situation. But, characteristically, the first expedient adopted was to cast blame on the agencies which supervised theatrical productions. The primary significance of the attack on G. Zhukovsky's opera *With All One's Heart* was the resulting shake-up in cultural organizations, particularly the Committee on Affairs of the Arts. Zhukovsky had already been awarded a Stalin Prize, First Class, for the opera when *Pravda* opened a violent attack on the work.[134] As a result of the outburst, the chairman of the Arts Committee was dismissed, the director of the Bolshoi Theater relieved of his post, and the Stalin Prize revoked. A flurry of meetings resulted, in which the Union of Soviet Composers, the Writers' Union, and the Arts Committee became targets for attack. Now Pogodin could repeat, though in milder form, the complaint about the deadening effects of bureaucratic control for which he had been rebuked at the Twelfth Plenum.[135]

Statements made at a conference on poetry in January 1953 were testimony of the suffering poets had endured during the party's postwar effort to wipe out traces of individualism from Soviet letters. Particularly noteworthy were Margarita Aliger's and Olga Berggolts' pleas against restraint of self-expression in lyric poetry. Commenting on the conference, *Literaturnaya gazeta* defended Berggolts against others who, it reported, discerned in her words a "hidden danger of individualism, egocentricity, subjectivism," and who believed the lyric poet must not "reveal himself" because a poet is "only a trumpet of the times." [136] This defense seemed a step in the direction of Zelinsky's theory of poetic self-revelation, condemned in 1947. When Olga Berggolts reproached poets for "forgetting themselves" and for "fear of expressing all the complexity, the unrepeatable uniqueness of a lyric character," she might aptly have cited the "cosmopolitan" Danin's article "We Want To See His Face," condemned at the Twelfth Plenum. Similarly, *Literaturnaya gazeta* itself had apparently adopted Yuzovsky's ill-starred criticism of the "inevitable victory" theory or borrowed a page from Malyugin's essay on Khmelyov; for in its report of the conference, it commented unfavorably on those who demand that the lyric poet "be always uniformly cheerful, invariably gay" and who immediately dub the slightest meditation or reflection "pessimism."

The reaction of various groups of intellectuals to Stalin's linguistics letters indicated that they interpreted the appearance of the letters as a sign that more generous attitudes might be adopted toward certain questions of theory and practice. The manner in which their efforts were held in check quickly marked the narrow limits of the relaxation. Stalin's denial that language belongs either to the "base" or to the "superstructure" provided an occasion for raising questions about the relation of art to these categories. When the question of aesthetics arose at one of the first philosophers' discussions of the linguistics letters, P. S. Trofimov contributed to a developing controversy with the argument that phenomena related to art are "complex and many-sided," that "art has in it something that can be called a nonsuperstructural element," and that it has aspects that "extend far beyond the limits of what we understand as 'superstructure.'"[137] Trofimov defended the materialist approach to aesthetics, however, and denied that his view meant that aesthetic values exist independently of content "as something eternal and unchangeable." What Trofimov's position could imply is best seen by placing it alongside Stalin's forceful reiteration of the traditional theoretical justification for demanding tendentious literature:

The superstructure is generated by the base, but this by no means signifies that it merely reflects the base, that it is passive, neutral and indifferent to the fate of its base, to the fate of classes, to the character of the system. On the contrary, having put in an appearance, it then becomes a most active force which contributes vigorously to the formation and consolidation of its base, takes all steps to assist the new order to drive the old base and the former classes into the dust and liquidate them.[138]

Stalin listed among components of the superstructure: "political, legal, religious, artistic, and philosophical views of society and their corresponding . . . institutions." Yet this statement did not preclude the argument that whereas "artistic views," aesthetics, and theories of art belong to the superstructure, art itself is superstructural only insofar as it embodies artistic, political, and other views, and that art in general is a "form of social consciousness" broader than the superstructure. This was roughly the position taken by Trofimov, Maseyev, and a few others.[139] It is significant that at a meeting of scholars in May 1951, R. V. Konstantinov, who shared Trofimov's views on aesthetics, objected to "an unqualified acceptance" of the term *partiinost* in literature and suggested substituting "Communist ideinost" or "Soviet patriotism." [140] Academician V. Vinogradov's address at the same meeting also contained some noteworthy passages. He warned against "ascribing belleslettres to the superstructure in general" without taking account of their specific characteristics, cited Engels on the danger of overemphasizing the content of literature and relegating questions of artistic form to the level of other social phenomena, and, finally, cited a rarely quoted passage from Marx — Marx's eloquent and impassioned defense of individual expression against the restrictions of Prussian censorship.[141] Those persons who argued for a broader interpretation of the place of art in society were not leading an open revolt against claims involving the necessary political involvement of art, nor did Stalin's formulations leave much room for maneuvering in this respect. Stalin had declared: "that which is inherent in all social phenomena, base and superstructure among them, is characteristic of language as a social phenomenon, namely: it serves society just as all other social phenomena serve it, base and superstructure included." [142] But Trofimov and the others, while paying ample tribute to the principle of partiinost, seemed to be endeavoring to win the acceptance of a less restrictive attitude toward the nature of the political functions of art, one that would justify giving greater attention to aesthetic values as such. The staunch defenders of party orthodoxy would have none of this, however. At the May meeting, both Yegolin, a party spokesman in cultural matters, and Yermilov, who always strives to adhere closely to the party line, criticized Trofimov's position. Accusing Trofimov and

Konstantinov of attributing to art characteristics that Stalin ascribed only to language, Yermilov made clear his real concern when he asserted that "the denial and slurring over of the definition of art as an ideological superstructure leads to a denial of the principle of Bolshevist partiinost, for at the basis of both of these distortions of the theory of socialist realism lies the denial of the social activeness of art." [143] The discussion continued spasmodically in the pages of *Voprosy filosofii* until April 1952. In the final issue for that year, the editors of the journal located art squarely in the superstructure and rejected the views of Trofimov, Maseyev, and the others, essentially on the grounds that Yermilov had stated so concisely.[144]

Stalin's strictures against Marr's rejection of comparative analysis in linguistics also provided an occasion for raising again the question of comparative methods in literary scholarship. While rejecting Veselovsky, G. S. Tikhomirov, for example, complained that the anticomparativist campaign had led to the undesirable extreme of rejecting comparative methods altogether, that "the very word 'influence' in critical literature has become the object of particularly harsh unpleasantness." [145] Tikhomirov's article, together with a pamphlet by A. I. Geletsky containing similar views, was attacked by the critic B. Ryurikov, who had also joined in the criticism of Trofimov.[146]

It is remarkable that the party, contrary to its usual practice, did not interfere in these controversies by issuing decrees or running editorials in *Pravda* or *Bolshevik*. It appears that party leaders were at this point pursuing a hands-off policy, relying on party stalwarts in various fields to keep things under control. This device made it possible for the "softening" signaled by the linguistic letters to spread gradually, without sensations and excesses.

Even though there was no apparent "external" pressure in certain significant controversies, the pull of the more orthodox against those pushing for a broadening of views was indicative of the larger trend of developments. There were other signs, from more authoritative sources, of the limits being drawn. Not long after Stalin's interference in the linguistics controversy, the party's four decrees on cultural matters were published in pamphlet form, as if to reinforce the point that they remained standard texts. *Pravda*'s attack in July 1951 on V. Sosyura's poem "Love the Ukraine" marked the beginning of an intensified campaign against manifestations of "bourgeois nationalism" within the various nationality groups of the USSR.[147] *Bolshevik* carefully linked this to an earlier campaign with the comment, "Cosmopolitanism is one of the forms of bourgeois nationalism." [148] When one of the most abused cosmopolitan critics, A. Gurvich, made a reappearance with a long article, "The Power of Positive Example," he was welcomed with a roar of outrage wholly disproportionate to the "errors" contained in his work.[149] It appears that the article had been handled with great care, for it was submitted to both Fadeyev and Surkov for approval before publication.[150] But a *Pravda* editorial accused Gurvich of slandering Russian and Soviet literature and of promulgating idealist aesthetics, though the charges here, and as repeated elsewhere, were strained and based on distorted evidence.[151] In his article, Gurvich pointed out that classical Russian literature is not rich in "positive" characters, and he unfortunately used the phrase "an unknown quantity" in referring to the "potentialities of the human spirit." On the latter point, Gurvich's mood and perspective were, at worst, reminiscent of Gorky's enraptured flights of humanitarian fancy or of Marx's utopian vision in *The German Ideology*. There seemed to be little in Gurvich's essay to violate the sensitivities even of the strictly orthodox. Whatever the motivation of the attack, it was another reminder that, if the cosmopolitan campaign had slowed down, it had not terminated. Because Gurvich had been thoroughly reviled before, he provided suitable material for making the point clearly and effectively.

The campaign against the no-conflict theory was the major product of Zhdanovism after the linguistics pronouncements, and the manner in which it arose and the character it assumed provided final proof that the "relaxation" in Soviet cultural life was being carefully restrained. An early document in the developing drive was *Literaturnaya gazeta*'s editorial, "Overcome the Lag in Dramaturgy." [152] One of the more significant passages from the editorial states:

The dogmatic demands of the critics often result in the fact that the portrayal of negative phenomena in our life should allegedly "not be permitted" in dramaturgy. "This does not happen," "this is not typical," "this is a distortion of life" assert the dogmatic critics here, there, and everywhere when they see in a drama a figure morally alien to us. And why? After all, these negative phenomena exist in real life. . . .

In addition to the remarks on negative phenomena, a noteworthy aspect of the editorial is that, in contrast to later practice, instead of placing the responsibility on writers' shoulders, it blamed critics and "certain officials" of the Arts Committee who "have established a close, restrictive framework for playwrights." In another passage it spoke of "the view *foisted on playwrights* that negative phenomena on the stage will necessarily be a distortion of reality." [153]

The next link in the chain of events was Anatoly Surov's rejection of Nikolai Virta's view, presented in an article written before *Literaturnaya gazeta*'s editorial appeared, that "apparently there is no longer any visible, vivid conflict, any clash of forces and concepts in life" and that plays would have to be built on "misunderstandings" rather than on complex dramatic clashes. [154] In his reply to Surov, Virta confessed his error, but the explanation of how he had reached such conclusions became an indictment of the controls imposed on playwrights. [155] In taking this tack, Virta had for support the authority of the *Literaturnaya gazeta* editorial and the example of the incident involving Zhukovsky's opera. Virta said that the theory of conflictless drama arose among playwrights after sober reflection "on the manner in which those of our plays which contain sharp life conflicts passed through the barbed-wire obstacles of the agencies in charge of repertory," where "everything living, true to life, sharp, fresh, and unstereotyped was combed out." He cited the history of his play *Our Daily Bread* as a case in point in a passage which conveys some sense of the writer's feeling toward the obstacles he faces:

The play was put on the stage long ago; its career in the theater was not an unhappy one, but no one knows what agonies the author of the play had to go through before it finally saw the footlights. It is hard to describe the tempestuous attack of some of the members of the (Arts) Committee when this "slander against the collective farms" reached their hands. The Committee "sessions" were not a very dignified spectacle — those sessions at which people who not an hour before had maintained that the play was "real" . . . stood on their heads when they found themselves face to face with the enraged Committee leadership, and started to berate the play so strongly that the author was left to ask himself the question: "Perhaps I really am a slanderer and deserve even worse than this horrible panning? . . ."

This lack of principle and dread "lest something come of it" if a play is approved could and did destroy many works of drama which deserved a better fate.[156]

Now dubbing his no-conflict theory "stupid and spurious," Virta proceeded to suggest that the conditions he had described were the cause of the prolonged silence of many playwrights who could not write the "dull, smooth little plays" in demand. Virta's *cri de coeur* was greeted with rejoicing by the poet Ilya Selvinsky, who exclaimed, "Yet all these torments of the playwrights are as roses and forget-me-nots by comparison with the thorns which have been the lot of the poet if he had the boldness to put his muse on the stage." [157]

On April 7, 1952, *Pravda* contributed the major document of the no-conflict campaign, in the form of a lead article.[158] The article is significant not only for the impetus but also for the calculated twist it gave to the developing campaign. For it marked an effort to curb excessive criticism of bureaucratic controls, to turn complaints such as Virta's back on their source, and in general to hold the currents of criticism in the proper channels. The editorial said that in seeking causes for the lag in dramaturgy the "weak guidance" of the Arts Committee and the Writers' Union must be noted, but that "the chief, decisive reason is the playwrights' and critics' misreading of certain questions of the theory and practice of socialist realism, particularly the question of conflict as the basis of drama." And it mentioned unfavorably the articles of Virta and Selvinsky. This aspect of the *Pravda* editorial was elaborated the following day by Surkov, who accused Virta of trying to justify himself by "representing the matter as though it was not he himself who got confused but 'chinovniki' [bureaucratic officials] who confused, disoriented and all but hounded him," which, said Surkov, "is to take the wrong line." And, he continued, "the absurd references to 'chinovniki' as the principal and well-nigh sole persons to blame for the confusion in opinions about the essence of dramatic conflict" only provide an opportunity for "philistine" playwrights to agitate for the acceptance of plays that have been rightly rejected.[159] Virta, it appears, had spoken too frankly, and his complaints about the excesses of Zhdanovism narrowly missed becoming an attack on institutionalized controls as such. Though bureaucrats did not remain above criticism, from this point on playwrights had to bear the brunt of the attack, and dissatisfaction could find an outlet only in general discussions of theories of representing "negative" types.

The *Pravda* editorial of April 7 was evidence that the no-conflict campaign would not culminate in any significant alteration of the postwar literary line. The editorial, it is true, boldly called for "Gogols and Shchedrins" and lashed out at critics who "rake over the coals" any writer who depicts negative aspects of Soviet life. But it was apparent that this was merely a reiteration of that principle of Zhdanovism which requires writers to expose and denounce forces that hinder the regime in the realization of its purposes. Characteristically, *Pravda* warned against overemphasizing the negative and advocated affirming the positive:

> Our dramatists must expose and mercilessly scourge the survivals of capitalism, the manifesting of political unconcern, bureaucracy, stagnation, servility, vainglory, arrogance, conceit, graft, an unconscientious approach to duties, a heedless attitude to socialist property; they must expose all that is vulgar and backward and hinders the progress of Soviet society.
>
> While truthfully portraying the shortcomings and contradictions that exist in life, the writer must actively affirm the positive basis of our socialist reality, must help the new to triumph. One cannot tolerate plays in which the negative characters dominate everything and, moreover, are portrayed more vividly and expressively than the heroes.[160]

That the call for Gogols and Shchedrins was a highly qualified one was demonstrated even more forcefully by a later editorial in *Kommunist* which, among other things, pointedly reminded readers that Zoshchenko's satire, with its "slander on Soviet man," has nothing in common with socialist realism.[161] Another of the party's persisting interests lay beneath its concern with the no-conflict theory. In various ways the party continuously seeks to instill in people's minds a sense of urgency, incites people to struggle and sacrifice in the name of party goals, and combats tendencies to settle back and enjoy what has been achieved, inclinations to "gather flowers," as Simonov put it. Literature is expected to help the party accomplish this. And, as Sofronov remarked, "To smooth out and varnish our life is to reduce the educational role of Soviet art. . . . Such an art soothes and lulls the vigilance of our people in their struggle against survivals of capitalism and stifles their desire to combat everything hostile to our life and ethics." [162] Thus the no-conflict episode, rather than developing into a broad discussion of the situation in literature, dissolved into yet another drive for political and ideological vigilance, and the dissatisfaction that Virta's and Selvinsky's articles signaled was turned into its opposite — a reaffirmation of the principles and practices of Zhdanovism. This may have had something to do with the fact that the plenary meeting of the board of the Writers' Union, announced by Surkov immediately after *Pravda* published its editorial, was never held. The occasion might have reflected, dimly but only too unmistakably, the discontent prevalent among writers. Or perhaps it merely became clear that there was really nothing more to be said.

By the time the Nineteenth Party Congress opened, it was evident enough that the stirrings which had hinted at some kind of relaxation in cultural policies only verified the aphorism, *plus ça change, plus c'est la même chose.* Leading articles in the party press on literature and art were distinguished from those of an earlier period only by their more vigorous denunciations of "embellishing reality" and their greater emphasis on artistic craftsmanship. The latter point was invariably accompanied by observations to the effect that poor artistic works cannot fulfill their educative functions, influence people's minds, help men in their struggles. The postwar policy remained essentially the same, though the party had rejected some of its crudest interpretations and had adopted a somewhat more realistic attitude toward its application. There now appeared to be a greater willingness to discuss shortcomings of current works in terms of form and style and to attend more to problems of literary technique in general; but the principle of narodnost, of "comprehensibility to the masses," and the attitude toward such things as "formalism" and "Western decadence" seemed to preclude any startling developments in literary practices. The party had warned extremists that showing certain less admirable aspects of Soviet life was not to be condemned out of hand; but clearly the negative phenomena revealed had to fit into approved categories. The party had also apparently ratified a widespread interest in humanizing "positive" types in fiction; but here, too, the continual emphasis on themes of patriotism, labor, social activity, and ideological awareness made it highly unlikely that the previous idealization would be discontinued. Indeed, literary publications did not fail to quote frequently the passage on "typicalness" from Malenkov's report to the party congress. It reads, in part:

In the Marxist-Leninist interpretation, the typical does not at all mean some statistical average. The typical should correspond to the essence of the given socio-historical phenomenon; it is not just the widespread, the frequently repeated or the commonplace. Deliberate exaggeration which gives sharpness to an image does not make the image atypical but shows and stresses the typical more fully. (The question of) typicalness is the chief sphere in which the Party spirit manifests itself in realistic art. The problem of the typical is always a political problem.[163]

This and similar statements have for years provided the theoretical justification for the unreality of socialist realism. Finally, there was no question of giving up the principle of partiinost in literature or even of applying a new label to the principle. The dissatisfaction and criticism that on occasion had been expressed with vehemence in previous years was but palely reflected in Malenkov's admission of certain "grave shortcomings" in literature and his references to "mediocre, dull works," "potboilers," and the like, or in Fadeyev's observation that in Soviet schools literature is too often "regarded as merely affording illustrative reading for history or for this or that sociological situation, without any allusion to the fact that literature is beautiful." [164] Although the voices of protest had been muffled, it did not require knowledge of the future to anticipate their re-emergence, given the occasion, in twos, threes, or in chorus, as circumstances permitted.

If the events of the first few postwar years pointed to a certain resilient quality within the Soviet literary community — a quality which produced counterpressures to the party's impositions from above — they also demonstrated the party's skill in holding its ground by absorbing these pressures and rendering them subservient to its own purposes. The answer to the increased freedom of the war period was Zhdanovism, which in turn created new problems and set in motion currents of reaction. But when dissatisfaction among the ranks of writers became acute, the party first squelched the discontented, then adopted their objections in a modified form. Indeed, the party method was reminiscent of that satirized by Mayakovsky in his poem "The Pillar":

> Criticism
>   from below —
>   that's poison.
> From above —
>   that's medicine!
> Well, can one
>   permit
>   the lower ranks,
> Everyone! —
>   to take to criticizing?!

In this manner, the party was able to keep discontent in check and to immunize the core of doctrine from contamination. The technique produced something less than a significant concession to discontented writers, though it did result in a more moderate form of Zhdanovism than that which had evolved by 1949. The Belik incident and, even more, the linguistics pronouncements were, in terms of Soviet practice, gentle methods of introducing a slight change in the atmosphere prevailing in intellectual circles, making it possible for those concerned to feel out carefully the approved limits of discussion and criticism while dealing with rather abstruse, but significant, topics. The developments during these years demonstrate the significance of the "artificial dialectic" as a means of controlling the tendencies toward extremes which seem inevitable in the Soviet system. But recalcitrance in the lower ranks played a role in the alterations that were made, though the regime took heed of the voices of protest less because they threatened to instigate an open revolt against current literary policies than because they focused attention on undeniable evidence that the regime's policies were leading to consequences which frustrated its very aims in establishing those policies. The tension between the demand for a literature of high political content and the necessity that literary works satisfy certain minimum aesthetic standards had once again produced a kind of "scissors crisis" in belles-lettres, characterized by a decline in artistic quality when devotion to political content is on the rise. But, since the regime refused to modify basic doctrinal tenets, it appeared likely that similar problems and similar protests would continue to emerge.

III ◇◇◇◇◇

The Quest for a Middle Way, 1953–1955

◇◇

The death of Stalin in March 1953 raised uncertainties about the future course of developments in the realm of literature as well as in other spheres of Soviet life. Would the new rulers adhere to the literary policies established by Stalin? Would they employ Stalin's techniques of control in dealing with the problems they inherited from the previous regime? Would they display a skill equal to Stalin's in pursuing their goals in belles-lettres? The developments during the years 1953–1955 are revealing both with respect to the force and persistence of the old patterns of behavior and to the new possibilities of aberrations from them.

During the three years after Stalin's death, the conflicts that had arisen in previous years moved more clearly into public view, becoming increasingly matters for open debate. The struggle between those who urged liberalization and those who resisted it seemed, despite significant reversals, to be moving toward some resolution based on a policy of comparative moderation, and events in 1955 indicated that the party had acquiesced in a further, though limited, tempering of Zhdanovism. But the situation in belles-lettres at the end of 1955 was at best unstable, and an astonishing interlude of freedom in 1956, discussed in the next chapter, was to precede what promised to be the more lasting "solution" to the literary struggles later imposed by the Khrushchev regime.

One of the most important events during the period under discussion was the Second All-Union Congress of Soviet Writers, the first such congress to be held in twenty years. Because certain aspects of this meeting are best understood when seen in terms of the experience of the First Congress of 1934, and because such comparison reveals more clearly some basic issues of Soviet literary politics, a digression from the analysis of developments in 1953–1955 is made in the following pages.

FROM THAW TO FROST

Almost immediately after Stalin's death there was a noticeable quickening in the discussion of the situation in belles-lettres. This did not at first extend beyond the limits established by the post-1950 form of Zhdanovism as proper for criticizing current literary practices or for examining such issues as the need for depicting "negative" aspects of Soviet reality, the desirability of "humanizing" literary works, and the propriety of self-expression. But a certain freshness was evident in the approach of many writers to these and related questions, and there were indications that the debate might surge beyond the channel cut for it a year or so before. Hints of a better life to come and promises of an increase in consumer goods clearly helped to foster these tendencies. The press underscored the point that greater attention was now being given to man and his well-being, and workers in the arts began to explore the implications of this for their own fields. In this atmosphere, the reaction against excessive stress on production themes and technological detail in literature grew more intense, and demands for literary representation of human problems and feelings became increasingly articulate. A suggestion of what was to come in the area of literary criticism might have been discerned in the first poems of Alexander Tvardovsky's cycle "Horizon beyond Horizon," which appeared in June 1953. In one of the poems, Tvardovsky complained that the current literary produce was so unpalatable that "one wants to scream," [1] and, in raising the question of the limitations imposed on writers by their own "internal" editors, he in effect directed attention to the external conditions which set up restraints and engendered fears among writers.

At the Fourteenth Plenum of the board of the Writers' Union, in October 1953, leading spokesmen for the literary bureaucracy gave their sanction to the emerging "frank discussion" among writers and critics. Although K. Simonov's and B. Lavrenyov's highly critical analyses of the situation in dramaturgy added little that was new to the fund of complaints that had accumulated since 1950 and even earlier, they at least endorsed current trends of criticism. Some of the specific points made by speakers are worth noting because they reveal the direction of these trends and the attitudes prevalent at this time and because they indicate that the limits of debate had begun to expand. Simonov, for example, denounced the practice of omitting certain plays from authors' collected works, referring to Alexander Afinogenov's *The Eccentric* and *Fear* as examples, and he queried with mock naïveté, "Whence comes this strange disposition of editors and critics to view republishing or discussing plays of the twenties and thirties as something on which they might burn themselves, and so to blow on their fingers in advance?" [2] In the same vein, he condemned the practice of glossing over complexities of the past and portraying people and conditions of the First Five Year Plan or of the thirties as no different from those of the present time. In the light of later events, it is of some interest that Simonov spoke favorably of L. Zorin's play *The Guests* and that Lavrenyov listed the play among those which evidenced "the growth of the skill and ideological strength of our drama." Also noteworthy was Simonov's reference to Ilf and Petrov, for the official attitude toward them, as toward Zoshchenko and Pasternak, makes it possible to use their names as one test of the astringency of literary policies. The republication in 1948 of Ilf and Petrov's satirical novels *The Twelve Chairs* and *The Golden Calf* had been declared a mistake shortly thereafter; but now Simonov expressed his "personal opinion" that the Writers' Union had been wrong in questioning the reprinting of these works. Furthermore, Fadeyev in his speech seemed to open the door to extensive criticism of the Writers' Union. He observed that democratic procedures had been neglected in the work of the union and that authors' individuality had been neglected, and he remarked on the absence of collegial leadership in the body — all of which had to be taken as belated self-criticism, in view of Fadeyev's lengthy service as the union's leading functionary.

Following the Fourteenth Plenum there appeared a succession of articles which examined the situation in belles-lettres with varying degrees of thoroughness and candor. Modestly indicating that he wished "to share with the reader thoughts about the writer's work," Ilya Ehrenburg, in an article published in October 1953,[3] summarized and stated in a more developed form ideas implicit in various essays and reviews that had appeared since Stalin's death. The article was impressive both as a case for humanism in belles-lettres and as a display on the part of a person prominent in Soviet society of a broad understanding of the writer's problems and tasks. The writer's proper realm is man's inner world, asserted Ehrenburg, and his task is the exploration of man's spiritual life, not the mere description of human activities and the external conditions of existence. Furthermore, a writer can concern himself only with what genuinely interests him, said Ehrenburg: he writes not to fulfill some external demand but "because he is compelled to tell people something he personally feels, because he has 'begun to ache' from his book. . . ." [4] Ehrenburg's elaboration of this point was actually only a different approach to the central thesis of Vladimir Pomerantsev's later argument on behalf of sincerity in literature. If Ehrenburg's article reflected current trends in its rejection of doctrinaire attitudes toward imaginative writing, it similarly revealed the threat to basic literary dogmas latent in these trends. Ehrenburg quite pointedly asserted that skill in Marxist analysis is not the essence of literary talent, and his suggestion that writers are persons with access to special knowledge of man, as well as his loose definition of tendentiousness as "passion," might well have appeared to alert theoreticians as a menace to the requirement of ideological uniformity and to the principle of partiinost. Moreover, whether Ehrenburg intended it or not, there was an implied criticism of forced rewriting in his insistence that successful works are those which are "natural" to a writer and in his scornful reference to the "cold, indifferent pages inserted in a story by some authors merely so that the critics will not say, 'But he did not describe this or that.' " [5] But Ehrenburg had not set out to explore at length fundamental theoretical and organizational questions, his tone was restrained, and his essay was overshadowed by other articles which appeared later on.

More sensational was Pomerantsev's essay, "On Sincerity in Literature," which appeared in the December 1953 issue of *Novy mir*.[6] In a fanciful interchange with a writer accused of hack work,

Pomerantsev attributed to the writer a remark which did not at all unfairly characterize recent trends in Soviet criticism: "Discussions of dullness and schematism have in a short time become just as fashionable and as hackneyed as the dullest book. For a long time you have abused me in private; and now critics have quickly caught on and this year have made *just another stereotype of criticism of stereotypes."* [7] With his forthright and biting attacks on current practices in literature and criticism, Pomerantsev was clearly trying to go beyond this and beyond the limits which even Ehrenburg had chosen to observe. Pomerantsev's long indictment of artificiality, didacticism, and schematism was a telling one, and his specific illustrations of discrepancies between the reality of life and reality as portrayed in literature were very revealing. But it was his stress on sincerity as a criterion of literary merit that later provoked the strongest protests. Pomerantsev's concise formulation of what was being said, in one way or another, by many others inevitably placed his article at the center of controversy. "The degree of sincerity," said Pomerantsev at one point, "that is, the directness of things, must be the first standard of evaluation." [8] If applied rigorously, this standard would, of course, undermine partiinost as the fundamental criterion for appraising literary work, and Pomerantsev's views smack of subjectivism and suggest pluralism — threats to ideinost and ideological conformity. Given the general tenor of the article, the remark, made in another context, that among Soviet writers "the uniformity of the Communist world view is taken for granted" [9] could not go far to quiet the doubts raised. Like other exponents of liberalization, Pomerantsev shied away from directly attacking the party's literary doctrine and controls. Rather, he blamed the general "conditions of literary life," which in his representation referred primarily to the unreasonable demands of dogmatic critics, whom the party "has repeatedly put in their place"; [10] and he reproached editors for preferring uncontroversial, "smooth" works, and writers for their own opportunism. The journal *Novy mir* in the early part of the next year followed this up with several articles, less important than Pomerantsev's, which in one way or another suggested re-evaluating "approved" literary works or questioned accepted modes of depicting reality.

The progress of the literary "thaw," whose onset was marked

by the Fourteenth Plenum, began to slacken noticeably even before the appearance in May of the work by Ehrenburg whose title has been widely used to characterize the period.[11] Chill breezes that arose early in 1954 suggested an imminent change in the ideological climate, though the wintry blast of Zhdanovism that came in June resulted only in a frost rather than in the deep freeze that would have been inevitable a few years before. There was a certain ambiguity in the situation that had established itself by the first part of 1954 and an evident uncertainty, even within the upper echelons of the literary bureaucracy, as to the proper limits of discussion. But an effort soon got under way to bring some order out of the chaos, an effort that began in a comparatively restrained manner. Once again the battle lines were drawn between the defenders of orthodoxy and those who stubbornly pursued more generous policies by squeezing through gaps in the ideological front. It is noteworthy that, in spite of the obviously unsatisfactory situation, the party did not interfere directly in the affairs of the literary community but left it to officials of the Writers' Union and other party stalwarts to handle the situation. The Central Committee did not issue a decree; the articles printed in party newspapers during the initial stages of the 1954 engagement were temperate in tone; and only after literary officials had initiated and nearly concluded their drive did the party press emerge with significant editorial commentary on the situation. Whether this reflected a division of opinion among top party leaders can only be a matter of conjecture. It may also have been one facet of the larger effort to encourage greater initiative in various spheres of Soviet life, including literature, and to curry popular favor by stressing "democratic" procedure while relying on subfunctionaries to maintain order and, if necessary, to transform themselves into scapegoats.

In various ways the developments of 1954 were reminiscent of control techniques employed during the period following the linguistics pronouncements of 1950. On the one hand, anything which seemed to call into question the party's final authority in belles-lettres was condemned, and authors who took too seriously the frequent demands for more satire or for showing the bad as well as the good in Soviet life were reproved. On the other hand, even the more orthodox were forced to admit serious shortcomings in belles-lettres, and they displayed a willingness to tolerate complaints that the Writers' Union and the Chief Drama Administration employed bureaucratic and undemocratic methods. Aram Khachaturyan's remark, "Creative problems cannot be solved by bureaucratic techniques," [12] could well be taken as the slogan of the day because it permitted a variety of conclusions ranging from "controls should be abolished" to "something should be done," the vaguer formulations gaining currency among literary bureaucrats. This may have soothed ruffled feelings, and it seemed to have the effect of diverting discussion from the more profound sources of discontent. It appeared that leading literary functionaries, while trying to put their house in order before the writers' congress planned for the fall of 1954, were offering as their program the pseudo-liberal policies which emerged after the "softening" of 1950: theirs was a "moderate" position, somewhere, let us say, between the viewpoint once defended by Belik and that represented by Pomerantsev. But the responsible officials of the literary community supplemented the tactics of diversion and the device of stealing their opponents' thunder with crude frontal attacks in the style of Zhdanovism. The policies which the leaders of the Writers' Union adopted and the methods they employed are best revealed by review of developments between January and August 1954.

Criticism of the Pomerantsev article and ultimately of the whole course of recent developments in literature began with an article in *Literaturnaya gazeta*, written by Vitaly Vasilevsky, which complained among other things that Pomerantsev had completely ignored the question of a writer's partiinost and Communist world view.[13] The next month, however, *Komsomolskaya pravda* printed a letter which criticized Vasilevsky and supported Pomerantsev; but the letter, written by four students and an instructor at Moscow University, observed that "a serious gap" in Pomerantsev's article was the lack of clarity on a number of important questions, "particularly on the partiinost of literature." [14] Shortly thereafter, the leadership of the literary world set out to clarify the situation. Perhaps because Vasilevsky's article had not had a sufficiently strong impact, the editor of *Literaturnaya gazeta* himself wrote a long article, though one very restrained in tone, which demonstrated the harmfulness of Pomerantsev's views.[15] And at the

Twelfth Congress of the Komsomol, A. Surkov observed that the editors of *Komsomolskaya pravda* "did not approach the task of defining their position in literary affairs with sufficient seriousness when they published the confused and in many ways strange 'readers' response' to V. Pomerantsev's article." [16] When an article by Surkov appeared in the May 25 issue of *Pravda*, it became clear that this affair was being taken seriously. [17] But even though the article broadened the attack and disclosed that the opposition to Pomerantsev's article was becoming more strident, the indictment was not so complete nor the tone so denunciatory as Surkov's speech to Moscow writers in June or his summation in the July issue of *Oktyabr*. In the *Pravda* article, Surkov attacked not only Pomerantsev but the whole group of articles that had been published in *Novy mir*. He declared that Pomerantsev's article "is essentially directed against the foundations of our literature — against its close link with life, against its Communist ideinost, against the Leninist principle of the partiinost of literature, against the most important requirements of socialist realism," and he claimed that it "orients writers toward turning mainly to the shady, negative aspects of our life." This was not very different from statements made after the "softening" of 1950, statements which warned against subverting partiinost and expressed alarm lest the call for "Gogols and Shchedrins" and for representing the whole of life result in an undesirably somber picture of Soviet reality. Surkov illustrated his own concern on the latter point by commenting unfavorably on Panfyorov's play *When We Are Beautiful* and novel *Mother Volga*, Zorin's play *The Guests*, and plays by Surov, Mariyengof, Virta, and Gorodetsky. Despite the fact that Surkov extended criticism to a long list of works, his general tone and the manner in which the campaign was being handled suggested that the literary leadership had undertaken to pursue a policy of moderation in some sense. One passage in the *Pravda* article made the point quite clearly, though it was couched in familiar polemical jargon: "we must with equal mercilessness protect it [literature] from the complacency of the boastful and conceited, from the leftist, bombasting assaults of the neo-RAPPist-type vulgarizers, and from the nihilist whine of petty-bourgeois panic-criers ready to slander all the wealth of experience we have accumulated." Surkov seemed to be prescribing adherence to policies and attitudes characteristic of post-1950 Zhdanovism.

Surkov's article in *Pravda* engendered a familiar response. Not only were the works specified by Surkov subjected to widespread criticism, but other harmful writing was discovered. At the same time, there was a quickening of activity among divisions of the Writers' Union as meetings were held to discuss the need for strengthening ideological work within the literary community. It is of some interest that Zoshchenko's name figures in reports of several meetings held in Leningrad. At a party meeting of writers early in June, V. Druzin, according to *Literaturnaya gazeta*, "condemned the behavior of M. Zoshchenko, who has drawn absolutely no conclusions from party criticism and has long concealed his real attitude toward the Central Committee's decree on the magazines *Zvezda* and *Leningrad*." [18] Shortly thereafter, Zoshchenko's "effort to justify his vicious position" was a second time condemned, unanimously, at a general meeting of Leningrad writers.[19] Zoshchenko was again rebuked by the writers' party organization when it met to consider a resolution on ideological work that had been adopted by the Leningrad *obkom* (regional party committee).[20] Given the changing tide of literary affairs, it was not surprising that when V. Yermilov appeared in *Pravda* with an elaboration of Surkov's themes he added a critique of some recent poems by Pasternak.[21] One test for astringency became complete when Surkov expressed a negative attitude toward the works of Ilf and Petrov in his speech at the Moscow conference in June.[22] However, the reversals that had occurred since the beginning of the year introduced some confusion into the process of putting the hierarchy of evils in order. Thus *Komsomolskaya pravda*, acknowledging its error in publishing a defense of Pomerantsev, compensated for that by making a thoroughgoing attack on Ehrenburg's *The Thaw*;[23] but Surkov disclosed at the June conference that Ehrenburg's work merited special treatment when he reprimanded the newspaper for "incorrectly placing the novel in the same category as L. Zorin's slanderous play *The Guests*." [24] In bursting into print with an extended attack on *The Thaw*,[25] Simonov may have been atoning for sins committed at the Fourteenth Plenum; but his position was somewhat peculiar in view of his earlier approval of Zorin's more pernicious work. Simonov devoted much space to an expression of dissatisfaction with *The Thaw*'s unflattering portrayal of conditions in Soviet art, as had *Komsomolskaya pravda*. But unlike the Komsomol publication, which asserted that there were no positive figures in *The Thaw* and that most of the characters were "spiritually broken and exhausted people," Simonov presented the rather curious argument that the work's basic defect was in portraying positive characters as rarities in Soviet society. Ehrenburg did not fail to take note of the discrepancy when he composed his rather evasive defense of *The Thaw*.[26] But even though these incidents point to a certain lack of coordination in specific cases, there could no longer be any doubt as to the main direction of trends in the realm of literary politics.

The leadership of the Writers' Union may have embraced a "moderate" position on questions of policy, but as it waged the literary battle its methods of attack and techniques of defamation grew ever more reminiscent of those employed during the peak of Zhdanovism. This became strikingly evident at the important open party meeting of Moscow writers in mid-June, the real turning point in the tide of affairs, where Surkov's speech showed a far greater degree of virulence than his *Pravda* article had. Surkov's remarks had by now a familiar ring, although he added a few new points. Most significant were the innovations he introduced into his criticism of the Pomerantsev article and his remarks on the "line" of the journal *Novy mir*. It initially appeared, he remarked, that the harmful articles in *Novy mir* were merely fortuitous phenomena, fruits of carelessness; but, he went on, "it has become clear that this was not a chance conjunction of circumstances, not an oversight, but the expression of a premeditated line — a line which has its predecessors in our literature." [27] Surkov specified the literary group Pereval as one of the predecessors. It may be recalled that in its own time this group was labeled "idealist" and "subjectivist" by leftist critics and later on was linked with the Trotskyite opposition. In his article of July — which was either the full text or an elaboration of the June speech — Surkov in the same context referred to the "cosmopolitan, nihilist" line of the "antipatriotic critics" who published in the journal *Literaturny kritik* during the thirties, and he claimed that Pomerantsev had made an open effort to rehabilitate this line.[28] Furthermore, *Literaturnaya gazeta*'s article on the June conference revealed that the editors of *Novy mir* had been called on the carpet even earlier. Reporting that the admission of error made on behalf of the journal by its deputy chief editor, A. Dementyev, had not pleased the conference, *Literaturnaya gazeta* indicated as well that the editors of the journal had defended their position at an earlier meeting of the secretariat of the Writers' Union and at a party conference of the union's board. This evidence of recalcitrance may explain the increasing ferocity of the campaign and the imposition of penalties. Those who erred might, for example, expect a fate similar to that of Panfyorov, who, after more than twenty years' service on *Oktyabr*, was removed from the editorial staff ostensibly because as chief editor he was responsible for the publication of a harmful footnote in one issue of the journal.[29]

Until late in June, the party press refrained from endeavoring to guide the literary discussion by interfering directly. An editorial in an issue of *Kommunist* that went to press late in the month commented extensively on the literary situation, but in a restrained manner.[30] It was symbolic of the trend, however, that the name of Stalin was again linked with Marx, Engels, and Lenin as a founder of that theory which the editorial urged all writers to study. While repeating what may be described as the Surkov line on various harmful literary works, the *Novy mir* articles, and Zoshchenko, the editorial took care to make it clear that the literary community itself had already expressed its unanimously negative judgment on these phenomena. The conclusions drawn from this survey of the literary scene were of some significance, however. Noting that the leaders and party organization of the Writers' Union had not been quick enough to take a "clear, principled position" on vital literary questions and had allowed discussion in the union and in the press to drift without guidance, the editorial added:

The most important task of the Union of Soviet Writers is to elucidate thoroughly the harm of those alien tendencies which have recently become particularly prominent in dramaturgy and criticism, to guide the discussion and solution of literary questions along the correct path, and to foster in the organization the necessary creative atmosphere.[31]

In brief, the officials of the union were enjoined to finish putting their house in order.

The union's leaders were not slow to follow the advice of *Kommunist*. The presidium meeting of August 11 was intended to place the discussion on the "correct path," indeed, to bring it to a close. The presidium passed a resolution which outlined and condemned the errors of the articles published by *Novy mir*.[32] Tvardovsky confessed his errors, in his own words, "unfortunately very belatedly, but quite honestly and sincerely." Nonetheless, he lost his post as chief editor of *Novy mir*, and Simonov once again took over the job.

An examination of the condemned *Novy mir* articles and the literary works that provoked the sharpest criticism will help to establish more precisely the character of the trends and countertrends that arose in the literary world during 1953–1954. Next in importance after Pomerantsev's article was F. Abramov's article on kolkhoz fiction.[33] Abramov's piece, which contained a remarkably outspoken criticism of the character of postwar literature on kolkhoz themes, was made possible by the recent party decisions to initiate a series of reforms in the countryside. In the light of these decisions, Abramov declared that many literary works embellished the realities of kolkhoz life and passed lightly over the actual difficulties that faced Soviet agriculture after the war. To illustrate his points, Abramov concentrated his critical fire on Semyon Babayevsky's novel *Cavalier of the Golden Star*, which had been awarded a Stalin Prize. In the novel, Babayevsky's hero, Sergei Tutarinov, returns from the battlefront to a countryside whose economy is in a state of disorder. Inspired by the announcement of the Fourth Five Year Plan, Tutarinov develops an ambitious project for constructing a power station and introducing electricity into the kolkhoz villages of the district. Tutarinov gains the support of the secretary of the district party committee for this scheme. It would seem, observed Abramov in his article, that in conditions of lagging agricultural productivity the first task would be to improve the work of the kolkhozes and, in addition, that only in this way would it be possible to acquire the material means necessary for building a power station. In the novel, however, only

Khokhlakov, the more practically minded chairman of the district executive committee, opposes Tutarinov, arguing that all energies must be concentrated on increasing the harvest. Khokhlakov is relieved of his post and, because of his "conservatism," he is later represented virtually as an "enemy of the people." Babayevsky's Tutarinov is typical of other rather incredible postwar literary heroes, the vigorous and dedicated patriots who set out, once the war had ended, to accomplish heroic deeds on the home front. Hence, it was significant that Abramov endeavored to dethrone Tutarinov and to rehabilitate Khokhlakov. Furthermore, Abramov objected to the bright tones Babayevsky had used throughout this novel and its sequel *Light over the Land,* and the critic scoffed at the portrayal of Tutarinov's life as "an uninterrupted triumphal procession along a path strewn with roses." [34] Tasks that in real life "demand great effort and persistent labor" are accomplished effortlessly in Babayevsky's romanticized kolkhoz scenes, complained Abramov in another passage.[35] Abramov's article was actually an exposé of the falsity in a group of previously approved works on kolkhoz themes, works by G. Nikolayeva, Ye. Maltsev, Yu. Laptev, and others, as well as those by Babayevsky. It turned out, however, that Abramov had misunderstood the implications of the party's new agricultural policy, for the presidium of the Writers' Union censured Abramov for " 'tearing into' all the more admirable Soviet prose works on the life of the kolkhoz peasantry during and since the war." [36] Abramov's article was in a sense an elaboration of a part of Pomerantsev's article, for Pomerantsev, too, criticized Babayevsky's novels, contrasting them unfavorably to Valentin Ovechkin's *District Routine.* Pomerantsev asserted that one could learn little from Babayevsky's novels about critical problems of kolkhoz life, and Tutarinov, he said, appears "less a hero than an angel on a cake." [37] But Ovechkin, he noted, not only portrayed living people in his work but boldly raised issues that other authors had carefully avoided.

The contrast between Babayevsky and Ovechkin was significant, for, in spite of the criticism of Pomerantsev and Abramov in 1954, the school of kolkhoz writing fostered by Ovechkin was destined to supersede the one represented by Babayevsky. No one could have seriously questioned Pomerantsev's point about the greater frankness of Ovechkin's work, which was generally accepted as a positive contribution to literature on kolkhoz themes. Short though it is, *District Routine*[38] is remarkable for its portrayal of defects in the work of the party apparatus in the countryside. Central to the work is a contrast between two different approaches to the management of kolkhozes in an average rural district in Russia. Borzov, the first secretary of the district party committee, is a typical bureaucrat who relies on routine administrative devices and a bullying manner to attain his goals. For him, the immediate needs of the government and expediency are considerations which override the claims of fairness and even of long-range planning; he is more concerned about observing bureaucratic procedures and preserving his good standing with the provincial party committee than about constructively seeking solutions to problems. Martynov, the second secretary of the district committee, and Opyonkin, the capable chairman of one of the few successful kolkhozes in the district, are presented as contrasts to Borzov. The divergent attitudes toward managing the district are illustrated by an argument that arises over Borzov's arbitrary decision to raise the grain-delivery quota of Opyonkin's kolkhoz in order to make up for kolkhozes whose deliveries lag behind. Martynov supports Opyonkin's objections to this decision, arguing that it is unjust, that it reduces the incentive of kolkhoz farmers, and that it is self-defeating in the long run. After a heated interchange, Borzov suggests that Martynov apply for a transfer to another district, where he will be able to operate according to the claims of "peasant justice," leaving Borzov free to continue work "in the proletarian manner." [39] It is noteworthy that because of his realism and concern for the interests of the kolkhoz peasantry Martynov, whom Ovechkin treats sympathetically, is somewhat reminiscent of Khokhlakov, whom Babayevsky represents as a negative figure. High-handed administrative methods come in for a considerable amount of criticism in Ovechkin's sketch. At one point Martynov says: "Nothing is worse for a kolkhoz chairman than not being certain that he will be abused only for a real cause, not being certain that in his difficult work, where some mistakes are inevitable, he won't be a victim of arbitrariness or high-handedness." [40] But elsewhere Martynov observes that "sometimes we fasten on a kolkhoz, as chairman, a rogue who shouldn't be allowed within shooting distance of public property," [41] and he suggests that a remedy might be to allow kolkhoz farmers a greater voice in the "elections" of their chairmen. In an equally forceful manner, Martynov criticizes the existence of a top-heavy bureaucracy with its surplus of "persons with super-extraordinary powers" whose tangible accomplishments are slight. Ovechkin's *District Routine*, the first of a series of sketches on kolkhoz life, appeared months before Stalin's death, but it was only after the party projected extensive agricultural reforms to overcome admitted defects in agriculture that Ovechkin's work moved into the literary limelight and set a new fashion in writing on kolkhoz themes.

The other *Novy mir* articles singled out for criticism in 1954 were less significant as indications of trends in creative writing. In reviewing a work by Marietta Shaginyan, well known in the Soviet Union as an essayist, Mikhail Lifshits accused Shaginyan of superficiality and haste in her efforts to write about virtually all aspects of contemporary Soviet life. Shaginyan's main defect, Lifshits concluded, is that she "is prepared to discourse on any subject while knowing absolutely nothing about it." [42] Probably because of the tone of the article more than anything else, Surkov charged Lifshits with using the shortcomings of Shaginyan's work as a device "for scoffing at a writer's active participation in life." [43] It was only one part of another article — Mark Shcheglov's review of Leonov's *Russian Forest* — that provoked the ire of the defenders of orthodoxy.[44] Shcheglov regarded Leonov's explanation of the origins of the novel's negative character, Granitsky, as inadequate. The critic's error, as it turned out, was his insistence that Granitsky was not merely a "survival" of the past, as Leonov would have it. Granitsky, said Shcheglov, had become what he was not only because of an early incident in his biography, one that occurred before the revolution, but rather because of various social conditions that existed after the revolution, some of which persist even today. Thus Shcheglov's error was of the same order as those committed by authors of the plays and novels that were attacked in 1954.

Surkov's journal article of July 1954 contained a brief but accurate summary of the principal objections brought against a number of literary works. Directing his attention specifically to several plays that had been labeled defective, Surkov complained that in these works "everything that is evil and rotten occurs among the leading groups of our society, and government and party workers, scientists and Soviet intellectuals appear as the principal negative characters." He added that "when the isolated incidents exposed in feuilletons become the basis for dozens of plays, the result is a one-sided, distorted view of the life of society." Surkov also observed indignantly that the problem of "highly placed papas and poorly trained children, or something of the sort" had lately become a "standard conflict." [45] Similar points figured among the objections which others raised against Panova's *Seasons of the Year* and Ehrenburg's *The Thaw*. And the works most frequently attacked and most thoroughly analyzed in the press — Zorin's *The Guests* and the novels of Panova and Ehrenburg — do have much in common. They all contain unappealing representations of Soviet bureaucrats, depict the development of bourgeois values among some segments of Soviet society, and present a contrast between the older generation of Soviet citizens and the generation born and raised under Soviet rule.

In *The Guests*, Zorin portrays and contrasts three generations of the Kirpichev family. The head of the family, Alexei Kirpichev, is a former comrade of Dzerzhinsky and a nationally famous hero of the revolution, a man of lofty principles and ideals. But his son Peter, who occupies a responsible post in the ministry of justice, is an unethical careerist who has been corrupted by a desire for power and prestige. Moreover, Peter and his family live in the grand manner of the Soviet privileged classes and have attitudes and tastes that are normally described as bourgeois in Soviet writing. But Zorin does not attempt to explain Peter simply as a "bourgeois survival" or a victim of an "alien ideology." Alexei Kirpichev's denunciation of Peter at the end of the play is interesting as a suggestion of the factors which formed the character of the latter:

I became, as they say, an important figure [says Alexei to Peter]. And did my life or hers [his wife's] change? Not at all. We only began to work harder. All the blessings fell to you. I thought that was a good thing — we suffered storms and tempests, let him have sun and roses. All sorts of people came to honor me. But I had no time for them, so they fell to you. Insignificant pygmies of people fawned on you because of your father, and you liked it. . . . I simply worked, worked alongside the great toilers of our land and didn't think how it feels to have power. But you tasted power when you were a child, and it poisoned you.[46]

The elder Kirpichev goes on to describe Peter as a "high-ranking magnate, gluttonous, arrogant, remote from the people." [47] Nor does Peter's son Tema promise to be any improvement over his father. The nineteen-year-old Tema, who has access to a chauffeur-driven car, a country dacha, and the other material benefits which accompany his father's position, leads the irresponsible life of a rich man's son; at one point Peter, not without a certain pride, refers to his son as an "habitué of restaurants" whom all the maîtres d'hôtel know.[48] Zorin pointedly reveals that Tema, a member of the Komsomol, has scant respect for old Kirpichev's stature as a revolutionary hero or for the values which the latter represents. But Tema is a student at the Institute of International Relations and obviously destined for a responsible position in government service.

The training of Soviet youth is also a theme of central importance in Vera Panova's *Seasons of the Year*.[49] The novel focuses on two families, the Bortasheviches and the Kupryanovs, and it reveals a paradox in the upbringing of the children of the families. Stepan Bortashevich is the director of a large factory and a respected figure in the provincial town where the action of the novel takes place; but he actually engages in criminal activities in order to meet the demands of his socially ambitious wife, who has not outgrown the bourgeois tastes which she acquired during the NEP period. When his nefarious deeds are exposed, Bortashevich commits suicide. But in spite of the comparative luxury in which they live and the pernicious influence of their mother, the Bortashevich children develop into admirable Soviet youths with a correct set of values. Dorofeya Kupryanova, on the other hand, is far less successful in raising her son Gennady, although her own values and background would seem to equip her admirably for the task. An uneducated peasant girl at the time of the revolution, Kupryanova worked hard through difficult years and became a responsible party member and ultimately a leading figure in the community. But her son is a *stilyag*, more interested in cars than communism; unable to settle down to productive labor, he wanders from one thing to another, feeling that life has cheated him. Gennady ultimately becomes involved with a gang of thieves, and only after he is nearly killed by one of the gang does he repent and begin to undergo a change for the better. Those who criticized the novel were particularly vexed by Panova's "objectivism," by her failure to make clear her attitude toward her characters. Thus V. Kochetov, who initiated the attack on the novel, queried:

What, then, is the reader called upon to feel in the end? He is called upon to pity Bortashevich's children, to pity and "understand" Dorofeya and her son, to wonder that excellent children grow up in the families of scoundrels, while in the families of those who have shed their blood for Soviet rule children grow up scoundrels, and to think: so that is how things are sometimes.[50]

Panova had not made her didactic intent clear enough, and she disconcerted some readers by showing that apparently good people may actually be rogues and that even a villain may have some admirable qualities.

As in the works of Panova and Zorin, the principal negative character in Ehrenburg's novel is a man who holds a responsible post — Zhuravlyov, the director of a factory. Zhuravlyov is hardworking and utterly devoted to the task of improving the production record of his factory. But at the same time he is ruthless, coldhearted, deficient in humaneness; he achieves his aims only by neglecting the welfare of the workers and by employing illegal and unjust methods. Ultimately he is exposed and deprived of his post, an event which carries forward Ehrenburg's main theme that a political "thaw" has occurred since Stalin's death, promising a better life to come. The novel, set in a provincial town, also depicts a group of people from various walks of life, people who do not for the most part seem to be particularly happy. The discontents of Ehrenburg's characters either arise from or are intensified by one or another of the less appealing aspects of contemporary Soviet reality, and their problems seem to reinforce the complaint voiced by one of them:

We have taken a lot of trouble over one half of the human being, but the other half is neglected. The result is that one half of the house is a slum. I remember that article of Gorky's I read long ago, while I was still at school; he said we needed our own Soviet humanism. The word has been forgotten, the task is still to be done. In those days it was only a presentiment, now it's time we tackled it.[51]

The novel, taken as a whole, strongly suggests that the negative characters represented in it, or the negative qualities of other characters, are in a significant measure products of the Soviet environment. Ehrenburg raises the question of differences between the generations by depicting the family of Andrei Pukhov, an old Bolshevik who is regarded by his children as an idealistic romantic. Sonya, Pukhov's daughter, is a serious-minded young engineer who is so imbued with the idea of selfless service to the socialist motherland, so accustomed to the notion that personal feelings must be regulated or repressed, and so suspicious of her own emotions that she jeopardizes her personal happiness. Volodya, Pukhov's son, is a disillusioned and cynical hack painter, a careerist who will paint anything to earn money and gain recognition. It is through Volodya that Ehrenburg criticizes the situation in the Soviet arts. "Raphael wouldn't be admitted to the Artists' Union," declares Volodya at one point, and elsewhere he observes: "Everybody's shouting about art and nobody cares a fig for it really, that's the sign of our time." [52] While discussing literature with an equally disillusioned actress, Volodya points out that a writer is not expected to have ideas: "What you're meant to look for in a book is ideology. If it's there what more d'you want? It's lunatics that have ideas." [53] As a contrast to Volodya, Ehrenburg presents the talented Saburov, a painter who is dedicated to his art, who paints only what interests him, and who lives in poverty, neglected by orthodox art critics and unrecognized by Soviet society. Ehrenburg's representation of conditions in the world of the arts called forth many objections, and Ehrenburg's sympathy for Saburov, as a contrast to Volodya, was declared misleading because Saburov, as *Komsomolskaya pravda* put it, "is a man without ideas, divorced from our life, escaping into the realm of 'pure' art, creating his paintings in an ivory tower." [54]

The criticism of Pasternak was a comparatively minor event among the literary incidents of 1954, but Yermilov's comments on a group of poems from the novel which Pasternak was then writing, *Doctor Zhivago,* are worth noting as evidence of the obstacles that Soviet writers may meet when they attempt to express their feelings and views in literary works. Yermilov was particularly offended by the following lines from "The Wedding":

> For life too is but a moment
> Only a dissolution
> Of our personalities into all others
> As if in offering.
>
> Only wedding revelry
> Bursting through the windows,
> Only a song, only a dream,
> Only a grey dove.[55]

Such pessimistic and decadent lines, said Yermilov, inculcate the attitude that it is absurd "to waste energy in the struggle for a better future for the homeland and for mankind," and they are incompatible with "educating our youth in a bright, clear, optimistic, and virile view of life as creative work, construction, action." Furthermore, Yermilov found in Pasternak's verse evidence of the error of Pomerantsev's views:

One cannot fail to note here that phenomena such as B. Pasternak's "The Wedding" show to an extreme degree the incorrectness of advancing the concept of "sincerity in literature" as the main and all-encompassing slogan of literary development. Even if the poem "The Wedding" is quite sincere, this does not preclude its being false in content.[56]

The principal merit of Yermilov's critique was that it illustrated clearly and simply one of the problems created by an orthodoxy which presumes the ability to ascertain whether a person's feelings about his experience are true or false.

In the light of past experience, it might have been expected that a dull pall of uniformity would again settle over the literary community after the presidium of the Writers' Union condemned the *Novy mir* articles and established an official attitude toward recent literary trends. It was some indication of the change in conditions since Stalin's death that the efforts of the literary bureaucracy to stifle cries of discontent rising from below fell short of the mark. To say that the August presidium meeting "brought to an end the widespread demand in the press for sincerity and freedom in literary creation" [57] is not quite accurate. Rather, the demand now had to be expressed in somewhat different terms, for the authority of the *Novy mir* articles had been demolished. It is worth noting, however, that even in September a Leningrad writer had to be rebuked for saying that the appearance of these articles had a "positive significance" because they had "stirred up" the literary community.[58] But even though the harmful character of the Pomerantsev article was generally admitted, at least in public, the struggle for greater freedom in literature and the debate over what amounted to the question of sincerity went on quite openly in the press. The most significant engagements occurred on two different fronts. On the one hand, there was a continuation of a controversy that had arisen over an article published by Olga Berggolts in April 1953.[59] The poetess had defended self-expression in poetry, the poet's lyric "I," and even sanctioned contemplative and melancholy moods in verse. Margarita Aliger had joined Berggolts, and both waged battle during the following year and a half. One climax was reached in October 1954, when Berggolts published a sharply worded rejoinder describing her opponents as people "who fear to express our life through their own hearts, who obviously mistrust themselves, who shy from the very terms 'personality,' 'individuality,' 'self-expression,' that is, from that without which poetry, and lyric poetry in particular, simply does not exist." [60] The second major controversy centered on the institutions having direct control over writers' activities and dealt largely with questions of organization and administration. But it represented a concrete effort to reduce pressures and to loosen administrative restraints; furthermore, manifestations of a sentiment favoring the abolition of the Writers' Union suggested that there were larger issues behind this facet of the debate. These two lines of discussion were very revealing with respect to several aspects of Soviet literary life, and some of the issues they raised will be considered later in other contexts.

Not long before the Second Congress of Soviet Writers opened, the poet Ilya Selvinsky managed within the confines of a comparatively short article to express his views on a number of the broader questions raised or suggested by the precongress discussions.[61] The article merits special attention both as a summary of what had gone before and as an introduction to the second writers' congress. It was a vivid and highly individual summing-up, certainly, but both the character of the precongress discussions and the actual response of a few writers to the article suggested that Selvinsky did not speak only for himself.

Selvinsky's article contained a long indictment of the bureaucratic practices of the Writers' Union. In particular, Selvinsky inveighed against the monopoly of control maintained by a few members of the secretariat, and he deplored the comparative impotence of the large body of writers and the sterility of the work of the commissions and creative (genre) sections of the Writers' Union. By way of illustration he recounted the history of his tragedy *Reading "Faust."* The play, according to its author, was received with considerable enthusiasm at a combined meeting of the poets' and playwrights' sections. Selvinsky continued:

The secretariat of the Writers' Union does not tire of assuring the association that its activities focus primarily on the creative sections. . . . Let us assume that this is so, not only on paper but also in actuality. In this case, is it not clear, after two creative sections displayed such fervor in their evaluation of the tragedy, that the secretariat should have given it at least some sort of consideration? However, the leaders of the union granted the favor of keeping silent. But they kept silent so energetically that in the course of six years (!) I was not able to publish my work. When it was finally included in a collection of my tragedies, the critics in a very organized manner . . . failed to notice it. . . .

Selvinsky explained that the play got into print only because of efforts on the part of Fadeyev, and he recounted a similar incident involving Aseyev, but one whose outcome was less fortunate. Because Selvinsky used this tale as a vehicle for raising larger problems, his detractors attempted to discredit the entire article and to evade the real issues it raised by claiming that he merely wrote because of personal pique. Displaying greater political acumen, *Literaturnaya gazeta* editorially supported Selvinsky on the score of his personal complaint and repeated the poet's assertion that not only he but a number of other writers had been unjustly neglected.[62] This reference to Selvinsky's views was made incidentally in a general editorial calling for variety in literature, and the newspaper did not specifically express its attitude toward the remainder of Selvinsky's article, though it had published it initially, of course. This aspect of the incident seemed to be another example of the practice, so much in vogue on the eve of the writers' congress, of admitting former wrongs in an effort to create an atmosphere of sweet reasonableness.

Although Selvinsky was clearly incensed by oligarchical rule in the Writers' Union, his fundamental concern was with the effects this had had on literary life in general. Selvinsky asserted that the monopoly of power in the Union led to a virtual monopoly in poetry itself:

Tvardovsky, Isakovsky, and Surkov are quite sufficient for the union's leaders. Having once and for all declared this school the universal one, they carefully eschew any deviation whatsoever, calling what is different "capricious" and what is complex "chaotic." [63]

And he added maliciously that "through the efforts of some comrades the formula Tvardovsky-Isakovsky-Surkov has been propagandized so vigorously that it has almost come to be accepted as a line from the Statutes of the Writers' Union." What has been the result? To begin with, dullness — "a single style, a single set of images, one and the same rhythmic patterns." At another point Selvinsky observed that in the cavalry "a horseman who can slip around the belly of a horse at full gallop and pop into the saddle again is not a mere prankster but a Dzhigit [a skillful Caucasian horseman]"; and he posed the question, a rather pathetic one in the light of Soviet literary history: "Why in poetry is a person who displays such 'fancy riding' in his use of words branded a formalist?" As a consequence of the uniformity imposed on poetry, the reader, according to Selvinsky, has become indifferent to poetry:

It used to be that he reveled in poetry; at any public recital of poets he listened enthusiastically and himself, then and there, came forward to speak from the rostrum. And now? Now he sits quietly, like an academician, at literary soirées and gets excited only at football matches.

As Selvinsky expanded his characterization of the situation in Soviet poetry in what is the most significant part of his article, he displayed a certain nostalgia for the twenties, a phenomenon not uncommon among Soviet writers when they lament the absence of vitality and variety in Soviet literary life:

We poets are beginning to lose contact with readers; that is the most terrible thing. At his literary soirées, Vladimir Mayakovsky used to devise a "purge of poets." He would enter the rostrum and start reading, let us say, Dorogoichenko's verses, calling their detail a "monotonous landscape." Then Dorogoichenko would step forward and, after defending himself in any way he could, would in his own turn read Mayakovsky's verses and criticize them for "egocentricity" and "incomprehensibility." After this, spectators would come to the rostrum and defend whomever they thought correct. All of this went on merrily and vivaciously. There was no officialism there, nor the practices of a ministry of literature, for Mayakovsky did not hold high posts in the literary directorate: he was an insignificant fellow — just a great poet, that's all. Now this tradition of Mayakovsky has been almost lost. We have learned to tear each other apart, but have forgotten how to criticize; it is not surprising that discussions organized by the Writers' Union are not as a rule successful. And how do we cultivate readers' taste? It is only dogmatists, not creative persons, who busy themselves with this.

Selvinsky's tirade was in fact a telling commentary on the effects of more than twenty years of Stalinist literary policies — a commentary on the stagnation induced by the expanding bureaucratic controls, by the exclusive hegemony granted to a single literary school, and by the policy of systematically extirpating every nonconformist tendency. It was under the burdensome legacy of two decades of Stalinism that the Second Writers' Congress would have to labor.

Although Selvinsky's article was almost alone in its scope and forcefulness, there were other discordant notes in the precongress discussion, and leaders of the Writers' Union expended considerable energy in trying to bring errant writers into line and to create a more comradely atmosphere before the opening of the congress. Although what their purposes were can only be a matter for speculation, it is worth noting that officials of the central Writers' Union made appearances at the writers' congresses of the several republics and at conferences of the lesser divisions of the union, meetings which were held to select delegates and to prepare for the forthcoming all-union congress. A report about the Moldavian Writers' Union reveals an attitude that officials of other branches of the organization may have shared, although the manner of its manifestation was quite probably unique to Moldavia. There the secretariat of the union demanded that the texts of all speeches to be made at the forthcoming Moldavian writers' congress be submitted beforehand for translation into Russian, and it noted that "any improvisation can only bring harm to the creative work of the congress." [64] Press reports continued to suggest, however, that the "open debate" among writers had not come to a close, and it may have been because the officials of the union encountered difficulties that the opening of the congress was several times postponed.

THE SECOND ALL-UNION CONGRESS OF SOVIET WRITERS

During the proceedings of the Second Writers' Congress, which began on December 15, 1954, the intention of the union's top leaders to pursue a policy of "moderation" and to mute controversy became even more apparent than it had been in previous months. The restrained and platitudinous greetings to writers from the Central Committee suggested what the general tone of the congress might be, and it is unlikely that party leaders had any reason to be disappointed by the major reports read at the gathering. During the discussions, several writers objected to the monotonous, uncontroversial nature of the main speeches, and Ovechkin's characterization of Simonov's coreport on prose might be applied to the other reports as well: "The coreport was suitably critical, suitably self-critical, suitably bold, and suitably cautious. All the proportions were observed." [65] Surkov said little in his general report on Soviet literature that would have created a stir had it been uttered three years earlier, and when he broached crucial problems he adopted the time-honored "on-the-one-hand-on-the-other" device. Surkov's position and the attitude he shared with the other major speakers can best be indicated by noting the manner in which he treated a few significant issues. It was not surprising that he justified previous "anticomparativist" and "anticosmopolitan" campaigns; but he did point out that the 1949–1950 phase of the struggle had been marred by the fact that some people used it to settle personal accounts.[66] Furthermore, he suggested that a general amnesty would be extended to those who had been guilty of mistakes of a cosmopolitan nature and had reconsidered their errors,[67] though in fact this process of rehabilitation had begun even before the congress opened. And while stressing the need to safeguard socialist realism from contamination by formalism and "pure-art" theories, Surkov on the other hand remarked upon the dangers of "primitivism," "vulgar sociologism," and "neo-RAPPism," referring specifically to the Belik incident in this context.[68] Typical of Surkov's whole approach to current problems was his effort to attribute to literary critics the guilt, on the one hand, for failing to expose the evils of the "no-conflict" theory and, on the other, for first delaying and for then being "insufficiently friendly" in dealing with writers who went from "conflictlessness" to the extreme of depicting reality "wholly in a somber light." [69] In their reports, Surkov and Simonov both illustrated the "friendly" mode of criticism by their comparatively temperate criticisms of the recent novels of Panova and Ehrenburg.

All the main speakers displayed considerable skill in contriving to gloss over or ignore the most significant aspects of precongress debates — in particular, the controversies over individuality in poetry and over the situation in the Writers' Union. Surkov did make a thinly veiled reference to the precongress discussion on poetry, though he did not refer explicitly to it or to its participants. Surkov asserted that "pure-art" theories appear in many forms — in the attempt to supplement socialist realism with the concept of "socialist symbolism," in statements about "the subjective nature of lyric poetry, allegedly only a form of self-revelation of the lyric subject," in statements which are "sometimes cloaked behind distortions of the views of Belinsky and other authorities." [70] Delegates to the congress had probably not forgotten that Selvinsky had been reproached several years earlier for raising the banner of socialist symbolism or that both Berggolts and Aliger had made skillful use of quotations from Belinsky to buttress their case for self-expression in poetry. When Samed Vurgun, in his report on poetry, touched upon the question of self-expression, he claimed that the whole dispute reduced itself to a question of terminology.[71] In his remarks on the Writers' Union, Surkov asserted that the "frequently severe" precongress criticism of the Writers' Union had been "aimed wholly at strengthening the union," and he declared that nowhere had the very principle of writers' organizations "as organs of the collective guidance of literature" been subjected to doubt.[72] The single exception, he noted, was a letter from a group of Moscow writers published in *Literaturnaya gazeta*. Surkov's characterization of the prevailing sentiment may have been basically correct.

There would be no reason to raise a question about it were it not that other articles in the press, while they did not openly say it, seemed to be inspired by the feeling that the literary community would benefit from the abolition of the union, that the press manifested concern over growing "nihilist" attitudes toward the union, and that Surkov made such a point of denying all this. Although Surkov avoided discussing two important strands of the precongress debate, his report gave expression, in its own way, to what would become the two main themes of the congress. In the first place, he conceded that the situation in belles-lettres was not wholly satisfactory, and he repeated the complaints common since 1950 about low literary standards, excessive didacticism, idealized heroes, gilded reality, and so on. Secondly, he acknowledged certain unwholesome aspects of Soviet literary life when he called for a better atmosphere in criticism, freer exchange of opinion, and curtailment of the practice of regarding a press review as a "final and categorical verdict on a literary work." [73]

A number of speakers at the congress made a more or less conscious effort to shatter the prevailing calm by probing further into issues touched upon in the major reports or by reviving some facets of precongress discussion. A significant divergence of attitude did manifest itself at the congress, though it was not one that took the broad form of a conflict between the "upper strata" of the literary community and the "rank and file." It is not clear, in fact, to what extent the rank and file were represented at the Congress. One complaint was made before the congress opened about a tendency for officials rather than ordinary members of the local writers' organizations to be selected as delegates to the congress;[74] but there is no conclusive evidence about how widespread this might have been or, in concrete terms, what effect it might have had on the proceedings of the congress. Nonetheless, the outlook of a group of leading writers was notably different from that of top literary functionaries. These writers sharply criticized the union's officials for policies and practices employed by the literary bureaucracy over a period of years, and they were far more outspoken than the union's directorate about the unsatisfactory situation in belles-lettres. It hardly seems that the dissenters were speaking for an organized opposition group united by a common purpose, although the charge of "clannishness" was inevitably raised. Ovechkin's vigorous denial that he was participating in an attempted palace revolution within the union failed to impress Boris Ryurikov, editor of *Literaturnaya gazeta*, who seemed to believe at the end of the congress that there had been some insidious intent underlying the criticism to which he and other literary bureaucrats had been subjected.[75] There was greater harmony among members of the literary directorate than among their critics, though the latter, while they indulged in a certain amount of squabbling among themselves, raised much the same issues and displayed similar attitudes toward them. That the dissident writers were able to express their views and to quarrel with the spokesmen for orthodoxy suggested that the trend toward liberalization had not yet exhausted itself, despite the obstacles thrown up by the literary bureaucracy on the eve of the congress. But perhaps more deeply significant were the limitations of the dissent. The rebellious contented themselves with bewailing a recent decline in Soviet letters and with analyzing the less fortunate aspects of "the general conditions of literary life." They did not attack fundamental dogmas of literary doctrine, and they by no means questioned the party's final authority.

A few writers were particularly outspoken about trends in belles-lettres that aroused the concern of many other speakers. Ovechkin observed that Surkov had apparently given Soviet literature of the last two decades an "average" grade of "good" or even "good, plus," whereas if Surkov would look more closely at the developments during this period, he would discover that "an alarming and dangerous thing has occurred — a lowering of standards." [76] And when Sholokhov referred to "the dreary torrent of colorless, mediocre literature which in recent years has been gushing from the pages of the journals and flooding our book market," his audience responded with applause.[77] Olga Berggolts' speech was one of the most notable, not only because of her vivid commentary on what had happened to Soviet literature, but also because she made an effort, though not a thoroughgoing one, to expose some sources of the difficulties. She remarked at one point:

Our theater has almost lost its theatricality, just as lyric poetry has lost a whole range of themes natural to it. Love has almost disappeared from lyric poetry, just as the naked body has disappeared from painting and movement from the cinema, where for the most part the characters sit, or stand, and talk, but most of all just sit and talk.[78]

Earlier in her speech Berggolts indicated why, in her view, this impoverishment of the arts had occurred. Referring in particular to lyric poetry, Berggolts again criticized the prevailing lack of consideration for the individuality and personality of the poet. The precongress discussion on poetry arose, she declared, because the situation was such that "the individuality of the poet had completely disappeared from poetry; it was replaced by excavators, scrapers, and canals, but man and his human feelings — the individuality of the poet — almost disappeared." She reiterated her belief that "without genuinely free expression by the poet of his individuality — a social and many-sided one — there is no lyric poetry, there is none and there can be none"; and she remarked sharply that, while critics call for "more poets, good and varied," it actually appears that they long for "a single poet, and preferably a dead one." Berggolts' second theme, repeated with variations throughout the speech, was that literature had been injured by disregard for the "criterion of artistry," by the practice of evaluating works "not from ideological and aesthetic viewpoints, not from the viewpoints of craftsmanship and artistry, but from completely different positions, frequently dictated by the needs of the moment; and often this evaluation was in the form of a directive from the secretariat." This last point was developed in various ways by other speakers who lamented a long list of ills in Soviet criticism — dogmatic critics, critics who "play it safe," divergence between "official" and private evaluations of works, and so on. During the course of the discussions a partial redress was made for the main speakers' failure to discuss frankly the earlier criticisms of the Writers' Union, and some opposition arose to the effort to foist on unnamed literary critics the burden of blame for present conditions of literary life. M. Sokolov took note of the "strange fact" that the major reports had not discussed the shortcomings of the work of the union, its board, and its presidium,[79] and S. Shchipachyov declared that Surkov had been wrong in blaming literary criticism as a whole for the spread of the no-conflict theory while "not uttering a single word about the fact that there were also zealous preachers of this theory among the leaders of the

Writers' Union," a remark that was greeted with applause.[80] Furthermore, the complaint about clannishness in the guidance of literary affairs raised by both V. Latsis and Aliger was in effect supported by a number of writers, among them S. Kirsanov, who closed his remarks on the subject with the tart comment: "There is a great difference between the collegiality of a broad circle of writers and the collegiality of a narrow circle of three or four persons in the secretariat." [81]

Although Fadeyev did not read a special report at the congress, his speech was actually a concise summary of what the proceedings of the congress signified in ideological terms, and in this respect it was more to the point than the summaries of the main speakers. Ryurikov and Simonov in their "concluding words," which focused on the more piquant remarks of Ovechkin and Sholokhov, demonstrated that they had been unconscionably abused, and Surkov combined this with an appeal for reasonableness. Fadeyev, it is true, had been less prominent in literary affairs since Surkov took over the post of first secretary in October 1953, and there were indications at the congress of some friction between the two. But the length of Fadeyev's speech and the coverage accorded it in the press indicated that Fadeyev, as chairman of the presidium and a member of the secretariat, still spoke with considerable authority. Thus it was significant that he unequivocally reaffirmed familiar literary dogmas and at the same time reproached Ovechkin, Aliger, Berggolts, Kaverin, and Sholokhov for ignoring the problem of ideological enemies and concentrating their critical fire "on those sides of our life which depend on us alone." [82] Fadeyev announced that he was personally inclined to support Berggolts in the precongress debate on lyric poetry, but it seemed that he took away with one hand what he had given with the other. His gloss on her position was expressed in acceptable clichés, and he advised Berggolts to drop the term "self-expression," which "sounds foolish in Russian, undoubtedly just because it was used at one time by decadents of all colors." [83] And even if there was some discord between Surkov and Fadeyev, they could agree on the need for ideological vigilance, the central theme of Fadeyev's speech. Fadeyev justified the campaigns against formalism, cosmopolitanism, and a series of other threats, as had Surkov, and he stressed the need to struggle against alien tendencies of the sort represented by Pomerantsev.

If the Second Congress provided no grounds for expecting a significant change in the literary policies outlined in the decree of 1946, it at least threatened no new "campaign" or a further tightening of ideological controls. Even though the widespread criticism of the conditions of literary life failed to produce a project for fundamental reform, there were at any rate indications that an amelioration of conditions might reasonably be expected. The resolutions of the congress listed a long series of defects in the work of the Writers' Union, although the program for dealing with these was contained in the single statement: "It is necessary that the new leadership of the union completely overcome all of these shortcomings." [84] The congress also adopted a new set of statutes for the Writers' Union. Though some of the theoretical formulations contained in the old statutes were revised to correspond to the new stage of Soviet history — the transition to communism — and a series of changes was made in organizational details, little was done in the new statutes to provide concrete guarantees against the deviations from democratic procedures or the other evils criticized before and during the Second Congress. The most significant changes in this respect were twofold: the addition of a provision for secret voting in the elections of the executive boards and the auditing commissions of the all-union and union-republic writers' organizations, and the explicit statement of a point assumed in the old statutes but disregarded throughout the postwar period — the accountability of the secretariat to the board and the presidium of the Writers' Union. The new statutes contained one change of somewhat greater interest — a modification of the definition of socialist realism. In the old statutes the passage dealing with socialist realism read as follows:

Socialist realism, the basic method of Soviet belles-lettres and literary criticism, demands of the artist truthful, historically concrete representation of reality in its revolutionary development.

At the same time, truthfulness and historical concreteness of artistic representation of reality must be combined with the task of ideologically remolding and training the laboring people in the spirit of socialism.[85]

In the revised statutes the second clause was omitted — the reason, explained Simonov, was that some persons found in it a justification for "improving on reality" [86] — and certain other changes were made as well. Now, after a statement to the effect that Soviet writers are guided by the method of socialist realism, the passage read simply: "Socialist realism demands of the writer truthful representation of reality in its revolutionary development." To this was attached a clause which somewhat strengthened the assurance contained in the old statutes that socialist realism affords exceptional opportunities for displaying variety and initiative in creative endeavor.[87] The revision of the definition of socialist realism disclosed perhaps better than anything else both the mood of the Second Congress and the scope of official tolerance of change. The elimination of the second clause cannot be considered a fundamental revision of doctrine, since it is a redundancy, a clarification of the meaning of the phrase "representation of reality in its revolutionary development," and there was certainly no evidence that anyone at the congress was prepared to relieve literature of its pedagogic tasks. But its elimination was a measure of the strong sentiment among writers at the congress against the character of the literary output of the immediate postwar years and a sign of the trend toward a less dogmatic application of Zhdanovist doctrines.

During the course of the proceedings of the congress there were other indications of improvements to come. The report of the auditing commission suggested that the efficiency of the administrative apparatus of the Writers' Union might be increased, even if the basic structure of the union was not to be changed.[88] Surkov's announcement of the founding of several new literary journals promised a certain quickening in Soviet literary life.[89] And Simonov made some points that were very similar to those contained in his speech at the Fourteenth Plenum in 1953: he objected to the practice of revising works written in an earlier period of Soviet history, called for the republication of works that had been long neglected, and indicated that the novels of Ilf and Petrov would be reprinted.[90] Finally, the extensive criticism that emerged at the congress and the forthrightness of its expression seemed to augur an invigoration of literary life.

Yet, taking all into account, the Second Congress was a rather dismal landmark in the history of Soviet culture, both because its proceedings were mainly negative in character, even in their liveliest moments, and because it documented the gradual narrowing of the scope of literary discussion that had occurred in the previous twenty years. But the acts of negation themselves hinted that the trend was being reversed, holding out some hope for a better future.

LOOKING BACKWARD

A comparison of the writers' congress of 1954 with the one held twenty years earlier reveals contrasts as well as similarities which are helpful in estimating the direction taken and the distance traveled during the intervening years. In this respect, some of the data provided by the two congresses have a certain symbolic significance. By the time of the Second Congress, the Writers' Union, whose membership more than doubled during the twenty-year period, had begun to show the effects of the increment of years. The data reveal that the average age of delegates to the Second Congress was significantly higher than that of delegates to the First Congress, and this appears to reflect a trend within the union's membership as a whole.[91] The very proceedings of the Second Congress expressed the middle-aged character of the gathering, for in them could be discerned a reflection not only of the experience of the past twenty years, with its frustrations and disenchantments, but also of the general consolidation of Soviet society that had taken place during that time. Significantly enough, the Second Congress was very much concerned with problems of institutional middle age and their effects — with ossification of the control system, overbureaucratization, oligarchical administration, and declining enthusiasm for the writers' organization among its members. Whereas the Second Congress as a whole seemed to be gazing regretfully, at times even bitterly, into the past, the First Congress had been anticipating the future with a certain hope and enthusiasm. Many speeches delivered at the First Congress reflected an eagerness and optimism aroused by a vision of a future socialist society and by a sense of the potentialities for cultural growth of an awakening people, and a certain confidence and sense of purpose seemed to derive from the belief that ties with the masses had been established, that the chasm between the intelligentsia and the people had been bridged. True, these were not unfamiliar themes even then, and the sincerity of the speakers cannot be measured any more than their motivations can be determined. But the affirmation of these or similar sentiments was often the most winning aspect of otherwise undistinguished speeches, and even in print many of the declarations have the ring of authenticity. Several events that preceded the First Congress may have contributed to the apparent optimism of the gathering. The Central Committee's decree of April 1932, which brought about the dissolution of the Russian Association of Proletarian Writers (RAPP) and the formation of the Writers' Union, aroused the anger of RAPP's leaders, but it evidently created a sense of relief among some groups of writers.[92] On its surface, the decree seemed to repudiate the doctrinaire policies that prevailed during the First Five-Year Plan, and it was in line with other changes in the party policy at that time. There was a certain similarity between the tactics employed in the decree and those which Stalin adopted in his "Dizzy with Success" speech of 1930, when he attempted to attribute to others the responsibility for the excesses of collectivization. RAPP, which had never been granted the party's official support, quickly became the scapegoat for all former misdeeds in literature, and its dissolution was represented as a concession to dissatisfied elements. Moreover, in asserting that the existing organizational structure in the literary world tended to alienate "those significant groups of writers who now sympathize with the aims of socialist reconstruction," the decree applied to belles-lettres the revised policy toward the old technical intelligentsia announced by Stalin in 1931.[93] Thus, when the First Congress met, toward the end of the brief quasi-liberal period of the early thirties, there were indications of better times ahead for Soviet literature. The situation following Stalin's death was perhaps analogous in some ways. Yet the Second Congress not only had twenty years of experience behind it; it also followed hard upon a setback in the struggle for liberalization.

Although in the broader purview of history the most significant difference between the two congresses may lie in their contrasting "moods," these qualities are highly elusive. Surely different impressions may be formed of events that stretched over a period of several days and consisted in each case of well over a hundred speeches by persons whose views on various questions were by no means identical. There is some point, therefore, in selecting one or two of the speeches made at the First Congress for closer examination, since in this way it is possible to indicate more precisely the path that has been traversed since 1934.

The narrowness of viewpoint and the apparent unanimity on fundamental questions that prevailed at the Second Congress, particularly within the top echelons of the Writers' Union, were among the most striking aspects of the event. This applies in considerable measure even to the persons who displayed attitudes not wholly in accord with those of the main speakers, for the former limited themselves to exposing the evils of a bureaucratic approach to literature and decrying the consequences of dogmatic applications of theories they all seemed to accept. Some of their remarks, it is true, implied far more generous views on matters of literary practice than the official ones. But the "dissenters" did not probe into the fundamentals of accepted literary doctrine in an effort to expose theoretical sources of error, much less political causes, nor did they elaborate a larger framework to support their more liberal outlook. Bukharin's report on poetry at the First Congress provides abundant material for contemplating the distance traveled between 1934 and 1954, for it reveals a breadth of viewpoint that is notably lacking in the main reports at the Second Congress. A comparison of Bukharin's speech with those of the later congress leaves the impression that during the intervening twenty years there had occurred a narrowing of the scope of ideas that could be explored in major speeches at important gatherings such as these. And it should be noted that Bukharin's appearance and the fundamentals of his report were approved by the party, though much emphasis was given to the point that no speech delivered at the congress was to be regarded as a "directive." [94] Bukharin's report is significant, however, not only because of the contrast between it and the reports of the later congress — especially striking in the case of its corresponding number in 1954, Samed Vurgun's vapid report on poetry — but also because of the controversy it provoked and the ultimate outcome of that controversy.

Like all the other speakers at the congress, Bukharin professed a utilitarian attitude toward the arts. But his was a much broader concept of utility than that which has since been accepted as dogma by Soviet literary officialdom. While stressing that *"objectively,* in the whole social relation . . . both science and art in general, and poetry in particular, play . . . a tremendously vital and at the same time practical role," Bukharin indicated that the "subjective experience" of the creative artist may be "completely disinterested in the sense of remoteness from all practice." [95] This was not unlike the theory of tendentiousness that Fedin had been reproached for propounding in 1944. Furthermore, while rejecting the formalist position as such, Bukharin asserted that techniques developed by the formalist school could be used in studying questions of literary form. Bukharin displayed concern about the low standards and "provincialism" of much Soviet poetry, particularly of "proletarian" poetry, and at one point he said:

Our poetry is sometimes elementary — often just with those people who are ideologically closest to us. Yet one of the signs of a significant work is the wealth of associations and feelings, thoughts and suggestions that it evokes. . . . But we not infrequently accept a rhymed slogan as poetry. You may mention Mayakovsky. But to a certain extent time has set its stamp on him too: for life has grown vastly more complex, and we must move forward. Culture, culture, and still more culture.[96]

Bukharin did not hesitate to praise Pasternak and Tikhonov, both at that time suspect from a "leftist" point of view, or to criticize a number of politically oriented poets. In the spirit of his belief that "the time of propaganda poetry in the style of Mayakovsky has already passed," he observed that such poets as Bedny and Bezymensky had become "old-fashioned." [97]

Bukharin's speech called forth many protests, and the poets he had criticized reacted with particular vigor. It is of interest that A. Surkov, whom Bukharin later called the leader of "the faction of the insulated," [98] opened the counterattack. Surkov asserted that Bukharin had "declared 'defective' the principal representatives of proletarian poetry" from a position of "abstract craftsmanship" and that he had mistakenly neglected social and ideological factors in his discussion of poetry.[99] Twenty years later, Surkov seemed to be stressing his final victory when he declared that the most daring innovations in the "fraternal literatures" of the USSR were being made by poets who had mastered the tradition of Mayakovsky.[100]

In his biting and witty "concluding word," Bukharin replied to his critics and reaffirmed his views.[101] He observed that he regarded Mayakovsky very highly, that in his report he had referred to the poet as a "classic," and that he was not opposed to tendentious poetry "in the good sense of that word." He continued: "I said that propaganda poetry itself must now change, that the conception of topicality has changed, that a mere rehash in verse of editorials and detailed operational slogans satisfies no one, that we must strive for a synthesis, for a powerful, rich, and variegated art." [102] A passage from Bukharin's initial report discloses more fully the character of his views on this point:

The entire diversity of life can and must serve as material for poetic creativity. Unity does not mean that everyone must sing the same song at the same time — now about beets, now about the "living man," now about the class struggle in the countryside, now about the Party card. Unity does not mean showing only ideal types and "villains" or abolishing — on paper — all contradictions and difficulties. Unity consists in a single *aspect,* the aspect of socialist construction. All the richness of life, all the tragedies and conflicts, the vacillations and defeats, the conflict of tendencies — all this must become the material for poetic creation.[103]

Some passages from the record of the Second Writers' Congress read like remorseful confessions of failure to heed Bukharin's admonition.

Olga Berggolts' remarks at the Second Congress on the poet's expression of his personality in lyric verse were directly related to the larger question that concerned Bukharin — the question of the character and function of belles-lettres in the new society — and her observations shed some light on the reasons why Bukharin's vision of a rich, diversified literature remain unrealized. But her analysis was in no sense complete; in particular, it omitted any reference to the historical factors behind that disappearance of poetic individuality which Berggolts presented as a cause of the impoverishment of poetry. Yury Olesha's speech at the First Congress was really a discussion of the same problem from a different point of view, and it starkly revealed the operation of forces engendering the situation to which Berggolts has devoted so much attention.

Olesha's remarks were a candid and sensitive commentary on a writer's struggle to adjust to the values and demands of the new order. He began by saying that in everyone there are good and bad elements and that he could not conceive of a man who is unable to understand what it means to be cowardly, vain, selfish. A writer, who is especially sensitive to these things, has a relationship to good and evil which is not a simple one: when he depicts a negative character, all that is negative in the writer rises to the surface and he even feels himself to be that character. Olesha went on to say that he was shaken when critics denounced one of his fictional characters who was to some extent an autobiographical representation:

I did not believe that a man with keen perception and an ability to see the world in his own way could be vulgar and worthless. I said to myself: Does this mean that all this ability, all these things of your own that you regard as strength are worthless and vulgar? Is it so? I wanted to believe that the comrades who had criticized me (they were Communist critics) were right, and I did believe them. I began to think that what I had taken to be wealth was really poverty.[104]

About the First Five-Year Plan, Olesha said:

This was not my theme. I might have gone to a construction project, lived at a factory among workers, described them in a sketch, even in a novel, but this was not my theme, not a theme which was a part of my blood, my breath. I would have lied, invented; I would not have had what is called inspiration. It is difficult for me to understand the worker, the revolutionary hero. I cannot be one. This is beyond my strength, beyond my understanding. Therefore I cannot write about it. I became afraid and began to think that I was not needed by anyone.[105]

Olesha's remarks vividly illustrate an attitude shared in various degrees by other non-Communist "fellow-travelers," as the literature and literary-political documents of the twenties and early thirties abundantly demonstrate. Many writers and critics who identified themselves with the party exercised little restraint in expressing their impatience with such views, which appeared to them idealistic and unnecessary. Some of the older party leaders — notably those who had advocated moderate policies in belles-lettres, such as Trotsky, Bukharin, Lunacharsky — displayed more sympathy toward unreconstructed intellectuals who were trying to reorient themselves. At a conference of the Press Section of the Central Committee in 1924, Trotsky, for example, remarked with particular reference to Boris Pilnyak, who later was badgered into capitulation: "To turn himself consciously about his own axis even a few degrees is, for the artist, a task of the greatest difficulty, often involving a profound, sometimes a fatal crisis." [106] At the congress, Olesha himself concluded on a note of hope. Indicating that he had become fascinated by Soviet youth, he said:

> I personally have given myself the task of writing about young people. . . . Somewhere in me there exists the conviction that Communism is not only an economic but also a moral system, and our young men and women will be the first embodiments of this side of Communism.
> I shall try to embody in these works all my sense of beauty, of refinement, my whole vision of the world . . . in order to show that the new socialist attitude toward the world is in the purest sense a human attitude. Such is my rejuvenation.[107]

Olesha first attempted to do this in a film scenario, "A Strict Youth." Some critics considered "bourgeois" the qualities which Olesha attributed to Communist youth, and the film, though made, was never shown.[108] Shortly thereafter Olesha disappeared from the Soviet literary scene. After the war he reappeared with a few minor stories and book reviews, but not until 1956 were some of his earlier and more significant works republished. Nonetheless, Olesha's fate was a happier one than those of writers such as Boris Pilnyak and Isaac Babel, who disappeared during the purges of the thirties. But Olesha's conception of the writer's calling and his views on integrity and individuality in writing were destined to be suppressed by an overwhelming opposition. It is this that gives a touch of irony to those occasions when speakers, such as Vurgun at the Second Congress, find it necessary to make a formal request for "variety of images, vivacity, and abundance of color" in literary works or to remind poets that they must express themselves in "the language of images." [109]

If the prominent role played by Bukharin's opponent, Surkov, symbolized the triumph of orthodoxy in belles-lettres, the greater uniformity of viewpoint displayed at the Second Congress reflected the impact of the regime's policies in literature during the preceding two decades. In actuality, the process of silencing nonconformist elements was well under way even by the time of the First Congress. Trotsky had already been exiled and Bukharin's influence drastically weakened by Stalin's attack on the "Right Opposition." The vicious attacks on Yevgeny Zamyatin and Boris Pilnyak in 1929 [110] — more or less the literary world's equivalent to the Shakhty and Industrial Party trials — proved to be only a prelude to the upheavals of the later thirties. In 1935, Count Mirsky was banished from Moscow, and the critic Alexander Voronsky, whose views on literary matters were in some ways close to Trotsky's, was exiled for a second time in 1937. The trend culminated in the antiformalist campaign in 1937, which provided the occasion for a full-scale purge in literature.[111] The consolidation that had taken place was signified in a way by the increase in party membership among delegates to the two congresses — from 52.8 percent in 1934 to 72.5 percent in 1954.[112] Perhaps of greater importance was an apparent change in attitude among nonparty writers, although the character of this can hardly be determined with precision. Even at the First Congress, Vsevolod Ivanov, once a member of the Serapion Brothers, declared that the conception of *bespartiinost* had changed: he asserted that none of those who had signed the Serapions' vigorous proclamation on the autonomy of art would now reject Zhdanov's views on tendentiousness in literature, and he reached the obvious conclusion, "we are approaching partiinost." [113] Twenty years later, the process had much more nearly approached its completion, or so it would seem. Valentin Katayev's testimonial at the Second Congress on the indispensability of partiinost to the writer was particularly impressive, not only because Katayev is not a party member, but because he had found it expedient to revise radically his novel *For the Power of the Soviets* after party criticism of it in 1950.

As well as differences there were, of course, similarities between the two congresses, some of which merit attention. It is clear enough that Zhdanovism may be dated from 1934, for the basic tasks of Soviet literature as outlined by Zhdanov in his speech at the First Congress were not modified in the following twenty-year period. On the other side of the coin, many of the criticisms of the situation in literature made at the two congresses were almost identical. Writers who differed on other points could at least agree, in 1934, that there had been a decline in the quality of belles-lettres during the period of the First Five-Year Plan. Referring to a statement by an official of the State Publishing House, Gorky indicated that 75 percent of the books published between 1928 and 1931 had not been worthy of a second edition, that is, were "very bad books." [114] As at the Second Congress, there were widespread demands that literature be "humanized." Pogodin's complaint that it was almost as if someone had declared love, joy, beauty, and pleasure "nonparty categories" was by no means an isolated expression of discontent.[115] Similarly, there were grumblings about methods of literary criticism and indications that the "atmosphere" in the literary community left something to be desired. Panteleimon Romanov, for example, complained that critics employ "the tone of a teacher to a third-grade student" in their relations with writers; Nikolai Pogodin objected to critics who operate on the principle, "either extol or malign"; and Vsevolod Ivanov vividly and rather crudely described the abnormal anxiety that writers experience over press reviews.[116] And Lev Kassil's lament about the dissociation between official and "corridor" criticism might well have been cited by Vera Ketlinskaya when, at the Second Congress, she took note of the difference between official opinion and public opinion of literary works.[117] Some of the evils that established themselves while the RAPP dominated literary life, and even before, had turned out to be remarkably persistent.

In providing a vantage point for surveying the fruit of twenty years of Zhdanovism, the Second Congress unavoidably directed attention to the larger meaning of the decision made by the party in 1932. Although the Central Committee's decree of that year purported to be a step toward liberalization, motivated by the belief that "the existing framework of literary organizations . . . has become too narrow and holds back the serious growth of literary creation," [118] it is evident that the impulse of the decree was in precisely the contrary direction. The decree was the expression of an urge toward uniformity, and it created an instrument to generate that condition — a single writers' organization under direct party supervision, an organization to supplant all existing independent literary groups. Its more tolerant attitude toward the "fellow-travelers" in literature was a guarantee that nonparty and non-proletarian writers would be allowed to participate in "socialist construction"; but the formation of the union marked the repudiation of the very concept "fellow-traveler," for in effect it eliminated such nice distinctions, leaving intact only the positions "for" and "against." Since Soviet society was officially said to be transforming itself into a solid bloc of nonparty members and Communists, identical claims might quite legitimately be made of all groups. The 1932 decree had "pointed out a common path for party and nonparty writers," as one delegate to the First Congress remarked,[119] and the canonization of socialist realism meant that a literary method as well as a political creed was being imposed on writers. In a speech at the First Congress memorable for its ironies and suggestions of hidden meaning, Isaac Babel said that out of respect for the reader he had become a great master of the "genre of silence"; and, quoting and giving his own interpretation to a remark of another speaker, he added that the party had deprived writers of only one right — that of writing badly, which, he observed, "was a very important right, and to take it away from us is no small thing." [120] Alexander Zharov drew out explicitly another of Babel's meanings when he asserted that writers had also been deprived of the right "to keep silence well." [121] In actuality, the party had denied writers the privilege of writing as they pleased about whatever interested them, and the whole force of the party's program was to wrench the writer's "axis of creativeness" from within the writer himself, to take from him that peace and freedom of which Blok spoke shortly before his death in 1921: "Not the outward peace, but the creative. Not the childish freedom, the freedom to be a liberal, but the freedom of creation, the secret freedom." [122] If what socialist realism required of writers was imprecise in specifically literary terms, its political emphasis was unmistakable; and if what it excluded was not defined exactly, it was apparent that manifestations in belles-lettres of a greater concern for literary values than for political purposes would be regarded as alien phenomena, outgrowths of idealism and formalism. Ilya Ehrenburg marked one of the dangers inherent in this emphasis when he said at the First Congress:

It often happens with us that cult of the most reactionary artistic form is disguised as the need to fight formalism. . . . In the attacks of some of our critics on quests for a new form, in this disdain for form, there is hidden the affirmation of a certain form, namely, a form that is derivative and profoundly bourgeois.[123]

Ehrenburg went on to say that neither *War and Peace* nor the novels of Balzac should be regarded as models for the new Soviet literature. Yet it is precisely such works which, since that time, have been so often singled out as models. In this part of his speech, Ehrenburg seemed to be echoing the views of Yevgeny Zamyatin, who had discerned these trends in the early twenties, predicted some of their consequences, and struggled vigorously against them. Urging the need for an experimental literature suited to the new age, Zamyatin once declared that the "best way to kill art is to canonize one form and one philosophy," [124] and on another occasion he wrote pungently: "The main thing is that there can be a real literature only where it is produced by madmen, hermits, heretics, dreamers, rebels, and skeptics, and not by painstaking and well-meaning officials." [125] The struggle between conservative and experimental tendencies in art that extended into the thirties arose with the revolution itself, or, more accurately, was cast into a new form by the revolution. And delegates to the Second Writers' Congress in 1954 might have profited from pondering the words written by an artist on January 5, 1918, in reply to an article warning the victorious proletariat of the dangers of futurism:

I have thought and I still think that the proletariat, having taken power into its own hands, will give art, in its broad meaning, the fullest opportunity to expand widely. It will give all true seekers of new forms in art the utmost opportunity to do this. . . . From pseudo-classicism and academism through impressionism to new forms and new quests.

. . . Rejected by the bourgeoisie, ignored by the "illustrious," artist-innovators, in spite of deprivations and failures, are continuing and will continue their work! Perhaps they are going astray now, but they have a burning desire to discover. And the proletariat itself will understand what is created by talent, what is fostered by love, what is beautiful, whether it be called "new" or "old." [126]

The outcome of the contest was to be determined by fiat, however. The decree of 1932, which created the conditions necessary for enforcing the Party's literary policies, was an essential element in the resolution of the struggle. It was at the same time an integral part of the emerging totalitarianism and the return to traditionalism that characterized the Soviet Union of the early thirties. The Stalinist counter-revolution triumphed in belles-lettres as it did elsewhere.

"TO GUIDE THE DISCUSSION . . ."

It quickly became evident that the Second Congress had not given final answers to burning questions of the day or laid down a firm line in literary affairs. Although the union's leaders proposed no revision of the basic tenets of Zhdanovism, they endeavored to generate the impression that these would be applied in a moderate manner; but they failed to define with precision the claims of this ostensibly moderate position or the limits that it established. It is true that ambiguity in varying degrees has always been a characteristic of Soviet literary policies. But as a policy moves away from an extreme toward some midway point, its uncertainties increase and it becomes more susceptible to misinterpretation, willful or otherwise. This possibility was increased in 1955 by the absence of forceful guidance from the party itself and by the fact that the "middle" ground had been designated at the Second Congress largely through negation — neither "vulgar sociologism" nor "pure art" theories, neither embellishment nor slander, neither all work nor all play, and so on. And during the months following the congress various tendencies and countertendencies manifested themselves in Soviet literary life as they had the year before the congress was held. Most important, there was a continuation of the struggle for liberalization that had gained strength after Stalin's death, the struggle that had been going on, though less openly, almost ever since Zhdanovism reappeared in a virulent form in 1946.

That the atmosphere of 1952, much less of 1949, had not reestablished itself was indicated both by the nature of the literary output and by the character of the problems which now captured the attention of literary critics. Some indication of what the recent trend had been was furnished by a conference of young writers in

January 1956, where manuscripts were read and evaluated and current literary problems discussed. Observing that love lyrics occupied an "increasingly large place" in the work of young poets, A. Makarov, in his coreport on poetry, displayed a concern shared by other authorities when he cautioned that love lyrics are "only one of the means of revealing a person's soul" and that "questions of love must not be artificially carried off to some special sphere isolated from the social activity and labor of the advanced Soviet man." [127] More direct was a later article by V. Azhayev in which the author, who had read the main report at the conference, summarized his impressions of the meeting and expressed his views more fully. After commenting at one point on the paucity of works devoted to working-class people and to labor themes, Azhayev said: "More than that, it is impossible not to see how, in recent years, these themes and problems have retreated if not to third, then to second place, yielding first place to problems of the everyday existence and family life of our people." [128]

The widespread interest aroused by Viktor Nekrasov's *In the Home Town*[129] and by Kseniya Lvova's *Yelena*[130] marked the changes that were occurring on the literary scene. Like much postwar fiction, Nekrasov's novel depicts the lives of Soviet soldiers who have just returned to civilian life. But the novel is not written according to formulas favored by many authors whose works dealt with similar subjects. Nekrasov's characters are not larger-than-life war heroes, nor do they return from battle with the intention of accomplishing stupendous deeds on the home front. They are ordinary men who find it difficult to adjust to civilian life and to begin their lives anew, and the novel deals sympathetically with them as they go through the process of making the adjustment. The plot of the novel is slight; the work achieves unity by focusing on the process by which Nikolai Mityasov overcomes his sense of purposelessness and lays the foundations for a meaningful existence. Mityasov's problems are complicated by the fact that his wife, Shura, has been living with another man during his absence. Although Mityasov is reunited with his wife, he eventually leaves her for another woman, whereupon Mityasov's friend Sergei, also a maladjusted war veteran, moves in with Shura. At the close of the novel the reader is left with the impression that the couples are now properly paired, that domestic bliss is inevitable, and that life in the future will proceed more smoothly. The reaction of Soviet critics to the novel was not, for the most part, a very favorable one. In the fall of 1955, Fadeyev neatly summarized the novel's basic weaknesses as they had been revealed in a series of articles published in *Literaturnaya gazeta*.[131] The central characters of the novel, said Fadeyev,

> are almost isolated from public life. Reality is examined by the author through the prism of their personal difficulties — everyday and family. . . . the author touches the large sphere of their laboring and toiling life only in passing. The novel lacks a sense of the spirit of the times; life flows on, but it is not transformed in the name of great purposes. The work of a Soviet writer has meaning only when it is illuminated by the great universal ideas of our century.[132]

Yet it was probably Nekrasov's skillful and restrained representation of the private, personal realm of experience that appealed to some of the readers of the novel.

With even greater justification, Fadeyev might have said something similar about Lvova's inferior novel *Yelena*, a tale of an extramarital love affair evidently written, as one of its critics tartly remarked, chiefly for the purpose of satisfying readers' "burning desire to read about love." [133] Yelena, the beautiful young heroine of the novel, is a talented chemist who is devoted to her work, and the reader is given the impression that she is to be regarded as a socially "positive" character. But during a temporary absence of her husband, Yelena finds time for an affair with a married man, Reshetov, who is described as a good party member and a capable scientist. Lvova eschews unpleasant problems in her book, allowing Yelena to escape some of the difficulties which her love affair has created. In the latter part of the novel, Yelena, who is now pregnant, is struck by an auto and consequently loses Reshetov's child. And when faced with choosing between Reshetov and her husband, Yelena is suddenly transferred to another part of the Soviet Union. Thus ends the first part of a work to which Lvova intended to add a sequel. It was not particularly surprising that *Komsomolskaya pravda* printed a review which took Lvova to task for "poeticizing vulgarity" [134] or that the novel was attacked in various other quarters. But the critics' reactions to the work were not unanimously negative, and at an important conference of writers in Moscow, Lvova herself stepped forward to defend her work and to justify her effort to show that "feelings and amorous experience make their claims in life." [135]

The recent trends in Soviet writing inevitably provoked discussions of the proper manner of treating love themes, problems of personal life, family relations, and the like, in literary works. Among the more interesting articles concerned with these or related topics was one by A. Shishkina which called for greater psychological depth in the portrayal of fictional characters.[136] Shishkina discerned in the works of young writers evidences of "empiricism" and incomplete understanding of human thoughts and feelings, and, while she approved the practice of devoting attention to the deeds of fictional heroes, Shishkina complained that authors restrict psychological analysis to questions of simple motivation: "The heroes of many novels reflect little on life, rarely ponder their feelings and actions, analyze them infrequently and sometimes helplessly as well." [137] The argument was all the more significant because of Shishkina's effort to demonstrate that she was by no means craftily encouraging a return to the "superfluous man" of the nineteenth century or anything of the sort, and she carefully distinguished between passive reflection which "destroys man's energy, paralyzes his will to action," and the creative self-analysis of Soviet literary heroes which is a part of the process "of enriching the spiritual life, of perfecting the feelings." [138] But while discussions of such questions and controversies over particular literary works revealed divergent opinions and considerable uncertainty about the proper stand to take, they did not issue in a general statement of policy or evoke an authoritative declaration to clarify the situation.

The effort to establish more generous attitudes in belles-lettres also manifested itself in discussions of literary theory and aesthetics. The point was repeatedly made in diverse ways that art has peculiar characteristics which distinguish it from other areas of human endeavor, that art is, after all, art and has tasks which are different from those of philosophy, history, and economics. The critic A. Petrosyan, for example, based a defense of one of Tendryakov's novels on such an argument when she claimed that critics found the work defective because their expectations were "justifiable only with regard to an article, a brochure, a report, or an essay on a prescribed theme," and she emphasized the point by asserting that "the artistic method of generalization is distinguished from scientific generalization by the fact that the typical or the regular [*zakonomernoye*], i.e., the general, finds its expression in the particular, the individual." [139] Nekrasov presented essentially the same views when he defended his novel *In the Home Town* at a Moscow writers' conference,[140] and similar arguments were made elsewhere. Thus the trend was following a pattern somewhat resembling that of the postlinguistics discussion, although problems could now be approached more directly, for the discussion did not have to be confined to analyzing the Marxist theory of ideologies or determining the place of art in the superstructure. Views similar to those which Olga Berggolts had defended for the past two years were now expressed more widely in the press, and in some elaborations they contributed to the discussion of the nature and function of art. The journal *Teatr*, in an editorial that was not exceptionally daring or liberal on the whole, criticized those who believe that artistic truth is born outside the artist, who think that the artist is merely a passive agent in reproducing reality and that the active interference of his unique individuality in the process necessarily entails the danger of subjectivism. Phenomena of reality become "facts of art" only through the "living soul" of the artist, said the editorial, though it was careful to elaborate the argument that the "creative subjectivity" must be of a "party nature," presumably lest anyone mistake these assertions as a defense of "sincerity" in the manner of Pomerantsev.[141]

Not all the guardians of orthodoxy viewed these developments with equanimity, and at least until the early autumn of 1955 there were occasional sharp outbursts against manifestations of ideological laxity. *Literaturnaya gazeta* gave some indication of the division of opinion among writers when calling editorially for greater ideological vigilance in the literary community:

Ideological vacillation can be seen among a number of writers, those who are not sufficiently grounded in theory. Thus at a party meeting of Moscow writers there were speeches which cast doubt on the usefulness of our struggle against cosmopolitanism. Among certain Leningrad writers there has appeared a tendency toward all-forgiveness on ideological questions, toward granting amnesty to the rotten and slanderous writings of Zoshchenko.[142]

At a conference of Moscow writers held the following month (May), Simonov was even more forthright. He condemned a recent tendency "to represent as 'excesses' and 'extravagancies' both the absolutely correct ideological struggle which was carried on against the erroneous articles published in *Novy mir* in 1953–1954 and the correct, sharp censure of the politically harmful tendencies that were particularly conspicuous in L. Zorin's play *The Guests*"; and he made a special point of emphasizing that "the principle of the partiinost of our literature . . . is not for us in any sense a matter of discussion." [143] Simonov also displayed some concern about the character of current writing, observing that the practice of embellishing reality had not been rejected in favor of dragging into view "a little more rubbish from the backyards of life," and he reminded his audience in addition that neither Pasternak's *Spektorsky* nor Olesha's *Envy* had determined the course of Soviet literature. The struggle against those who demand "ideal" heroes, continued Simonov, had not been waged under the banner of "living man" theories, "with their rotten justification of a schizophrenia allegedly inherent in man, with their false assertion that every man is in his own way right, that it is necessary to accept him as he is and, having understood him, to forgive him."

A thundering, wide-ranging editorial in an issue of *Voprosy filosofii* that went to press late in August disclosed that the editors of that journal shared with Simonov what were really misgivings about the increased attention being devoted to psychological analysis in literature.[144] In reaction to the former impoverishment of man's spiritual life, stated the editorial, there has arisen a theory that "it is completely unnecessary to show Soviet man in all the spheres of his activity, and particularly in his work"; at a recent writers' conference, it declared, one writer went so far as to say that "it is possible to create a splendid image of our contemporary, of the active fighter for Communism, even if during the whole novel or story he lies in a dressing-gown on a couch and occupies himself only with his own thoughts and feelings." [145] And after interpreting Shishkina's article in a distorted manner, *Voprosy filosofii* was able to present it virtually as an effort to provide theoretical justification for depicting Soviet Oblomovs. This ultra-orthodox editorial railed against a whole series of articles which had agitated during the past two years for conditions permitting greater individuality and originality in works of art: in all of them it discerned threats of subjectivism. In its effort to preserve a pure understanding of partiinost and ideinost, the editorial sharply attacked A. Lebedev's statement, "Art is called upon to reflect and appraise reality aesthetically." [146] Art, stormed the editorial, "is called upon to reflect reality not aesthetically but *truthfully*. These are two completely different things." [147]

Partly because of a discussion carried on in a Georgian youth newspaper, the relation of art and reality received increasing attention during the summer of 1955. In July, *Literaturnaya gazeta* devoted a long editorial to the matter, demonstrating that some of the participants in the discussion were denying art's cognitive functions. Thus a certain V. Kvachakhiya had written, according to *Literaturnaya gazeta*: "The aim of science is to give knowledge to society. The aim of art is to cultivate the spiritual and emotional world of man, to satisfy his aesthetic needs." [148] This and similar views were reactions to the oversimplified theory that art is only a means of illustrating ideas, said *Literaturnaya gazeta*; but, the editors emphasized, the reaction was extreme, for such views cast doubt on art's ability "to cognize reality, to reveal the laws of life in typical, artistic images." But *Literaturnaya gazeta* displayed an attitude less rigid than that of the later *Voprosy filosofii* editorial. For the newspaper repudiated a formula it had previously advocated — that art "represents in artistic images the results of the process of cognizing reality" — on the grounds that this can justify "illustrative-type" art, and it disclosed that it now regarded artistic creation as "specifically artistic cognition of reality." With the passage of time and after a change of chief editors, a further softening of *Literaturnaya gazeta*'s viewpoint took place, or so it appeared in November, when the newspaper attacked the editorial in *Voprosy filosofii*. Reprimanding the philosophical journal for its exaggerated concern about alleged manifestations of subjectivism, the editors of *Literaturnaya gazeta* pointed out that there is an obvious difference between "a writer's subjective (in the sense of personal), individual view" and subjectivism as "a definite world view," and they defended Shishkina's article, although they noted that it contained "certain inaccuracies":

For example, there was no reason for the critic to use the term "self-analysis," which subjectivists have misused; but the general tenor of the work and its main idea are fruitful. . . . Protesting against dull, superficial works which do not show man with his actions, thoughts, and feelings, the critic calls for deeper psychological description of characters, for showing how man analyzes his conduct, for conveying the complexity of his experience.[149]

In conclusion, *Literaturnaya gazeta* declared that the authors of the *Voprosy filosofii* editorial had unwittingly become "apologists for illustrative-type art" and had erred in ignoring "the specific nature of a literary work."

Thus, during the year following the Second Writers' Congress there was a certain disorder within the literary community which indicated that the leadership of the Writers' Union had not wholly succeeded in fulfilling *Kommunist*'s earlier injunction to "guide the discussion and solution of literary questions along the correct path." At a writers' conference in October, Valentin Ovechkin accurately characterized the situation with his laconic remark: "A certain confusion has recently appeared in our criticism. This is from an addiction to official evaluations. Now there are no such evaluations, but there is literature. Thus it happens that the shop is full of goods, but there is no inventory." [150] It was evidently in an effort to clarify the situation that *Kommunist* published an editorial on problems of literature and art in the last days of 1955.

The *Kommunist* editorial, "Toward the Question of the Typical in Literature and Art," [151] had a sensational quality because of its strong insinuation that the theses enunciated by Malenkov at the Nineteenth Party Congress were to be repudiated. Thus one passage from the opening section reads:

Unfortunately it is necessary to state that in recent years certain pedantic and erroneous views on the typical have spread among workers of literature and the arts. Widespread acceptance was gained by formulas equating the typical with the essence of a given social and historical phenomenon and describing it as the basic sphere in which partiinost is manifested in realistic art; it is asserted that the problem of the typical is always a political problem and that only conscious exaggeration of a character discloses and brings out its typicalness.[152]

To suggest that these oft-quoted maxims from Malenkov's speech were actually incorrect was to hint at a significant revision of literary doctrine, for Malenkov had merely given concise formulation to ideas that had long had "widespread acceptance" in the Soviet Union, at least among literary bureaucrats and party officials. But if the article initially aroused such great expectations, it provided little to sustain them either in its treatment of the relation of art to other categories of ideology or in its treatment of typicalness and partiinost in literature.

A fundamental concern of the article was the problem that had come to the fore in 1950 and after — that of low aesthetic standards and dullness in art. The underlying reason for this concern was the very one that had given rise to anxiety on the earlier occasions, as the following statement indicates:

The depth of typification determines not only the cognitive but also the socially active, educational role of literature and art, their capacity to arouse intense feelings of love, hatred, and contempt, and the desire to imitate beloved heroes and to follow their example. To reproduce the essential aspects of life not schematically, but rather in vivid, concretely felt, and aesthetically impressive images, affecting not only the reason but the emotions — this is the essence of the complex process of artistic typification of the phenomena of life.[153]

Kommunist observed that "mediocre, inartistic works" were being produced and that many novels and stories were "peopled not with live individuals but with moralizing manikins." [154] The reason for this, said the journal, was that the thesis which states that the typical is "an artistic generalization of what is most characteristic of life" had been given a "one-sided and pedantic interpretation." The definition of typicalness which resulted fosters "illustrating general principles instead of making artistic discoveries," fails to take into account "the specific nature of artistic cognition," and neglects the qualities that distinguish art from "other forms of ideology." [155] Here the journal revealed that its own position was similar to that adopted by *Literaturnaya gazeta* not long before: Art, said *Kommunist*, "is a specific form of ideology. Artistic cognition of life is governed by its own laws, which differ substantially from those of scientific cognition. . . . Unlike science, art reflects the laws of life in images, that is, in a concretely felt form, portraying the universal via the individual." [156] Although *Kommunist* presented its arguments in a manner which suggested that it was saying something significantly different from what had been said three years earlier, important distinctions between its position and views enunciated in 1952 or in 1947 — or in 1937, for that matter — are not readily discernible. Much attention was paid to the difference between scientific and artistic cognition after the linguistics pronouncements in 1950, and even during the height of Zhdanovism innumerable theoretical essays acknowledged the distinction between "thinking in images" and "thinking in concepts" and examined the problem of universals in their particular artistic embodiments. In practical criticism, too, certain differences between a journal article or propaganda tract and a work of art, though propagandistic art, had always been recognized. It will be recalled that in 1947 Simonov's *Smoke of the Fatherland* was condemned because the basic idea of the work was realized "not in artistic images but . . . in declaratory judgments pronounced by the author" and because its hero was not a three-dimensional figure but a "moralizing *intelligent*." [157] Indeed, it appeared that *Kommunist*'s theoretical exercise on this point was little more than another call for the creation of "vivid images of Soviet man," although in the literary-political context of 1955 the calculated emphasis of the article had a special significance. *Kommunist* also pointed out that the formula under attack caused artistic standards to be neglected in critical evaluations of fictional characters. Although Onegin and Pechorin appear to have the same social-class "essence," said *Kommunist* by way of illustration, "each is an individual with his own passions, destiny, and so on." [158] Here the journal's argument was directed against an evil not unlike the one that Fadeyev had remarked upon at the Nineteenth Congress when he said that literary works were too often regarded as "illustrative reading for history or for this or that sociological situation, without any allusion to the fact that literature is beautiful." At any rate, this part of the *Kommunist* article should have given some comfort to those who had been arguing since 1950 for individuality and deeper psychological analysis in the portrayal of fictional characters, and it seemed to give retrospective support to those who had complained during the postlinguistics debate on aesthetics that art was too often ascribed to the superstructure "in general," without consideration for its peculiar characteristics. *Kommunist*'s discussion of the nature of art did little more than reiterate and give theoretical justification to claims that had been made both before and after 1950, but it carried the force of a rebuff to *Voprosy filosofii* and those who shared that journal's views. Thus it consolidated gains made in the realm of literary practice since 1950 and since Stalin's death.

Kommunist also displayed a very familiar concern about the practice of idealizing reality, and it made a show of rejecting justifications for deliberate exaggeration. But in fact the journal merely reaffirmed what it ostensibly set out to deny. There are many techniques of typification, argued *Kommunist*, and it is a mistake to reduce them all to the single one, exaggeration. In contrast to this erroneous view, *Kommunist* announced that "exaggeration is not one of the devices of typification, but rather fuses with the very concept of typification." [159] It is true that *Kommunist* took note of "various dubious arguments concerning the typical exceptional hero, where 'exceptional' means uncommon," but this was immediately followed by the statement: "But the uncommon is typical in realistic art if it reflects the germs of the new, which are always potentially mass phenomena." [160] This and *Kommunist*'s assertion that literature must "with irresistible artistry" depict "the all-conquering power, greatness, and beauty of the new and progressive" [161] were directed toward the same end as Zhdanov's claim that literature must provide "a glimpse of our tomorrow," a claim that has for two decades provided justification for idealizing reality. *Kommunist* also disclosed its awareness that exaggeration can cut two ways when it added a caution against hyperbolic illustration of the negative sides of life. In short, the only perceptible difference between Malenkov's and *Kommunist*'s views on this question was the manner in which they were phrased.

Kommunist's critique of the thesis that the typical is "the basic sphere in which partiinost manifests itself in realistic art" was primarily directed toward the problem of how to interpret works of pre-Soviet writers and of contemporary non-Communist authors abroad, and the views of the journal gave added impetus to changes in attitude toward Western writers that had begun to manifest themselves several months before.[162] Here the journal advocated a more substantial modification of policy than it had on other matters, though there was no evidence of any revision of the theory of partiinost. *Kommunist* argued that equating typicalness and partiinost encourages an antihistorical approach to literature: it fosters a tendency, said the journal, to regard all realistic artists of all epochs as "party men" and to place all "progressive" artists in the same party camp. Although this was apparently intended to indicate that greater freedom of interpretation would be tolerated in literary scholarship and criticism, it should be noted that objections to instances of particularly blatant distortion were not novel. Even in 1949, for example, *Literaturnaya gazeta* reproached M. Dobrynin for attempting to transform Chekhov "almost into an ideological comrade-in-arms of the Marxists." [163] But more than that, *Kommunist*'s argument had the effect of tightening the conception of partiinost, as the journal itself indicated:

one cannot simply divide all artists into two politically opposed parties. The advocates of such a division point out that there has always been reactionary and progressive art. This is quite correct; but the incorrect conclusion drawn from this equates progressiveness with partiinost. The concrete content of the term partiinost disappears in such a definition. . . .[164]

Kommunist's argument entailed the familiar presupposition that great works of art necessarily manifest narodnost: great artists have always expressed the aspirations of the people, and their works, by truthfully portraying reality, have aided the people in the struggle against the exploiting classes even though the artists themselves may not have consciously adopted the viewpoint of the masses. Lenin gave this understanding of narodnost a "new historical content," asserted *Kommunist*, by singling out Communist partiinost as "the basis for the creation of truly popular art." [165] The implication of this is that the exactions and restrictions imposed on artists in the name of partiinost are really only manifestations of a purer and more adequate understanding of what artists have always done. With reference to "progressive realist artists" in capitalist countries who do not accept the principle of partiinost, the journal asserted that it was wrong to say that they cannot create vivid, typical images or contribute to progress, though it indicated that their services would be greatly enhanced if they supported the proletarian cause more directly.[166] *Kommunist* clearly was not endeavoring to broaden the concept of partiinost itself, and the journal did not neglect to stress the point that it is through Communist partiinost that the artist can "find the path to that artistic truth without which no truly great work of art is possible." [167]

The party accommodatingly provided a concrete illustration of the revised theory of typicalness only a few days after the above issue of *Kommunist* had gone to press. On January 5, 1956, *Pravda* condemned Pogodin's play *We Three Went to the Virgin Lands*, and on the following day, the editors of *Komsomolskaya pravda*, who had approved the play on December 13, revised their opinion. The play, which was produced on the stage at the Central Children's Theater, had been presented on television as well. The movement toward re-evaluation, however it was instigated, actually began shortly before the *Pravda* editorial appeared. On December 19, *Sovetskaya kultura* announced that it had changed its original estimation of the play because of critical letters it had received after the television showing on December 10. On the day that *Pravda* attacked the play, *Literaturnaya gazeta* published a report of a writers' conference at which Pogodin admitted that the work had some "false accents" and declared his intention to correct the shortcomings.[168] But it is worth noting that this was the first time since Stalin's death that *Pravda* had attempted to legislate opinion on a particular work by means of a denunciatory editorial.

The three protagonists of Pogodin's play are young factory workers who decide to answer the party's appeal for volunteers to go to the virgin lands. In a soliloquy in the play's first scene, one of them, Rakitkin, analyzes his decision to volunteer, asking himself whether it was motivated by a desire to escape some trouble he was in:

Answer me: Why did you so quickly agree to fly off to those waste lands? Was it just fear of a possible trial? No, I swear it wasn't! Out there, in the open spaces, I'll begin life over again. The past is dead. Everyone will drink — but I won't. I'll be respectable, almost saintly, I swear it. And then no one will be able to say that Rakitkin is on the brink of hooliganism. . . . The past is dead! [169]

Once on the sovkhoz, the three comrades meet other young volunteers, and it quickly becomes apparent that almost all of them have come to the virgin lands for personal reasons and that they are at first disillusioned by the life they find awaiting them. A seamstress named Nelly, for example, is chiefly interested in finding a husband, and early in the play she thinks enviously of her less adventurous friends at home: "Right now my friends are sitting at the hairdresser's having their hair waved, while I lie miserably on bare planks all evening. . . . And there's no virgin land here, just snow up to your neck, storms, and wolves. You're lost, Nelly." [170] Of the young volunteers, only Tamara came to the virgin lands dreaming of "superhuman heroism," and she did so because, in her own words, she "thought life was like a technicolor movie." [171] But the play reveals the strength of the young people as well as their inadequacies in coming to grips with the difficulties of their new life, and it ends on a note of optimism. Nonetheless, Pogodin had not chosen ideal Komsomol types for heroes, nor had he represented their motives in going to the virgin lands as "pure" ones. This apparently vexed some people. *Pravda* complained that Pogodin's heroes are "chance-met people who in no way characterize the main body of Soviet youth" and that they go to the undeveloped lands only to "improve either their characters or their biographies"; furthermore, Pogodin failed to show "the organizing role of the Soviet collective" in reforming and educating people. *Pravda*'s own view of the situation was that in real life the volunteers are the flower of Soviet youth and that they are moved to go to the virgin lands not by self-interest or a desire to escape their pasts but by "the exalted romance of a labor exploit, of selfless service to the socialist motherland." [172] But there was ample evidence to indicate that *Pravda*'s representation of the situation was an oversimplified one. V. Kadrin's survey of fiction and essays about the virgin lands pointed to diverse conditions, not all of which approximated the party's ideal.[173] Kadrin commented on the variety of people's motivations in going to these outlying areas, the mixture of good and bad types, the hardships and disappointments experienced, the problems of hooliganism and drunkenness. Moreover, the critic indicated that some authors refused to write about the virgin lands because there was too much about which it was "not pleasant to write" and because they would inevitably be reproached for producing a "gloomy picture." [174] Of more interest in some ways were Pogodin's notes on his trip to the virgin lands to gather materials, originally for a scenario; for he apparently anticipated taking some sort of risk and provided an apologia in advance. Pogodin observed that "the great majority of readers" would probably question the purpose of showing such things as drunkenness and would object to representations of "uncultured persons" who do not conform to the highest ideal; but if the writer adjusts to such standards, said Pogodin, the result will be a representation of "some kind of real but at the same time unrecognizeable life." And the playwright went on:

According to this highest ideal, the best of the best young people, whom it is customary to call "envoys of the Motherland," go to the virgin lands. Why such an exalted attestation, I cannot understand. As it must be in life, the exceptional people sustain it; but there are vast numbers of neither the best nor the worst, people who are not distributed according to categories but who are moving — they grow, lag behind, stumble, meet with life's catastrophes — in a word, they constitute a huge sea of life.[175]

More important than whether Pogodin or *Pravda* was right about the objective situation was the principle that *Pravda* implicitly reaffirmed by its attack. It is the party, not the individual writer, that determines the nature of the "typical," and if "specifically artistic cognition of reality" produces an image that conflicts with the party's interpretation of reality, it is the former that must be modified.

The *Kommunist* editorial of December revealed that the party leadership was trying to dissociate itself from the worst excesses of Stalinist practices in belles-lettres, but without surrendering or weakening the dogmas which constitute the theoretical basis of the control system in literature. The strength of writers' reactions against postwar literary practices, as it was revealed in 1953 and 1954, was undoubtedly one of the factors which convinced party leaders of the expediency of reassuring dissatisfied elements in the literary intelligentsia by dramatizing the party's support of a position of moderation. But the *Kommunist* editorial was above all significant as a maneuver which epitomized the tactics employed by the literary bureaucracy during the preceding two years. These tactics were patterned after devices employed skillfully and successfully in 1950–1952 to save the core of literary doctrine from violation — devices such as routing the opposition, adopting some of the opposition's views in an emasculated form, and hinting at a forthcoming revision of literary policies. *Kommunist* was following in this tradition when it labored mightily to bow just perceptibly to current trends. True, it granted some benefits to scholars and others concerned with non-Communist writers, and, if concrete achievement is a measure of intent, this was the principal purpose of the article. Beyond this, *Kommunist* took note of evils that had been officially admitted long before, and it provided retroactive theoretical support for gains already made in the realm of literary practice. In doing this, *Kommunist* emphasized that the party had rejected rigidly doctrinaire views in favor of somewhat more generous interpretations of basic literary dogmas. But *Kommunist* did this in a manner which tended to create the illusion that past policies were being modified in a significant way. Instead, the article marked an effort to shield the party's literary theories from attack and to keep debate within limits, for to repudiate the most extreme formulations of policy was to provide security, in the form of slight concessions to the discontented, against a counterattack on essentials of the policy. This, too, was reminiscent of a stratagem employed in 1950–1952.

Trends since Stalin's death, however, demonstrated that the devices which a few years before made it possible to reduce pressure for liberalization no longer operated with the same effectiveness. The discontent that in the past burst only occasionally through the veil of unanimity was now emerging ever more frequently into full light. It was becoming evident that to pursue a policy of moderation in a generally relaxed atmosphere while enforcing time-honored literary dogmas was no easy task. In the milder climate of 1956, as events were soon to suggest, some writers either unwittingly misinterpreted the position which the party had taken in the *Kommunist* editorial or decided to use it as an opportunity to push the party further toward liberalization than it had intended to go. It was an indication of the changed conditions at the end of 1955 that party-minded critics failed to detect immediately the harmfulness of Kadrin's article and Pogodin's play, for both contained materials not wholly in accord with the party's views on a subject dear to its heart. This was only a part of the evidence that pointed to a growing rift between actual literary practices and official literary dogma. During the next year, following the Twentieth Party Congress, these tendencies acquired sufficient force to raise the threat that the rift might develop into a deep and unbridgeable chasm.

IV ✧✧✧✧✧

The Challenge of 1956

✧✧

The ideological confusion that manifested itself in 1956, after the Twentieth Party Congress, greatly exceeded that which arose following Stalin's death. The denigration of Stalin at the Twentieth Congress and the renunciation of parts of the Stalinist heritage provoked questions about the essentials of party policies and, indeed, about the very foundations of Soviet society, though party leaders tried as best they could to forestall this development. Khrushchev's defamation of Stalin, vivid as it was, traced the dictator's degeneration only from 1934 and was in other respects qualified, and the Central Committee's clarifying resolution of June represented an effort to shield the Soviet system itself from searching criticism.[1] But the momentous pronouncements of party leaders at the congress, shocking as they may have been to some Soviet citizens, could hardly have failed to arouse expectations of a brighter future. The surge of hope and sense of release that some writers experienced are reflected in remarks about the congress written by Olga Berggolts in April, on the occasion of Lenin's birthday. How often, Berggolts exclaimed, have historians and writers "depicted the past, present, and future path of our people as an express way paved with sugared asphalt! How often and how long have many of us been imprisoned by doctrinaire, dogmatic stereotypes. . . ." And in the congress the poetess perhaps discerned an affirmation of attitudes she had urged in recent years, for she declared triumphantly that the congress had opened to "literature, poetry, the cinema, and the theater just that scope for thought and imagination, that scope for individual inclinations, which Lenin bequeathed to art." [2] But the discussion that emerged during the summer and fall of 1956 threatened to extend beyond, if not to call into question, that "great truth, the party's truth and Lenin's," which Berggolts coupled with "lofty individual craftsmanship" as the "single law" of Soviet writers. The issues raised were not actually new ones, for they centered on problems that had troubled the literary community during the whole of the postwar period. What is remarkable is that the reaction against Stalinist policies took the form of highly articulate searchings which reached toward the ultimate causes of admitted evils. Taken as a whole, writers' criticisms, demands, and visions — as they were articulated not only in articles but in novels, plays, and poems — threatened to become, whether it was intended or not, a forceful indictment of the essentials of Soviet literary doctrine and of the very fundamentals of the control system. The literary discussion did not, of course, move in a single direction: the familiar pattern of conflict between prophets of orthodoxy and advocates of liberalization emerged through the flux of events and grew increasingly distinct as the year 1956 drew to a close.

The major purpose of the following discussion is to outline the central issues raised during the literary ferment of 1956. Though in some sense this constitutes a summary of much that has gone before, it provides a necessary background for analyzing the literary policies of the party during the ensuing three years, and it perhaps affords a prospect on the more distant future, for the legacy of 1956 will plague the regime in one way or another for years to come.

Early in the unfolding literary debate of 1956 it became apparent that, directly or indirectly, doubt was being cast on the validity of the hitherto sacrosanct trinity of the official theory of art — partiinost, ideinost, and narodnost. What was loosely called "withdrawal from party positions" first manifested itself, according to a later report, "in speeches by certain writers at meetings with readers." [3] As this suggests, discontented writers found it possible to develop their views more frankly in speeches than they could in printed essays — and more frankly than the Soviet press chose to reveal in its rare and brief references to such speeches. Even so, the polemical articles that were published, together with the reactions of the guardians of orthodoxy, provide more than a bare clue to the scope of private thinking and discussion.

Most menacing from the viewpoint of the party were the assaults on the very principle of partiinost. As early as May, *Literaturnaya gazeta* sounded the alarm, asserting that some people "are forgetting about the partiinost of literature" and disclosing that at writers' conferences speakers had declared "in an alien voice" that literature should not be a "servant of politics." [4] Many months later, during the drive to restore order in the literary household, charges of antiparty thinking became fairly common. An editorial in *Kommunist*, for example, denouncing writers and artists who demanded "anarchic freedom" from control, admitted that attacks were made on party guidance itself. [5] The discussion as it progressed in the press, however, did not produce direct attacks on partiinost as a guiding principle, and it may be that few writers actually hoped or even wished to do away with the general notion of party guidance. Rather, they complained about unduly narrow interpretations of partiinost and even more vociferously about the stultifying "administrative methods" used to realize it; while doing so, they seduously emphasized the distinction between "party guidance" (good) and "petty tutelage" (bad). This occasioned a ruthless probing of the problem by Tvardovsky in 1945, at the Tenth Plenum of the board of the Writers' Union, when he questioned the possibility of organizing literary successes. But because in 1956 writers' complaints took the form of attacks on virtually everything that partiinost had come to mean in terms of the institutional devices that made its application effective, the alarm of party officialdom was understandable.

The most important article dealing with the question of controls, written by B. Nazarov and O. Gridneva, appeared in *Voprosy filosofii*. [6] Though its specific subject was dramaturgy and the theater, its significance extended to all the arts. Lashing out at regulation of the arts by administrative techniques, command, and "the application of all kinds of repression," the authors rejected the whole idea of guidance by directive and cast doubt on the postwar decrees by arguing that it was Stalin's personality cult which gave birth to the conviction that "it is possible to attain success in art by instructions, orders, decrees, and resolutions." [7]

Undoubtedly emboldened by recent discussion of the need to re-write early Soviet history with greater attention to fact, Nazarov and Gridneva made effective use of Lunacharsky's statements and of quotations from the party's policy declarations at a time (during the NEP) when it was pursuing a moderate course of compromise in the cultural realm. While rejecting the idea that theatrical affairs should be freed from governmental regulation, the authors pointed out that such regulation can be direct or indirect, and they advocated transferring the responsibility for supervising the theater from the Ministry of Culture to a new "public organization" similar to the Writers' Union, in order to give the theatrical world a measure of self-government. The experience of the Writers' Union and other professional organizations hardly suggests that such a change would in itself be enough to eradicate the causes of dis-content. But it is of some interest that the proposed solution took this form, the more so when it is viewed in conjunction with an-other theme of the article and against the background of widespread dissatisfaction in the other arts. For the authors asserted that the imposition of "harsh controls not only over works of art but also over the creative process itself signified a loss of trust in the artistic intelligentsia," [8] and a sense of injury over the party's alleged lack of confidence in artists was strongly expressed elsewhere in the article. That the reaction was to demand "self-government" sug-gests that the art intelligentsia may have begun to define its own interests more clearly, to gain strength as an "interest group," and that urges toward pluralism may have been increasing. If workers in the arts share a sense of alienation and seek beyond their own fields to find the common basis of discontent, their stirrings might over a period of time become an increasingly serious challenge to monolithic party rule. On the other hand, it has long been the policy of the party to fractionalize the intelligentsia and to deprive intellectuals of a common forum for voicing their discontents. It is significant in this respect that Nazarov and Gridneva claimed that only members of the intelligentsia holding administrative posts had been trusted and that full confidence was still accorded only to "officials of administrative agencies, among whom there are to this day not a few 'play-safe-ites.' " [9] This not only points to one of the cleavages within the intelligentsia, hence to a success of party policies, but it also directs attention to that vast structure of controls whose purpose is to restrain urges toward autonomy in the lower ranks and to preserve the party's ultimate authority.

Startling as it was, this outburst against party controls was limited in ways characteristic of many other articles written after the Twentieth Congress. Most notably, Nazarov and Gridneva argued that repression and harmful techniques of controlling the arts emerged in the mid-thirties and that in the theater this was marked by the creation of the Committee on Affairs of the Arts in 1936. While it is quite true that the mid-thirties prepared for the final victory of Stalinist cultural policies — a victory not properly celebrated until the bacchanalia of postwar Zhdanovism — the policies that led to the difficulties described in the article have their sources in earlier periods of Soviet history. Jumping back to the golden era of the NEP to find contrasts to later evils, the authors remained understandably silent about events in the arts during the First Five-Year Plan. Without rehearsing the history of the period, something of its atmosphere may be suggested by recalling a remark which Gorky made in 1930 with reference to the Pilnyak case and other such incidents:

We have formed a stupid habit of dragging people up the bell-tower of fame and throwing them down into dirt and filth after a little while. I won't give examples of such absurd and brutal treatment of people; they are known to everyone. They remind me of the lynchings of petty thieves in 1917–18. . . . And it is thoroughly exasperating that precisely these bigoted, barbarous, rapacious persecutions of men come to mind whenever you see how eagerly and lustfully everybody pounces on a person in order to capture his position after he has been debased and destroyed.[10]

Against Gorky's statement, Nazarov and Gridneva's recommendation of Leninism becomes somewhat less persuasive:

Right up to the middle of the thirties the party, proceeding from Leninist principles, led an unflagging struggle for realistic art. The chief method used in this struggle was guidance based on patient, comradely criticism. . . .[11]

But it was quickly made evident that the article in the philosophical journal had attributed too much to the Stalinist personality cult as it was. *Pravda* and *Izvestiya* simultaneously printed articles which criticized Nazarov and Gridneva's effort, and *Voprosy filosofii* repudiated the article in its next issue.[12] The official attitude on the question of party controls and the postwar cultural decrees, as it emerged toward the end of 1956, was stated most succinctly by B. Ryurikov in *Kommunist*. Ryurikov defended the decrees and in effect argued, not without justification, that they were a logical outgrowth of Leninism:

The party's scientific Marxist policies in the province of literature and art — policies formed over a period of decades — found their expression in the postwar resolutions . . . on ideological questions. In these documents there are isolated inaccuracies, insufficiently grounded evaluations and characterizations. But in the main, the documents — in which are expressed such bases for the development of our art as ideinost, service to the people, recognition of the lofty social role of art — preserve their whole significance today. They have played a large positive role in the spiritual life of our society and they continue to be powerful ideological weapons of the party.[13]

It is apparent that a threat to partiinost was similarly discerned in Konstantin Simonov's rather quixotic efforts to induce a revision of attitude toward the first version of Fadeyev's *Young Guard*. Fadeyev's novel, it will be recalled, was criticized for giving a gloomy impression of the first phase of Soviet defense against the Germans and for underplaying the guiding role of the party in the underground resistance to the invaders. For a number of reasons, Simonov appeared to be on fairly solid ground in demanding a reconsideration of the case. A revision in the interpretation of the first years of the war had been underway since the spring of 1955, when a reaction was initiated against "embellishing" the events of those years.[14] And with the denigration of Stalin in 1956, increasing stress was placed on the role of the masses in history and on the virtue of initiative. In his first attempt in the summer of 1956, not long after Fadeyev's suicide, Simonov, though he broached the question of fact, observed that this question was really irrelevant since Fadeyev's novel was, after all, a novel and not an historical chronicle, and he suggested that the first version "had a greater inner unity and was closer to [Fadeyev's] original intent." [15] However, this argument failed to impress the editors of *Pravda*, who among other things objected to Simonov's effort "to oppose some sort of 'inner unity' to the historical truth." [16] Nonetheless, Simonov developed his argument more fully in the December issue of *Novy mir*.[17] One of Simonov's main points was the quite reasonable one that the novel in its first version demonstrated more convincingly, if less directly, the impact of the party's educational efforts on youth precisely because the young people in the novel were able to act effectively without immediate supervision and direction by party leaders. Simonov's ensuing attack on the "normative" aesthetics which formulates rules about how certain classes of people must or must not be portrayed was hardly novel in itself; but because the criticism was directed against the editorial in the party press which had opened the Fadeyev incident — and against what had been represented as the party's impersonal opinion — Simonov's analysis seemed to contain a threat to the party's right to determine the nature of reality. The claim that Stalin himself had inspired the editorial was an obvious opening for escape, and through it Simonov made his exit — or so it might be argued. But at the same time Simonov, with considerable display of emotion, cast doubt on the wisdom of requiring writers to revise their work. Simonov's position, if accepted, would not only cancel out the widely publicized moral of the Fadeyev incident but tend to negate two basic principles of the theory of controls. Hence the response of *Kommunist*'s editors was not wholly surprising, even in its charge of anti-Soviet thinking:

K. Simonov tries to make it appear that A. Fadeyev, . . . having accepted party criticism and creatively revised the novel *Young Guard*, only impoverished the work. . . . Why was it necessary for K. Simonov to cast doubt on the freedom of authorship of one of our outstanding writers? Was it not in order to revive and rehash old tendencies, long ago condemned, which in the final analysis are directed toward the "liberation" of literature from "party tutelage," toward the preaching of so-called freedom of creation, about which bourgeois liberals abroad are now shouting so much? [18]

As always, the party was showing itself to be extremely sensitive to every significant challenge, open or implicit, to its ultimate authority in the arts. The incident was an evil portent for authors who were demanding recognition of the right to portray the truth of life as they perceive it.

If partiinost was questioned, at least in certain of its institutional embodiments, socialist realism was subjected to even more searching criticism. To distinguish between the two is, of course, somewhat artificial, for as *Literaturnaya gazeta* pointed out, attacks on socialist realism "in the last analysis lead to one thing — the denial of partiinost and ideinost in literature." [19] But skepticism about socialist realism raises special problems having to do with diversity of literary styles and, even more important, with the dogma of ideinost, or the ideological conformity that is allegedly a requisite for high artistic accomplishment.

Because socialist realism was canonized in the thirties, it was almost inevitable that the doctrine would be attacked as one of the pernicious outgrowths of Stalinism. The extent to which criticism was carried is indicated by press reports that at one conference a speaker declared socialist realism "bankrupt" and proposed that it be "abolished." [20] A revealing analysis of the threat that reared its head in all the arts was provided by the well-known painter V. Serov:

> The danger is that the mistakes bound up with the cult of the individual leader are being exaggeratedly represented as well nigh the ideological foundation of Soviet art. Persons seeking to pass off the concept of socialist realism as an offspring of the cult of the individual are jostling their way in under the banner of just criticism aimed at eliminating the effects of the cult.
>
> They are not beyond revising even the principles of realism in general, presuming that the time has come to restore the rights of citizenship to any modernist, formalist trends. . . . They are trying to persuade us that consistent realism in Soviet art was artificially and forcibly imposed upon the artist.[21]

Counterarguments took two forms. It was asserted, on the one hand, that socialist realism emerged as a product of historical forces, that it existed before a name was found for it in the thirties, and that it "was not 'established' but won out in free creative competition with other methods." [22] The other defense was to acknowledge past errors and narrow-minded interpretations in order to preserve the principle itself. This was a central theme in Simonov's article of December. At one point he argued, for example, that it would be wrong to substitute the phrase "literature of the epoch of socialism" for socialist realism because the former would include with good works all the falsifications which in the postwar years "were very often declared models of socialist realism," something that caused confusion not only among Soviet writers but among "like-minded writers in countries of the socialist camp." "It is time to eliminate this confusion," Simonov added, "and thereby fully to rehabilitate the method of socialist realism in the eyes of all who in a fit of bewilderment or bitter disappointment were rashly inclined to renounce it." [23] The officially sanctioned policy that evolved toward the end of 1956 was aimed at salvaging the reputation of socialist realism by renouncing some of the potboilers formerly held up as models and admitting that socialist realism could embrace a greater degree of diversity than had been tolerated in the recent past. This policy was based on the recognition by responsible literary functionaries that, in the words of a Soviet historian writing on the question of partiinost, "the sectarian-dogmatic tendency and the nihilist tendency nourish one another." [24] The approach was not in principle different from that which Surkov adopted in 1954 when he indicated that a moderate policy must be followed, a policy of opposition to "new-RAPPist-type vulgarizers," on the one hand, and to "panic criers" who would slander the whole of Soviet literature, on the other.

The year 1956 was marked by extensive, though not indiscriminate, rehabilitations of the reputations of Soviet writers, most of them deceased, who during the past twenty years or more had been consigned to various levels of the Soviet literary purgatory. At the same time, a movement to reappraise the Soviet literary past gathered momentum among critics and scholars. Many of these developments enjoyed official sanction, and, insofar as they did, they may be regarded as part of the effort to preserve the essence of Soviet literary doctrine while eliminating some of its most ludicrous applications in the realm of literary history. The spate of literary rehabilitations that occurred after the Twentieth Congress would have been unthinkable in 1954, when tentative steps in this direction were first taken; for in 1956 the movement resulted not only in the reprinting of Ilf and Petrov's satirical novels, but in the republication of selected works of Isaac Babel and Yury Olesha and the resurrection of the names, if not always the works, of many other authors who had long been referred to with disfavor.[25] Moreover, the rehabilitations included persons identified with condemned literary groups, such as the Pereval. Even the party journal *Kommunist* published an article which cautiously supported a more objective approach to the Soviet literary heritage. Pointing out that

Zhdanov's speeches of 1946 contained an "inadequate description" of the Serapion Brothers, the article hinted in addition that a revision of the traditional attitude toward the Proletkult and the RAPP might be in the offing.[26] It was sometimes mentioned in the press that rehabilitated persons had been associated with literary groups that were later condemned, and there were other indications that the evaluation of these groups might be modified. There was a danger, of course, that these developments might strengthen the affection that some Soviet writers felt for the years of the NEP, when divergent literary currents had not yet been channeled into a single stream and effective instruments had not yet been devised for enforcing partiinost in the arts. Thus it was hardly surprising that the authors of the *Kommunist* article repeated the warning, frequently heard during these months, that it is incorrect

to make the antihistorical assertion advanced by some writers that only the twenties were a "paradise lost" in Soviet literature because literature then was distinguished by "unsurpassed diversity." Everyone knows that, along with remarkable examples of revolutionary art, the literature of those years included various formalist, naturalist, decadent "writings" that did not enrich Soviet literature. . . .[27]

Because the authors had enumerated some of the pernicious effects of Stalin's cult of personality on literature, they were careful to underscore their opposition to attacks on partiinost, socialist realism, and the fundamentals of Marxist-Leninist aesthetics and to reject all doubts about "the indisputable achievements of Soviet art."

While there was a willingness in responsible quarters to concede that socialist realism must be interpreted more generously, what this would mean in specific terms for those currently engaged in writing remained in doubt. Thus the authors of an article in *Kommunist* asked suggestively whether socialist realism does not embrace "works which cannot be included unconditionally and fully in the category of realism," but they gave as examples only works in which romantic elements predominate.[28] In view of the repeated discussions of this matter over a period of years, by 1956 there could no longer have been any serious doubt that socialist realism includes elements of romanticism. The meaning of socialist realism might be broadened quite simply, for it is necessary only to conclude that one school or another is realistic in its essence — a service that I. Grabar attempted to perform for the graphic arts with respect to impressionism, only to provoke formidable opposition.[29] And, in general, such attempts were countered by references to Lenin and the Proletkult incident and to Lenin's views on modern art. The more elaborate argument that behind various "schools" of art there are concealed ideological and ultimately class interests was implied in numerous warnings against manifestations of a "conciliatory attitude toward the phenomena of bourgeois art, which is part of an attempt to carry the thesis of the peaceful coexistence of countries with differing social-political systems into the realm of ideology." [30]

The threats to ideological orthodoxy that the party-minded discerned in attempts to broaden the meaning of socialist realism were in some measure engendered by the party itself. For the party had not only tolerated but upon occasion had advanced views which fostered "conciliatory" attitudes and tacitly raised a significant ideological problem in belles-lettres, one which revealed distinctly an old weakness in the ideological armor plate. While arguing that a correct world view is the prerequisite for accurately representing reality, Soviet literary ideologists have had to develop theories to explain how a writer such as Balzac, whose political views could not even be considered "progressive" for his time, could depict reality so truthfully as to win the approbation of Marx and Engels. The problem becomes more apparent when it is admitted, as *Kommunist* did in 1955, that contemporary non-Marxist writers, who cannot be unaware of the existence of a highly developed and correct world view, are nonetheless able to portray reality so accurately that their works are worthy of the attention of Soviet readers. Ideology would seem to become irrelevant to the representation of reality in literary works. In an article which marked the changing attitude toward Western writers, printed in September 1955, Fadeyev displayed his awareness of the problem. Referring to Engels' comments on Balzac, Fadeyev observed that some people place a "simplified interpretation" on the passage, contending that the question is one of contradiction *between* a writer's creative method and his world view. The correct interpretation, urged Fadeyev rather indecisively, is that there may be contradictions *within* a writer's world view.[31]

Fadeyev's defense of the relevance of ideology to artistic creativity will not bear close scrutiny even within the framework of Soviet aesthetic theory, and it is of interest that in 1956 one scholar expressed dissatisfaction with it.[32]

The challenge to orthodoxy that emerged in the arts was only one manifestation of a malaise that afflicted other realms of Soviet society and the whole socialist camp as well. If the stirrings among Soviet youth were particularly striking, so were the forms by which they found expression. The press reported a sudden upsurge of student interest in literature, the organization of literary circles in institutes and universities, and the appearance of unofficial handwritten or typewritten journals (one of which was called "Heresy"). Brief though they were, such reports — which included complaints about decadent tendencies in student writing and even the assertion that some students had fallen under "enemy influences" — indicated that the disquiet was extensive.[33] Revealing evidence of the nature of the ideological threat appeared in an article published by *Vestnik vyshei shkoly* which complained that "there has arisen among some students a so-called 'gnoseology trend,' which advocates an idealistic interpretation of Marxist-Leninist philosophy and denies that dialectical materialism is a world outlook and historical materialism a philosophical science." [34] Among the party's responses to these developments was an organized campaign to steer student activities in the "correct direction" by placing the discussion groups and unofficial journals under party or Komsomol guidance. Similarly, a serious challenge to ideological unity manifested itself in the Communist countries in the form of devastating criticism of socialist realism, notably by Hungarian and Polish writers. Soviet policy emphasizes close cultural ties among countries of the socialist camp, and should artists in Poland, for example, succeed in banishing socialist realism or even in establishing a broader interpretation of it than that which prevails in the USSR, Soviet artists and audience alike, having discovered that rather surprising artistic practices are not incompatible with socialism, might begin to wonder whether one of the national paths to communism does not have certain advantages over their own. The vigor with which Soviet officialdom denounced attacks on socialist realism is understandable as an effort to check a developing ideological pluralism.

During 1955 and even more vigorously in 1956, doubts were voiced about a number of practices usually rationalized in terms of the principle of narodnost, doubts that touched upon several distinct but related questions. Many writers expressed dissatisfaction with the crude oversimplification with which narodnost had become identified. Ilya Ehrenburg, for example, while affirming his belief that "every artist strives to be understood by as many of his contemporaries as possible," pointed out that "this does not mean that all works of art must be perfectly comprehensible to all readers, viewers, or listeners the moment they appear." [35] But when Ehrenburg expressed his feeling that "we sometimes use the word 'formalism' loosely," he failed to provide his readers with the larger perspective on the problem that he might have if he had cited remarks on the dangers of the struggle against formalism that he made some twenty-two years earlier, at the First Writers' Congress.

That the possibilities open to Soviet artists had been unduly restricted and that the Soviet public had been provided with much inferior work were themes which appeared with increasing frequency after Stalin's death. But what was striking in 1956 was the growing concern revealed in the press about the effect this had had on the Soviet public, a concern that went beyond references to the declining public interest in contemporary prose, poetry, and theater. Some commentators admitted that the arts had contributed far less than claimed to the enrichment of man's spiritual life and to that "complete emancipation of all human senses" which was the utopian vision of both Marx and Lenin. In an essay on poetry, for example, one critic penned a biting analysis of the "reader-vulgarizer" who, nourished on "rhymed productions" that pass for poetry and schooled by "bad critics," has a primitive conception of poetry and approaches the other arts just as crudely, expecting paintings to be photographs and musical compositions to be songs consisting of familiar and easily remembered motifs.[36] Such readers, the critic asserted, do not understand metaphor, hyperbole, or poetic imagery and are only vexed by genuine poetry; they prefer verse in which "every line is understandable, predigested," verse

which "does not require any exertion of thought"; and, worst of
all, they bombard editors with complaining letters when journals
publish poetry which is more than "rhymed prose, rhymed information." [37] Similar points about the situation in the dramatic
arts were made by G. Georgiyevsky, a theater director, who observed that for years the press and persons associated with the
theater had persuaded people that "schematism, rhetoric, mere
illustrations" are what art should be. If a part of the audience
learned to stay away, he said, another part — "the most submissive,
uncultivated, and naive" — developed the habit of verifying their
theater experiences not against life "but against the theater itself, so
to speak — by faithfulness to the standards then prevalent in dramaturgy and on the stage. They stopped seeking the truth of life in
art and became habituated to the notion that the theater is a place
for conventionalized action, heroes 'generalized' into clichés, and
prettified happy endings." [38] Georgiyevsky's conclusion is significant, for it is undoubtedly applicable to all of art:

> to these theaters today still come people whose taste we formerly spoiled
> and who are merely returning to us what we once gave them. Here, as in
> other spheres, the law of inertia operates. It is not an accident that we now
> speak of eradicating the *consequences* of the mistakes committed in various
> spheres of ideology. For it is one thing to understand some thought, idea,
> or thesis, and quite another to reconstruct one's thinking, one's psychology.
> This process is taking place on both sides of the footlights, but it will take
> time for the new trends, so eagerly greeted today by the people, actually to
> be embodied in art and for the people who have been trained to be satisfied
> with surrogates and substitutes in art to disappear completely.[39]

The authors of the *Voprosy filosofii* article on dramaturgy, whether
they intended to do so or not, probed even further into the question of the method by which taste and aesthetic values are cultivated, though they did not elaborate their views very fully. Claiming that the Soviet people have unequivocally spoken for realism in
art, the authors declared that "this does not at all mean that they
have repudiated the right 'to judge about everything' or to enjoy
all the fruits of art, not just those which someone acknowledges
as suitable for consumption." [40] The authors further asserted that
"the higher a person's cultural level, the stronger will be his urge
to examine everything independently, the more vigorously will he
defend his right 'to judge about everything,' " a remark which im-

plies that autonomy of judgment is an integral part of education and cultural growth. Such autonomy is meaningful only when there are genuine alternatives to choose between, which might mean occasional contact with difficult and disturbing works of art. In answer to this, the editors of the philosophical journal wrote:

Correctly speaking of the important role of the Soviet community, of the opinion of the people, in the development of art, the authors are inclined to forget that the development of this public opinion must not be regarded simply as a "spontaneous" phenomenon. The opinion of the people always, in all epochs, developed and develops under the influence of the various social ideas and teachings elaborated by ideologues of the various classes. The opinion of the Soviet people is formed and developed under the guidance of the people's advanced segment, its avant-garde — the Communist Party. . . .[41]

Although the party apparently wishes to establish conditions permitting the exercise of greater initiative on the part of its citizens, it is not yet evident that it has granted them scope to determine for themselves "what is created by talent, what is fostered by love, what is beautiful."

As on former occasions, disquiet about low aesthetic standards in art was reflected in efforts to find a theoretical basis for dealing with aesthetic problems as such. The conference on aesthetics organized in 1956 by the journal *Voprosy filosofii* was concerned with matters no less recondite than those which arose after the linguistics pronouncements, when discussion centered on the question of art's position in the superstructure and its possible status as a broader form of social consciousness. But, as on the earlier occasion, underlying the debate in 1956 over the definition of "aesthetics" and its relation to the "theory of art" were issues of a more mundane character.[42] One of the two major speakers, G. B. Puzis, presented the thesis that aesthetics is properly the study of beauty and its laws, whether in art or in nature; but the theory of art, he argued, is concerned with all the elements that appear in art — aesthetic, economic, political, moral, and such. The editors of *Voprosy filosofii*, in a commentary accompanying the report of the conference, made it clear that Puzis' thesis was unacceptable to them. One of the reasons they gave was that it "isolates aesthetics from actual practice and obliterates the cognitive function of art, its role in the struggle against everything negative in life which

impedes the gradual development of society." [43] A. P. Belik, a
representative of the journal, had already put the point rather more
bluntly, at the cost of misrepresenting Puzis' viewpoint: "It is
profoundly mistaken," said Belik, "to reduce the whole plenitude of
art's contents to the beautiful, for such a reduction unavoidably
brings us back to the theory of 'art for art's sake,' which restricts
the contents of art to the aesthetic and the beautiful." [44] The editors of *Voprosy filosofii* lent their support to the more ambiguous
position of the other main speaker, G. A. Nedoshivin, who offered
an indecisive definition of aesthetics and argued that to admit of a
disjunction between aesthetics and theory of art is unsound. The
significance of the "broader" view which denies that aesthetics is
merely a study of the beautiful was fully revealed in the following
number of the philosophical journal, which contained an article
that made the usual identification of art's aesthetic properties and
"ethical" or political factors, thus demonstrating that art mobilizes
men's thoughts and feelings for the struggle of the new against
the old.[45] The philosophers' discussion was in its own way an
example of the persisting vigilance lest theoretical groundings be
provided for an aesthetic standard that might supplant partiinost
as the ultimate criterion for evaluating art.

The more or less straightforward efforts to modify aesthetic
theory were by no means the only threat to orthodoxy in this
sphere. Many articles which dealt in one way or another with the
larger purposes of literature and the proper tasks of the writer reflected attitudes toward art that implicitly challenged official
doctrine. The reaction in 1956 against the narrowness of that conception of utility which is a defining feature of Soviet literary
theory was remarkable because of its extent and its forcefulness.
True, the reaction itself was not wholly new. Much that was said
could be regarded as an elaboration of attitudes revealed in certain
articles published during 1953 and 1954 or, more particularly, in
Olga Berggolts' polemical outbursts. For articles that appeared in
1956 provide moving evidence of Soviet writers' longing to portray
life truthfully; and in some of them, writers, critics, and scholars
call for genuine diversity of form and content, argue that literary
works must reveal the full complexity of human experience, and
defend the right of authors, and of poets in particular, to express

the whole range of human emotions — a reversion, in effect, to the defamed theories of "self-expression." An article by the critic S. Shtut, published in *Novy mir*, contains a pithy, vigorous statement of the more generous viewpoint. Decrying the fact that "tragedy, satire, doubt, and meditation" had been declared incompatible with socialist realism, Shtut asserted that a work need not provide a final answer to problems that it treats and declared that it was time to exercise the privilege "of evaluating according to its merits *every* book that in some way has made life happier and more meaningful." [46] Elsewhere the same critic propounded views which recall Olesha's wistful comments on the intricacy of the writer's task:

Truth in art is complex. It is sometimes deficient, contradictory; it is a neighbor to error; it struggles with the artist's subjective limitations, with the defects of his political and philosophical world view; sometimes it conquers them completely, sometimes partially; sometimes it emerges from these skirmishes severely wounded. But even wounded and bloodied, it is truth all the same. And not simply truth, but the truth of discovery or, what is the same, the discovery of truth. And this ability to discover a truth unknown to anyone before constitutes the very core of the creative individuality.[47]

Perhaps less colorfully, with greater or lesser force and consistency, other writers and critics touched upon related themes in exploring the question of originality in belles-lettres, in urging writers to "speak with their own voice." What this direction of thought may ultimately imply can best be demonstrated in connection with a work in which it was expressed with particular clarity, although undeniably in an atypical manner — an unabashedly romantic work entitled *The Golden Rose*,[48] which contains the reflections on writing of Konstantin Paustovsky, a writer of the older generation (born in 1892). As one reviewer acutely observed, the work is an elaboration of an attitude presented concisely in one of Paustovsky's short stories: "You must admit that leisurely meditation and intent contemplation of life in all its details are at certain times just as right for every person in our land as sleep, the reading of books, and a person's favorite work." [49] One of the noteworthy features of *The Golden Rose* is that its author speaks of literature without relying on Marxist jargon and of writing as a calling to which a person might — and should — commit himself wholly. This is not to say that Paustovsky advocates a radical theory of art for art's sake, that he endeavors to set belles-lettres off against life, to separate literature from human values. On the contrary, he urges that it is precisely the writer's task to capture and preserve in art, for the sake of his fellow men, the wealth and variety of human experience as he knows it, that the writer is a person who cannot live without "transmitting to people with unstinting generosity the whole vast profusion of thoughts and feelings which fill him." [50] What is actually the essence of Paustovsky's conception of the writer's function is revealed most succinctly in a digression on van Gogh, which gives some indication of the book's spirit as well. Van Gogh, says Paustovsky,

was always astonished by nature's faultless correlation of colors and the inexhaustible variety of their mutations, by that coloration of the earth which continually changes but is equally beautiful in all seasons and in all climes.

By an exercise of will he stopped the incessant flux of colors, that we might enter into their beauty.

How is it possible in the face of this to assert that van Gogh was indifferent to man! He gave man the best thing he possessed — his capacity for living on an earth that gleams with all possible colors in the most subtle modulations.[51]

Paustovsky's viewpoint raises the same problem that Pomerantsev's criterion of "sincerity" did: it might encourage subjectivism and foster ideological pluralism. It is significant that others who wrote on related questions frequently seemed less concerned that a writer's subjectivity be of a "party nature" than that it be the writer's own.

Paustovsky's work, which appeared in 1955, was usually described as controversial when it was mentioned at all; the comparatively few critics who discussed the work approached it with some caution, when they did not actually rebuke Paustovsky for some of his views. What bothered some people is revealed clearly enough in the question of T. Trifonova, who wondered whether it is possible to discuss art without illuminating "such general problems of aesthetics as the problem of the narodnost and partiinost of art." [52] As it might have been expected, Trifonova also touched upon the question of the educative functions of art in discussing both *The Golden Rose* and *A Turbulent Youth*, the second part of Paustovsky's autobiography: "The influence of art," she said, "is connected with what Chernyshevsky called a 'judgment on life' and Belinsky defined as the artist's 'fervor.' With K. Paustovsky the judgment sometimes remains very much in the background and the fervor hidden behind highly refined but sometimes chilly . . . craftsmanship." [53] But what is more, Paustovsky's highly individual work reflects a more widespread reaction against illiberal conceptions of the political and pedagogic tasks of art, and the author's attitude seems close in spirit to the view which Fedin had expounded in 1944 — that an artist does not consciously strive to produce politically tendentious works. Indeed, the instances of apolitical thinking, the manifestations of individualism, and the evidence of a rebirth of humanism were reminiscent of developments in the literary community toward the end of the war; but the forces which produced them seemed even more robust in the year of Stalin's disgrace.

Works of imaginative literature registered perhaps more sensitively than the articles discussed above the currents that were sweeping the Soviet literary community in 1956. Although Soviet disputation on ideological questions takes place in rather rarefied atmosphere, issues fought out on this level are still significant as indications of policy trends precisely because of the Soviet habit of rationalizing practice in terms of doctrine. Yet even when the issues are formally resolved and ideological conformity is secured, the possibility remains that actual practice may deviate in varying degrees from established theory. This happened in belles-lettres during 1956. It appeared that the principles of the postwar decrees were becoming increasingly irrelevant to emergent literary trends and that at least a portion of the literary output was in spirit antagonistic to the larger purposes of the control system. A consideration of some salient features of developments in Soviet literature during 1956 will indicate the character of the problems facing the regime in this sphere.[54]

Currents of thought that had found outlets in belles-lettres in 1953–1954 were represented even more vividly in some works that appeared in 1956. Ehrenburg, with his unexpected extension of *The Thaw* into a second part, once again provided a suitable label for a new period of ferment.[55] He carried on with themes presented in the first part of the work, criticizing narrow-minded views on art and emphasizing the changes for the better that were occurring in Soviet society. But he took care to clarify his views on several matters that had disturbed critics two years earlier. In the second part of the novel it is made unmistakably apparent that the talented and sensitive painter Saburov is not an artist in an "ivory tower": Ehrenburg reveals that Saburov is closely identified with the life of the toiling masses and that his paintings inspire workers to greater sacrifice in the struggle for the realization of the good society. Furthermore, Ehrenburg rewards Saburov by allowing him to achieve public recognition. But the fortunes of the hack painter, Volodya Pukhov, are on the decline; thoroughly demoralized, Volodya has begun to suffer the full consequences of his cynicism and lack of principle. Ehrenburg's treatment of a new figure, Vyrubin, is indicative of the character of the second installment as a whole. The reader is told that Vyrubin, who had been unjustly arrested many years before, spent seven years in prison and ten in exile before his case was reviewed and the charges against him declared false. But Vyrubin discloses that during the difficult years of imprisonment and exile, neither he nor most of his comrades in misfortune ever lost faith that justice would ultimately win out. Vyrubin is represented as a gentle person whose sufferings were beneficial to the development of his character and whose undeserved punishment for some reason prevented him from growing old in spirit. It is not necessary to dwell longer on Ehrenburg's novel, for material contained in other works is more significant in terms of social criticism, which is our principal concern here.

As noted earlier, the more orthodox elements of the literary community had been distressed by the fact that in a number of works — *The Thaw*, Panova's *Seasons of the Year*, and Zorin's *The Guests* among them — social evils were not only depicted but, it was alleged, shown to be widespread, even "typical," and, furthermore, that the evils were not represented as "bourgeois survivals" but appeared in some way or other to be products of Soviet society itself. Yet such phenomena are apparent in a number of works published in 1956. Among the most striking examples are Daniil Granin's story "One's Own Opinion" [56] and Vladimir Dudintsev's novel *Not by Bread Alone*,[57] both published in the journal *Novy mir*.

Granin's story is remarkable because of its concentrated and straightforward presentation of the theme that the pressures of the Soviet bureaucracy force those who are a part of it into a pattern of hypocrisy, falsehood, and deceit. The story in effect develops a motif that appeared in Zorin's play *The Guests*, in the self-justifying words of the unprincipled bureaucrat Peter Kirpichev:

A position of responsibility is a severe master. It has a moral code of its own. You want to be kind, gentle — and it won't let you. The governmental mechanism, you see, is like an orchestra: if you want to play in it, you have to follow the baton, fall into rhythm.[58]

The central character in Granin's story, Minayev, has fabricated his career through subterfuge and deception, by misrepresenting his own opinions, suppressing the views of others, and defeating naive and well-meaning "innovators" who tilt at persons entrenched in the bureaucracy. Once an enthusiast in opposition himself, Minayev quickly learned the futility of struggling against insuperable odds and set out to attain a position of strength by the devious means requisite, that he might then speak in his own voice and so redeem his sins:

He taught himself to be patient and to keep silent, in the name of the day when he would be able to do what should be done. . . . He voted 'for' when his conscience told him to vote against. He spoke words that he didn't believe. He praised what should have been criticized. When this became utterly intolerable, he kept silent. Silence is the most convenient form of lying. It comes to terms with the conscience, it cunningly reserves the right to maintain one's own opinion and, possibly, to speak it sometime. Only not now. Not as the head of a workshop and not as the head of a technical department and not as the chief engineer of a factory. And not at the defense of a dissertation. Still too soon. Every time it was still too soon! [59]

The story concludes with Minayev's dismal realization that the road has no end, that no position is secure, that he will go on justifying his stratagems in the name of a tomorrow that will never dawn. Nor is Minayev represented as a unique figure. In the story, Minayev himself concludes that only two people say what they actually believe — the naive, honest engineer-in-revolt and the "base, thoroughly base" party instructor who could speak his own mind precisely because everybody else "thought one thing and said another." [60] When the editors of *Partiinaya zhizn* criticized the story, they treated Granin kindly in saying that "whether the author of the story intended it or not, objectively his story seems to assert that it is not Minayev's fault that he has become a time-server and a double-dealer, but that the fault lies with life itself, with our reality." The editors were also annoyed because the single party official in the story is described as incompetent and malicious, because there are no positive characters who struggle against the evils shown, and because the story "creates a mood of hopelessness and futility" with respect to this struggle and does not contain "a single ray of hope." [61] It is quite true that the story lacks the inevitably happy ending characteristic of works of earlier years, even of Granin's own novel *Those Who Seek*,[62] which aroused considerable interest when it appeared in 1954. Indeed, Granin's story "One's Own Opinion" was a step in the direction of fulfilling a task which the author set for himself at a readers' conference in Leningrad months before. Asked why in *Those Who Seek* he had not shown how "negative" types originate, Granin replied:

This is a very complex problem and for me a very difficult one; I know I did not fully solve it in the novel. To solve this problem is, in the last analysis, most important for the educative influence of a book. One must expose the germs of that evil which crops up in our midst, in people who were born under Soviet rule and are unacquainted with capitalist society.[63]

Granin's story added to the evidence that in 1956 writers felt freer to probe further into social problems which even two years earlier they had broached with some caution.

Although Dudintsev's novel *Not by Bread Alone* is more broadly conceived than "One's Own Opinion," it has certain elements in common with Granin's story. The main plot of the novel is built around a "conflict" that is familiar in Soviet fiction: it concerns an inventor, Lopatkin, who carries on a struggle, in this case virtually singlehanded, against obstructionists in the bureaucracy. Although Lopatkin is portrayed as a rather unusual personality, to say the least, Dudintsev indicates that Lopatkin's predicament is not unique by depicting two other figures who have already been defeated in similar struggles. The theme of the nonconforming "little man" — in this case a strong and stubborn character, to be sure — who carries on a lonely and just battle against apparently insuperable social forces is central in the work. Like Granin's story, the novel suggests that the ethical code of those in high positions does not correspond to the ideal of socialist morality, for in the novel the bureaucracy is populated by shrewd, unprincipled manipulators for whom human values are of incidental importance — qualities epitomized in the figure of Drozdov. But Drozdov is presented as a product of his environment. He represents a class of tough, hard-working, but narrow-minded administrators who have risen to the top because they could meet the demands of a system which requires industrial growth at any cost; they do not draw back, as men of more generous mold might, from the distasteful maneuvers which their own survival requires. Some critics were scandalized because the novel seems to treat Drozdov and his ilk as a common Soviet type, and it was urged in opposition to this that Drozdov "is typical not as a new 'antisocial type' that has developed in Soviet society, but as a representative of an old breed of bureaucrats that is gradually dying out." [64] There is a notable paucity of "positive" characters among the bureaucrats depicted in the novel, and the few worthy figures who do occupy positions of responsibility — Galitsky is the principal one — are admirable not because of their mastery of Marxist-Leninist philosophy but simply because of their human qualities and their sense of justice. Dudintsev indicates that men like Lopatkin and Galitsky are not isolated types in Soviet society, but he suggests that they are often suspiciously regarded as "idealists" with apolitical tendencies. The work also contains some rather incidental, though vivid, evidence of differences of living standards between the upper and lower strata of Soviet society.

But what is more striking is the novel's criticism of the bourgeois ideals of the Soviet philistine. Thus it develops motifs that appear in Zorin's play, where one character refers to a Soviet bureaucrat as a "high-ranking magnate" and another character describes her attitude toward such bureaucrats as "similar to a class feeling" and rails against people who lead lives "in which the main thing is not labor but position, not achievement but acquisition," lives which are "narrow, complacent, uninspired, radically different from the life which I and millions like me live. . . ." [65] Dudintsev's preaching of devotion to a task even to the point of asceticism, illustrated by Lopatkin's rejection of material comfort for the sake of an ideal, and the contrast the author draws between Lopatkin's "courageous madness" and the timid "good sense" of philistines are among the aspects of the novel which some critics found objectionable. In developing this theme, Dudintsev is not merely criticizing philistinism. Lopatkin is more than an imaginative engineer: he becomes a symbol for the creative impulse that moves the writer and the artist as well. The novel glorifies selfless devotion to a vision and unwavering dedication to the pursuit of goals that contribute to the social good, a good which may not be truly represented by those who speak in the name of the "collective," by entrenched bureaucrats with whom the dedicated must wage a relentless battle. The termination of the tale fails to bring with it a resolution of the fundamental conflict. Lopatkin has won the immediate contest, but his enemies have been neither vanquished nor weakened, and the struggle will go on.

Dudintsev's novel aroused great excitement in the Soviet Union, and if it "touched the minds and hearts of readers," as one critic declared,[66] it also evoked contrary reactions, obviously giving rise to vexation in some quarters. Opinion as it was represented in press commentary toward the end of the year and early in 1957 showed an increasingly marked divergence from the attitude expressed by a reviewer who wrote in an October issue of *Trud* that Dudintsev's novel is characterized "by deep portrayal of the truth of life." [67] Soon the novel would become a major target of attack. But it was the widespread discussion, public and private, that the novel provoked which made the appearance of the work particularly significant.

One effect of the reaction to the novel was to reveal that other writers shared with Selvinsky the nostalgia he expressed in 1954 for the days when public participation in literary life was livelier, and some persons hopefully discerned signs of a revival in the developments of 1956. At a public discussion held in the Moscow writers' club, Vsevolod Ivanov declared "portentous" the "exceptional attention" given by readers to Dudintsev's novel, and he expressed his joy because of this and because "today's crowded meeting reminds me of the days of my youth, when Soviet literature was being formed and when the Polytechnic Museum was the forum of the new literature. It would be very fine should our club become such a forum for contemporary Soviet literature." [68] A similar viewpoint, elaborated some months earlier by a drama critic in an article on the theater, may be cited to bring one aspect of the Dudintsev affair into sharper focus:

We frequently have to deal with plays against which one cannot raise an objection, for they contain a useful idea, do not violate the truth of life, do not destroy our correct ideas about this or that question, but add nothing new to these correct ideas. We must demand that in a play Soviet playwrights say something new, something never before said on a given topic. Let the play give birth to discussion in the theater; let arguments arise about a theme that is treated profoundly. [69]

The discussion to which Dudintsev's novel gave birth disclosed the potentialities inherent in a work which does say something new, a work which, as the reviewer for *Trud* thought, "is imbued with a profound and original view on life." The danger in this, of course, goes beyond the contents of such a work, for literary discussions of controversial books may easily become discussions of broader social and political questions.

There can be no doubt that Dudintsev's novel inspired discussions of broader issues. Press accounts of the meeting at the Moscow writers' club in October provide revealing evidence of this. The report in *Literaturnaya gazeta* contains the following passage:

K. Paustovsky went on to tell of his trip to Europe on the liner "Pobeda," on which he chanced to meet with certain "responsible" [*nomenklaturnye*] workers who, in his opinion, are akin to Drozdov. From these observations K. Paustovsky drew a series of incorrect conclusions and generalizations to the effect that Drozdovs are a mass phenomenon. [70]

Paustovsky's speech was not published in the Soviet press. But a stenograph of the speech, transcribed by someone present at the Moscow meeting, appeared in *L'Express* in France and in *Novoye russkoye slovo* in the United States. The report may explain why Paustovsky's performance was so vigorously condemned in later months, for the speech as reported in the Western press is an astonishing denunciation of the Soviet state bourgeoisie. Announcing that "there are thousands of Drozdovs" and that he wanted to talk about them, Paustovsky went on:

This is not merely a matter of describing a few careerists. It's not simply a matter of careerists. It's all much more complex and more important than that. The problem is that in our country a completely new social stratum exists with impunity and even flourishes up to a certain point — a new petty-bourgeois caste. It is a new population of rapacious and propertied persons who have nothing in common with the Revolution, with our regime, or with socialism.[71]

Paustovsky then recounted several anecdotes, based on observations made during his European tour, which he intended as illustrations of the arrogance and vulgarity of this new "caste." Though Paustovsky linked these people with the Stalinist personality cult, he charged the whole group, not only Stalin, with the destruction of unorthodox artistic talent: "If it weren't for the Drozdovs, such people as Meyerhold, Babel, Artyom Vesyoly, and many others would still be living amongst us. They were destroyed by the Drozdovs. And they were destroyed in the name of the stinking comfort of these Drozdovs." Simonov's reply to Paustovsky is further evidence of the direction taken by the discussion, which, as *Literaturnaya gazeta* indicated in its summary, slighted the question of literary craftsmanship:

If we locate Drozdov on a specific level [said Simonov] and believe that Drozdovs are only found traveling first class and in specific positions of privilege, as K. Paustovsky suggested, we dishonor too many people without any foundation and at the same time unjustifiably pardon too many people. To speak of the liner "Pobeda," there were Drozdovs on various levels and in all three classes, including the one where writers traveled. But each of these classes had its own Galitskys as well. . . .

There are not a few people who are prepared to use the term "Drozdov" to ill purpose. They pretend that the novel criticizes whole strata of the party and governmental apparatus. In reality, Drozdov is a distinct type in the governmental apparatus, and all the healthy forces in that very apparatus everywhere lead a relentless fight against his type.[72]

The turn which the public discussion took perhaps provides some basis for speculating about what was being said by those whose views the press did not record. Whatever that may have been, the occurrence inevitably evokes the memory of an earlier period of Russian history when, because of censorship and limitations on political activity, belles-lettres became a vehicle for discussing social problems and, as such, a means of political activity, however limited. Analogies in history may obscure more than they reveal, but it is at least suggestive to recall Annenkov's comment on the social significance of art during the period of severe tsarist repression a little more than a hundred years ago: "People of this epoch saw in a concern with art the only path left to them which led to public affairs of some sort: art was virtually the salvation of people, for it permitted people to conceive of themselves as freely thinking human beings." [73] The Soviet regime may well have had reason to be concerned about what a reviewer writing for *Izvestiya* decried as the "unwholesome stock-jobbing" that had allegedly arisen in connection with *Not by Bread Alone*.[74]

In the realm of poetry, the work closest to Dudintsev's novel in theme is Semyon Kirsanov's "Seven Days of the Week." [75] Kirsanov's poem is an attack on a dehumanized bureaucracy that stifles creative thought and initiative, and at the same time it is a plea for the freedom and trust that are conditions of creativeness. The poem, a surrealistic and grotesque fantasy, deals with an inventor's unavailing struggle during the course of a week to win acceptance of his plan to produce new human hearts for people whose hearts have become defective. Having drawn up a blueprint for the hearts, the inventor tries to interest a governmental ministry in his project, but he is met with indifference on the part of bureaucrats, who impose a fine on him as a reminder that no thoughts may be born without directives. But the inventor persists and, with the permission of the party district committee, produces a model of the new heart. Kirsanov's characterization of the functions of the heart is significant as an indication of the moral and humanistic impulses underlying the poem. For the heart, says the poet, is to serve as a means of communicating vital emotions — excitement, joy, pain, love; it is to be a means of establishing contact among people, of joining people in a community of feeling. A heart of this sort will be sympathetic to every kind of appeal; it will not deceive, lie, or vent its spite on the weak. The acute need for this heart is emphasized: "It is awaited everywhere/ It is awaited in the *ispolkom* [the executive committee of a soviet] and in the law court." [76] But the inventor's efforts come to nought when, on the fifth day of the week, the model heart is inspected by a commission of government officials, who are described in terms of the qualities they represent — "the Double-Faced One," "the Indifferent One." The commission rejects the invention:

> Such hearts are not needed for public consumption.
> And in general our market does not require novelties.
> We need useful hearts, hearts like iron locks,
> Uncomplicated, convenient, capable of fulfilling every command.[77]

And the commission warns that in the future a penalty will be imposed for such "seekings." Kirsanov then — in a satirical reference to governmental efforts to regulate human emotions — has the inventor appeal to the Committee of Lofty Feelings, Sector of Urgent Business, Division of Humanity.

For a brief moment the inventor experiences a surge of hope, when he thinks he discerns "the Country" smiling with approval on him; but an official interposes himself between the inventor and his vision, and the hope dies. The final irony occurs when the inventor discovers that his idea has been stolen and that the newspapers are celebrating someone else as an "innovator," an inventor of hearts now being advertised for sale at department stores. But what kind of hearts are these? They are cheap counterfeit hearts — hearts of tin and rubber, heart-shaped flasks of sweet perfume, and albums of facile verse. His notion of a living heart, the inventor bitterly muses, has become a "velvety freak," and, what is worse, the public has been taken in by the deception:

> A lie in the form of a heart was being brazenly handed out,
> And the public succumbed to the fraud.
> And a man without a heart gave his poor girl friend
> A little heart in the shape of a copper brooch.[78]

The inventor has struggled in vain, and his only comfort is that the next Monday, a new week, may bring greater accomplishments.

In this poem Kirsanov repeatedly makes a plea for a grant of trust from the Country, a plea that is coupled with a defense of those who seek to serve a common human good and a condemnation of the corrupt callousness of obstructionists. In this the poem reflects a mood generally shared by authors of the "critical" literature of 1956. Kirsanov makes his plea with especial forthrightness in the opening and closing sections of the poem, where at the same time he expresses hopes with respect to the Country that are disappointed by the actions of the Country's official representatives. In his introduction, Kirsanov addresses the Land of Soviets, referring to it as the embodiment of freedom and appealing to it to speak out clearly in freedom's name:

> And so say: I shall not reject any requests. . . .
> I need everyone, and every dreamer
> Perishing from thirst is dear to me.
> Soullessness is hateful to me, as to you!
> So that there will be no further threat of it,
> I shall deny defense to no one!
> Conceive plans, reflect, seek,
> I shall not shut the door to you,
> And I hand you my trust, like a mandate! [79]

Elsewhere the poet refers to a longing for "faith and trust" and "not to live like a petitioner/ Before a silent door." [80] At the close of the poem, too, Kirsanov voices the hope that the Country will give scope to ideas and destroy "dead soullessness."

In attacking spiritual apathy and official indifference, Kirsanov hardly draws a flattering picture of Soviet reality, and his distinction between the Country and officials who speak in its name verges on heresy. It was perhaps to be expected that Kirsanov's appeal for creative freedom, trust, and tolerance, like the petitions of the protagonist of his poem, would fall on deaf ears. The poem provoked the wrath of Soviet officialdom and became a major target of attack a few months after its publication.

Another poem which elicited official denunciation was Margarita Aliger's "The Most Important Thing," written in 1948 but first published in November 1956.[81] The poem is a profoundly heretical one, for it shatters the official image of the new Soviet man. The forcefulness of this short poem is partly the result of the ironic contrast around which it is built. Aliger first characterizes the official view of the new man, imagining that an unknown caller, an ordinary Soviet man, comes to tea. The poetess at first sees in the visitor all the attributes of the new man. He is the builder of bridges and cities, the author of whole libraries of books, the embodiment of all desirable moral qualities:

> How persevering and relentless he is,
> How noble and strong.
> It was he who crushed the fascists,
> And he who will build communism.
> He will not fail the Plan,
> He will make his own — such is he!

Aliger refers to him as "a giant/ The hero of the legends and of the ages," as one who is needed by all mankind. But when the visitor dissembles and tries to extricate himself, the poetess suddenly sees him for what he is — a liar who slanders his friend, a coward who flees from difficulties. The lofty illusion has been punctured, the heroic giant reduced to a cowering dwarf:

> Leave him to the fierce frost!
> Let snow cover him over.
> He is not needed by humanity,
> Worthless is this man.

This outburst is more an expression of an intense revulsion against the extravagant glorification of Soviet man encouraged by the regime than it is an indication of a lack of humanity or absence of hope on Aliger's part. In the closing lines of the poem, she says that if this man is worth anything at all he will discover for himself some "chemical compound" which, like acid, will destroy the reprehensible "accidental" features of his character, which "will kill the villain in the hero/ And the scoundrel in the giant." The Soviet people, Aliger concludes, believe that man may become great and good; it is for this that they are striving.

The appearance of the second volume of the almanac *Literaturnaya Moskva* toward the end of 1956 was one of the outstanding literary events of the year. The volume contains a novel, a play, and several short stories, poems, and articles which, when read together, afford revealing insights into the mood of dissident writers. This issue of *Literaturnaya Moskva* excited the anger of party spokesmen, who criticized the almanac even more harshly than they did *Novy mir*, which published the works by Granin, Dudintsev, and Kirsanov discussed above. A consideration of two of the short stories will be sufficient to indicate the critical tendencies which the almanac represented and to suggest the reasons for the angry attack which it provoked.

Official critics censured Alexander Yashin's "Levers" [82] with particular severity because the story deals directly with the party, depicting it as the source of a variety of evils. As the story opens, four party members are sitting in the administrative office of a collective farm, informally and frankly discussing the problems of the farm and the treatment they receive at the hands of the party authorities who are their immediate superiors — the members of the district committee. District officials, they complain, are ignorant of the real situation on the farm and make impossible demands. The relationship between the district committee and the farm is a wholly one-sided one: order after order comes from the district secretary, who refuses to heed the advice of the farmers themselves, declaring them to be mere "levers" of the party in the countryside. The farmers particularly resent the district secretary's failure to trust them. And they dislike his cold, officious manner; he evidently feels, they say, that the party would lose authority if he were to act like an ordinary human being or speak to them straightforwardly and simply. The point of the story comes when the men who have been complaining open their own party meeting. The atmosphere abruptly changes, and the frank discussion ends. The farmers now imitate the manner of the district secretary: they make long ritualistic speeches and repeat the very words of the secretary to which only a moment before they had bitterly objected. They have lost their simplicity and humanity in spite of themselves, partly out of fear of making mistakes or behaving improperly. When, with a certain relief, the farmers close their meeting, the atmosphere once again changes, and they become themselves. "And again they were," in the closing words of the story, "pure, warm-hearted, straightforward people and not levers." The story was offensive to party officialdom because it shows that ordinary people feel that a gulf separates them even from the next higher level of the party, and it suggests that a similar gap separates other levels of the party hierarchy. More than that, the story depicts the party as a dehumanizing force and rank-and-file party members as its victims.

Though it attracted less attention, Yury Nagibin's "Light in the Window" [83] is in some ways a more significant story than Yashin's. The protagonists of this very short but highly symbolic story are the director of a Soviet sanatorium, a cleaning woman, and a high-ranking official who never makes an appearance. The director, Vasily Petrovich, has reserved in the sanatorium a spacious, well-appointed apartment, complete with billiard table and television set, for the exclusive use of a bureaucratic superior — referred to simply as "himself" — in case the official should ever make a visit. Nastya, the cleaning woman, has been assigned the task, in addition to her regular duties, of cleaning the apartment thoroughly each day, so that it will always be in impeccable order. The director sometimes regrets the time and effort spent on the upkeep of the apartment, and he is inclined at times, out of generosity and sympathy, to open the unused rooms to patients crowded into inconvenient quarters. But Vasily Petrovich represses his human impulses, the bureaucrat conquering the man, and the rooms remain unused. Nastya, who might be expected to resent the existence of the apartment, at first has no doubts about the propriety of the director's behavior or the usefulness of her labors. On the contrary, she takes great pleasure in caring for the apartment, indulging in fantasies about what she imagines to be the extraordinary qualities of a man who is able to elicit so much concern. But when days lengthen into weeks and weeks into months, until more than a year has passed and still the rooms have never been used, Nastya's joy turns into hatred. Feeling that she has been deceived by the official she has never seen, she is overwhelmed with contempt for him, and she now thinks it "the cruelest injustice" that the rooms are held in reserve for him. It is important to note that Nagibin describes Nastya in such a way that she appears to typify the basic goodness and generosity of the simple common man. The story concludes with Nastya's rebellion. Late one night, the director sees lights in the windows of the guest apartment, and, looking in, he finds Nastya sitting before the television set with the two children of the janitor, who is in the adjoining room playing at the billiard table. The director has a momentary, half-conscious feeling that this is good and as it should be. But a surge of anger supplants the initial feeling, and Vasily Petrovich, stamping his feet, rages noisily at the intruders, as if hoping "that his furious indignation would reach the ears of the one whose rights were so rudely violated." Nagibin closes his story with these words:

It can't be known whether *himself* heard him, but the trespassers remained deaf to the director's anger. Leading the children by the hand, they walked past the director with serene and stern dignity.

And looking at their stubborn, almost triumphant faces, Vasily Petrovich suddenly stopped short, fell silent, noting with astonishment a strange, new, unfamiliar feeling which rose and grew within him, penetrating to the tips of his fingers, a feeling of unbearable disgust with himself.

In depicting the bureaucratic hierarchy as a corrupting force, a system that victimizes those caught up in it, stifling their natural human sympathies, Nagibin presents an analysis of Soviet reality very much like that made by Granin, Yashin, and others writing in a critical vein in 1956. But in "Light in the Window" Nagibin goes further than most other writers. For he openly suggests that the common people — symbolized by Nastya — have been deceived by leaders to whom they honestly and naively gave their trust, faith, and love. But taught by bitter experience, they have at last seen through the ruse, and they are not likely to be taken in so easily again. Though they may obey in stubborn silence (Nastya and the janitor leave the forbidden rooms without resistance or complaint), they are aware of their moral superiority and resentful of injustices, which may provoke flashes of rebelliousness within them.

Because the party is highly sensitive to transgressions of the proper limits of self-criticism, works like Dudintsev's novel and Granin's or Yashin's story are the first to draw sharp critical fire when campaigns to heighten ideological vigilance get under way, and they are the first to suffer the impact of the prepublication screening process that takes place in editorial offices — the first victims, in short, of the control system in literature. For this reason it is meaningful to consider another broad trend in Soviet writing that has gathered force in recent years, one that may have a greater claim to permanence than the more overtly critical trend, at least if generally moderate policies prevail in belles-lettres and in other spheres of Soviet life. For convenience this trend may be referred to as the new humanism in Soviet letters, and its effect is also to contravene, though less immediately and directly, some of the presuppositions and purposes of the literary control system.

The pressure for "humanizing" belles-lettres, already reflected in the literary output of 1955, gained in strength during 1956. Writers were evidently inspired by the sense that the time had come, as Ehrenburg said in the first installment of *The Thaw*, for the creation of a genuine Soviet humanism and by the hope that in the future human relationships would be infused with greater generosity, tolerance, and compassion. This mood was stated explicitly in a passage in Nikolai Pogodin's play *Petrarch's Sonnet* where one of the characters, referring to that injunction to hate the enemy which is an essential feature of the official definition of socialist humanism, says:

> . . . I consider class hatred a sacred and noble feeling. But in reality we no longer have hostile classes. Who is there to hate? one asks. There are scoundrels, thieves, riffraff. They perhaps deserve contempt, and sometimes even compassion. But I am now speaking of great hatred. Whom in my country must I hate? Maybe it is time to learn to love.[84]

The humanistic trend was expressed in poetry by outpourings of intimate feeling and apolitical appreciations of nature; in other realms of belles-lettres it took the form of treating problems of personal and private life. One critic characterized the drift accurately enough when he complained that of late "emotions of love have assumed an excessively large place in poetry, as family problems have in prose," all as a reaction, he observed, to the one-sided emphasis "at the end of the 1940s" on production themes and the like.[85] Writers were moving further and further away from old formulas in dealing with problems of love and marital relations, and they sometimes included in their treatment of these subjects a defense of people's right to a personal, private life, free from outside supervision and interference. Two outstanding examples of this current of writing were *Petrarch's Sonnet* and S. Alyoshin's play *Woman Alone*.

Petrarch's Sonnet is memorable above all for its vigorous defense of the view that an important part of a man's inner life lies beyond the area in which the party may legitimately exercise control. Though Pogodin develops his argument by contrasting two concepts of love — an intolerant one and a generous one — he makes it sufficiently clear in the course of the play that he is speaking not only of love but of a whole range of human emotions. The plot centers about a middle-aged married engineer, Sukhodolov, who becomes enamored of a young girl, Maiya. Sukhodolov's love is pure, and his relationship with Maiya is a platonic one. But the snooping Klara, who is incapable of imagining such a relationship, reports Sukhodolov's feelings to a party official, Pavel Mikhailovich, implying that Sukhodolov is guilty of immoral behavior. From this point on, much of the play is concerned with depicting the antithetical views held by different characters. Klara defends, in the name of Communist morality and party orthodoxy, a narrow-minded, dogmatic attitude not only toward love but toward emotions in general; feelings, she argues, must be regulated, held within defined limits. Ironically, Klara is a public lecturer on cultural topics, employed by the Society for the Dissemination of Cultural and Political Knowledge. The tolerant, humane viewpoint is represented by the party official, Pavel Mikhailovich, and by Sukhodolov, who summarizes the attitude they share when he says:

there are some things that one cannot tell the party. If it were a political matter, cut off my head. . . . I give my whole soul to the party, will give my life. But a man can have certain intimate sides to his life which he will not reveal to anyone. He simply is not obliged to. There is no such rule.[86]

Ultimately, Sukhodolov is exonerated. But the play concludes with the implication that Sukhodolov will maintain his relationship with Maiya and that their love may be consummated.

Alyoshin's play *Woman Alone*,[87] which concerns the dissolution of two marriages, defends people's right to seek happiness in their own way, even when this entails breaking up a family. The author makes a halfhearted attempt to give the work some "social significance" in the officially approved sense by introducing something which resembles a "production" theme in the play; but this subplot has little to do with the main action and is quickly dropped. The plot of the play is simple and its central problem a familiar one. Sergei Platonov, an engineer, falls in love with his assistant, Varya, a married woman many years his junior. After a certain amount of soul searching, Platonov deserts his wife and daughter, and Varya leaves her husband. In several respects Alyoshin's treatment of the subject is interesting as a deviation from what have long been norms in Soviet writing on family themes. The dominant motifs of the play are the transience of human attachments and the threat of loneliness. These motifs emerge early in the play with the appearance of a minor figure, Margarita, who represents the loneliness that will be the lot either of Varya or of Sergei's wife, Maria. In one interchange, when Varya asks Margarita whether she has been married, the latter replies:

. . . I was. Three times. And all three times I gave it up. Each time I was outraged by the very same thing. Why is everything so good at first and so bad later on? Where does love go, anyway? It's like water and sand.[88]

Margarita indicates, however, that she has grown wiser about what marriage actually involves but that it is too late, and now "this doesn't matter to anyone." Again, it is a minor character, Lida, who puts Maria's predicament in stark perspective after Maria has been deserted by her husband. Lida, who has also been abandoned by her husband, finds solace in vodka and casual relations with men. When she appears at the end of the play begging Maria for drink, Lida defends her right to live as she sees fit:

You think I don't see that everyone condemns me? . . . I know how people talk: "Today she has one man, tomorrow another, and so on." . . . But I think it's better to be with them than to be alone. . . . During the day I work as a timekeeper, and at night I make merry. So there you are. . . . Let them condemn me, those who have always hidden behind their husbands' backs. Some of them don't feel any love, and they don't care. They only want to be supported. They only want the title "a married woman." . . . But I'm better than they. I don't hang on to anyone. And I can ruin myself as I please — this way or that. I want to drink vodka — and I will! I have the right.[89]

The unhappy Maria indicates that she understands that drink and self-destruction can present themselves as escapes from suffering, but she defiantly announces her rejection of such solutions. Thus the play ends with a declaration of strength and courage, though rousing optimism is hardly the dominant tone of the work. The image of three lonely women is likely to dominate the reader's or viewer's memory of the play, and Maria's grief and the suggestion that Varya and Sergei may not be happy together further modify the play's brighter notes. Alyoshin's tolerant attitude toward most of his characters is also noteworthy. He does nothing to prevent the reader from sympathizing with the three unhappy women or with Varya and Sergei.

Pogodin's and Alyoshin's plays both stirred up controversies.

Alyoshin's, indeed, was produced only after the stubborn objections of the Ministry of Culture and the Chief Administration of Theaters were overcome.[90] But the plays evidently struck responsive chords in Soviet audiences, and it is some indication of the strength and persistence of the moods they expressed that Moscow theaters were still playing them to well-filled houses in 1959.

Of the works published in 1956, several which were written by young authors or which deal with Soviet youth are of particular interest for what they disclose about the attitudes of a younger group of writers and at least a part of the younger generation in the Soviet Union. The attitudes revealed in these works are a facet of the renascence of humanism in belles-lettres, but they are especially significant because they relate to Soviet youth. Over a long period of time, the tendencies deriving from them may bring about important changes in the character of Soviet literary output and contribute to the broader changes taking place in Soviet society. These tendencies inevitably affect the party's policies in literature, at least indirectly, since the regime is forced to cope with them as they emerge in literature in an attempt to hold them within officially approved channels. To indicate the nature of the attitudes which these trends represent, it will suffice to consider two works — a poem by the young poet Yevgeny Yevtushenko and a novel about teen-agers by Lyubov Kabo.

Yevtushenko's long poem "Zima Station," [91] completed in 1956 when the poet was twenty-three years old, provides some evidence of the impact of de-Stalinization on the younger members of the intelligentsia. It reflects both the sense of shock that de-Stalinization initially produced and the hope and enthusiasm that it revived in some quarters. But above all the work is memorable for the open-minded attitude that the poet reveals, for his dissatisfaction with pat answers, his disgust with falsehood and deceit, and his unrelenting determination to seek truth, which is conceived as something complex and difficult.

The opening passage of the poem reflects the confusion into which the poet has been thrown by the death of Stalin. Shocked by the realization that the past was not what he had taken it to be, he sees that he must re-evaluate his beliefs and seek his own answers to the questions that trouble him:

> I know that others would give willing answers
> To all my questions — "How?" and "What?" and "Why?"
> But suddenly it turned out that I
> Must find these answers for myself.[92]

Full of doubts, anxious and upset, the poet returns from Moscow to his native Siberian village — a railway transfer point, Zima — to search for his answers and to rediscover himself.

With a keen eye for the details of everyday living, Yevtushenko paints a vivid and not very appealing picture of life in his home town. His interest in the ordinary life of the common man is in itself noteworthy, for it is characteristic of a group of younger writers who are perhaps reacting against the prettified representations of reality and the false heroism of much of the literature of the postwar period. Much about Zima shocks and repels the poet — the rawness and crudity of life there, the personal suffering that he witnesses, the injustice and inhumanity of representatives of Soviet officialdom. But even though the environment furnishes little consolation, Yevtushenko's experiences in his native district contribute to his search and to his understanding.

In a dingy restaurant Yevtushenko meets a Moscow journalist and pours out his heart to him. The journalist, a symbol of the cynical disillusionment which could conceivably be Yevtushenko's own fate, chides the poet for his naïveté, speaking disparagingly of the role of writers and uttering the most politically pointed lines in the poem:

> . . . And what is a writer today?
> He is not the creator, but the guardian of thoughts.
> Yes, change, yes, but behind the speeches
> There's some kind of shady game.
> We talk about what yesterday we kept quiet,
> And keep quiet about what we did yesterday.[93]

Yevtushenko rejects the journalist's cynicism, but he is carried a step further in his own reflections when he attends a show given by a third-rate juggler and magician. Significantly, the audience is enraptured by the performance and — like Nastya in Nagibin's story — taken in by the cheap, stale tricks. Yevtushenko, however, is led to reflect:

> How much of this kind of thing I've seen!
> I've seen so many old tricks,

> Only staged in a new, expensive way,
> And at so many performances like this
> I've applauded, though not too much, with the others.
> I've seen so many decorated spoons,
> When you couldn't find groats to make soup with,
> And I thought about truth and falsehood,
> And the transformation of truth into falsehood.
>   . . . We are all guilty . . .
> Of the empty verses, the countless quotations,
> The stereotyped endings of speeches.[94]

But Yevtushenko's musings lead him no further in this direction. He rejects pessimism and cynicism, and he denies that he is merely indulging in carping criticism. True devotion to one's country, he asserts, must be based on something more than thoughtless acceptance: "Today we need not blind love/ But thoughtful, searching love!" [95] A deep-seated idealism is the fundamental impulse behind the poem, and Yevtushenko not only emphasizes the need to live for a purpose but claims the right to examine the purposes for himself: "We don't want to live as the winds may blow/ We must understand our 'why.' " [96]

The theme of the search for truth is the central one in the poem, and it is with this theme that it ends. About to return to Moscow, the poet, looking down on Zima from a hill, thinks he hears the village say to him:

> "Today you are not alone in the world
> In your searchings, aspirations, struggle.
> Don't grieve, my son, that you've not answered
> That question which has been put to you.
> Be patient, observe, listen.
> Seek, seek. Roam the whole wide world.
> Yes, truth is good, and happiness is better,
> But still, without truth there can be no happiness.
> Go into the world, holding your head high,
> Looking always forward with heart and eye,
> And on your face —
>   the lash of wet pine needles,
> And on your eyelashes —
>   tears and storm.
> Love people — and you will understand them.
> Remember —
>   I shall be watching you.
> If it is hard — return to me.
> Now go!"
>   And so I went.
>   And so I go.[97]

Though the poet's visit did not produce answers, it did bring the conviction that truth is to be found only through persistent questioning, not in easy, ready-made formulas, and that the quest must go on. Determined not to be deceived again, the poet insists on his right to look behind fine phrases and flashy surfaces. The poet's determination to pursue truth and the idealism which is the basis of his rejection of deceit and falsehood hark back in a sense to the spirit of the early revolutionary period of Soviet history, though his is an idealism mellowed somewhat by experience.

Lyubov Kabo's novel *On a Difficult March*[98] suggests that the questioning and confusion, even disillusionment and cynicism, of some Soviet youth have their origin in something far more profound than the re-evaluation of Stalin's career: the sources are deeply embedded in Soviet reality itself — in the educational system in particular — and they give rise to forces which touch not a few individuals but whole groups of Soviet youngsters. Though the novel is first and foremost a polemic on education, directed chiefly against conventional, unimaginative, and uninspiring methods of teaching in secondary schools, it deals with a number of other important matters. The attention the author gives to adolescent students' boredom with the hackneyed phrases and stereotyped ideas of official orthodoxy and her portrayal of their perception of hypocrisy and falsehood are especially significant. Some of the sixteen- and seventeen-year-old students at the boys' school where much of the action of the novel takes place are both angered and perplexed when they come across conscious and calculated distortions of the truth. One of the most vivid statements on this subject occurs during a classroom discussion of a novel about the Soviet countryside written by an unnamed author who has won Stalin prizes for his literary efforts (the reference may well be to Babayevsky). One of the boys bursts out:

Anyway — the book is rotten. . . . I couldn't read it. It made me sick. Really, why is it that in the book it's one thing, and in life something else? Last summer I was at my uncle's place on a collective farm: the farmers there haven't been paid for three years. Can you imagine? And it's already been seven years since the war! That's what they should write about! Half the houses in the village are empty there. Should they write about why this happens, or shouldn't they? They should! But instead, writers slobber over everything. . . . They slobber, mix in some syrup — and it's disgusting to read. No, tell me, I'm asking seriously: why don't they write the truth? [99]

Though the discrepancy between reality as the students experience it and reality as the agents of officialdom represent it engenders apathy or cynicism in some students, it distresses the more thoughtful ones and stimulates them to raise basic questions. At the end of a scene in which the students are shown scoffing and jeering at a florid, falsified press account of an event in which they have participated, one of the youths asks with anxious insistence: "Just tell me one thing. In what should I believe?" [100] One of the teachers repeatedly voices his concern not about the doubts that a few students have, but about their indifference to fine phrases and about the debasement of words — a teacher's principal tool — through callous misuse of them by persons in positions of authority. The problem, as he sees it, involves more than words alone. At one point he says: "We're teaching indifference to words, that's what we're doing. And indifference to words brings with it indifference to what those words signify." [101]

Kabo obviously believes that the values which the Soviet regime officially espouses are threatened by the actual lack of concern for those values on the part of persons whose responsibility it is to inculcate them. She sees a similar threat in the growing prosperity of Soviet society, or, more accurately, in what has accompanied it — the spread of tastes and attitudes that have traditionally been regarded as bourgeois. An excessive interest in material comfort and the easy life, Kabo argues, leads to the spoiling of children and hinders the development of that self-sacrificing, morally strong, loyal citizen which it is the task of the Soviet educational system to produce. In one interesting section of the novel, this question is discussed at a meeting of parents and their sons with one of the teachers. The teacher says to the parents in a half-joking manner, "Comrades, listening to you, I begin to fear for Communism," and he continues:

"Really, I do! As time goes on, material well-being will increase, and you will begin to see our children driving to school in their own cars or flying in some kind of helicopter." With a wave of his hand he quieted the growing animation of the boys. "We may assume that this will not happen soon, but it will happen! But look, even now they [the schoolboys] have an utterly parasitical conception of Communism." [102]

Like the authors of many works published during the post-Stalin literary thaw, Kabo is highly critical of materialism and philistinism — particularly as manifested by the privileged groups in Soviet society — for she sees them as distortions of what the Soviet system is supposed to stand for.

The representation in literary works of disillusioned idealism, together with the bourgeois features of Soviet life, as a kind of dry rot which affects the younger generation, giving rise to indifference or cynicism, is significant for what it reveals not only about Soviet society but about the viewpoint of the authors themselves. It indicates that some writers have preserved that high-mindedness and firm attachment to the humanitarian values of Marxism which they attribute to certain of the fictional characters portrayed in their works. An intense idealism that has been preserved despite disappointments and setbacks may, when it comes up against petti-ness and corruption, become a source of criticism and questioning of the most penetrating kind, and perhaps this constitutes a greater threat to the forces interested in preserving the status quo in Soviet society than do apathy or indifference. However this may be, in 1956 these tendencies presented serious challenges to the party.

Partly in response to persistent pressure from below after the death of Stalin, partly out of its own recognition of the need for reforms in Soviet culture, the party, from the end of 1955, per-mitted the official position in literary matters to move farther in the direction of liberalization than it had at any other time since the war. This trend, which received a powerful stimulus from the Twentieth Party Congress, quickly made itself felt in the arts, creating a sense of reawakening that was greeted by many artists, writers, and critics with an eagerness that was both inspiring and touching. One drama critic, writing in a buoyant mood about the new atmosphere evident not only in the theater, but in literature, music, and graphic art, pointed to what was perhaps the strongest impulse behind the sense of spiritual renewal that stirred many writers. Attempting to characterize the spirit underlying the 1955–1956 season in the arts, the critic said:

> An active, energetic, and — most important — common desire for the new was one of the marks of the past year. . . .

But it would seem that stronger and firmer in us than the desire for the new was the desire for truth. Let it be severe. Let it be wounding. But for that truth with which Soviet art cannot bear to be in the slightest disagreement.[103]

Significant numbers of writers were inspired by the possibility of expressing ideas and sentiments which they had long repressed, and in the events of 1956 they saw a foreshadowing of the emergence of an honest, bold, realistic, and humanitarian literature. If they criticized rigid controls in literature and corruption and dishonesty in their environment, they did so not out of disloyalty, but out of a desire to serve their country sincerely, without making compromises with their art, without violating their integrity as human beings. Yet the writers and critics who were most excited by the new possibilities were nonetheless acutely aware of the precariousness of the situation. They repeatedly cautioned that the recent achievements were at best the bare foundations of a better future, and they hinted that important battles were yet to be fought. Such warnings were obviously inspired by a fear that the new trends might be stifled by the resistance they had provoked in certain quarters. Writing in that vein, one critic said, referring to the dogmatic, narrow-minded attitudes toward poetry characteristic of the recent past:

And although this narrowness is now being overcome, it is, all the same, being overcome slowly and hesitantly. So that we shall be cured of this chronic ailment once and for all, so that in the future we shall not be tormented by distressing relapses and traces of the old, we must speak of all this openly and frankly.[104]

But only a few months after these lines were written it became increasingly difficult to speak out openly and frankly. The dangers involved in allowing writers greater scope to decide for themselves how they should fulfill their tasks became apparent quickly. The literary discussion that followed the Twentieth Congress occasioned the sort of questioning about essentials of Soviet literary doctrine that the party had always tried to prevent, and the more relaxed conditions permitted the publication of works which cast doubt on the literary doctrine, at least by implication, and which in content and spirit were incompatible with the larger aims of the control system. The party's relaxation of controls in 1956 stimulated a restlessness among writers that challenged the authority of the party in literature and, what was worse from the viewpoint of party leaders, reinforced similar challenges to party authority in other spheres of Soviet life.

V ⬦⬦⬦⬦⬦

The Drive for "Consolidation," 1957–1959

⬦⬦⬦

Another turn in the zigzag course of Soviet literary politics occurred in 1957, when the party initiated a drive to divert the forces unleashed in 1956 into the channel of orthodoxy. The drive to "consolidate the ranks of writers on the basis of principle," as the effort was frequently described, moved through several phases, absorbing most of the energies of literary officialdom during 1957 and the following two years. If in the first months of 1957 successes were comparatively few, they increased perceptibly with the growing strength of the drive in the spring. New energies injected into the effort in the summer produced a triumph of orthodoxy by the end of the year, though it was a triumph based on a somewhat uneasy balance of forces. During 1958 the activities of literary officials were largely directed toward stabilizing the victory of the preceding year, and by the time of the Third Congress of Soviet Writers in 1959 the foundations of the Khrushchev settlement in literary affairs had been firmly laid.

Threats to orthodoxy had met with opposition throughout 1956; but there was a noticeable change of atmosphere after the middle of November, when Khrushchev warned students about "unhealthy phenomena" in their midst and Molotov defended socialist realism at an artists' conference.[1] Undoubtedly the new trend was a reflection of alarm in the top echelons of the party over developments in the satellite countries. The abortive Hungarian revolution, because of the role that writers played in precipitating it, threw into sharp relief the serious implications of unrest among the Soviet literary intelligentsia, and party leaders probably drew from the experience the lesson echoed by the editors of *Kommunist* when they observed: "The events in Hungary have demonstrated the consequences of disregarding Leninist adherence to principle in questions of the guidance of literature and art." [2]

The ensuing campaign for ideological vigilance initially took the form of organized meetings of writers throughout the Soviet Union. What began to happen, and what the party expected to happen, was indicated by the terse comment of a *Kommunist* editorial: "Soviet writers are giving a decisive rebuff to all efforts to lead literature from its general path. The meetings that have recently taken place in writers' organizations testify to this." [3] Not only were the works published in *Novy mir* and the second volume of *Literaturnaya Moskva* subjected to increasingly severe attacks, but attempts during the preceding year to "rehabilitate" works such as Zorin's play *The Guests* were repudiated. [4] As the campaign grew in strength, editorials and speeches began to sound distressingly like those which presaged the emergence of postwar Zhdanovism, emphasizing as they did the urgency of relentless ideological struggle at a time when the world is divided into two camps. Even some of the lesser niceties of polemical discourse and defamation began to reappear. The main speaker at one important writers' gathering warned that this was not a time "to rest by a quiet stream," [5] much as Simonov in 1947 had censured those who were inclined to "lie down and rest a little" or "gather flowers"; and a speaker at another conference, accusing Pasternak of "inner emigration," berated the poet for preferring life "in an ivory tower" to intercourse with people. [6] Nor did the ritual of recantation go unobserved for long, as an account of a party meeting of writers in Leningrad discloses. [7] Olga Berggolts sent to the meeting a letter in which she acknowledged criticism for remarks which were not published but which one speaker described as a revision of the postwar decrees on ideological questions; these remarks, according to the report, had already been "unanimously condemned at a previous party meeting." Similarly, Vera Ketlinskaya, reportedly ill, sent to the gathering a statement in which she clarified her views on a number of basic questions as well as her attitude toward Dudintsev's novel; the statement was not accepted as satisfactory, however, because in it "there could not be felt a sincere admission by V. Ketlinskaya of her errors."

The return to orthodoxy was prompted by statements issued on the highest levels, statements which were, however, tempered by admissions that in previous years there had been shortcomings in certain details, though not in the principles, of the party's cultural policies. An editorial published by *Kommunist* in February 1957 outlined the position of the party in a typical way.[8] While conceding that during the period of the personality cult of Stalin there had been evidences of guidance by administrative injunction and of "unjustifiably harsh criticism," the editorial asserted that the main line followed in the guidance of literature and the arts represented the application in this realm of Marxist-Leninist principles expressed in the Central Committee decrees of 1946–1948. Observing that certain statements in the decrees had become dated or required more precise formulation, the editorial nonetheless reaffirmed the basic tenets of the decrees, and in a familiar manner it attempted to attribute responsibility for "distorting" the decrees to writers and artists themselves — to "timeservers" and persons lacking in profundity. This remained the position of the party throughout the period under discussion.

Though the direction of official policy could no longer be mistaken, the drive toward orthodoxy met with resistance, manifested with startling vigor by a group of writers at a session of the executive board of the Moscow writers' association, held in March 1957. As it was to be expected, the speaker who read the principal report at the meeting commented unfavorably on the controversial works published in *Novy mir* and *Literaturnaya Moskva*. According to the account of the proceedings in *Literaturnaya gazeta*, V. Kaverin, an editor of *Literaturnaya Moskva*, led the counterattack on the main speaker, demonstrating "bitter intolerance of criticism" and even threatening "to take his opponent to court."[9] Kaverin's position was supported by other writers, including Aliger and Kirsanov, and among those listed as exhibiting "intolerance of criticism" were Kabo and Yevtushenko, both authors of unorthodox works published in 1956. Dudintsev, whose impassioned remarks about *Not by Bread Alone* were regarded by *Literaturnaya gazeta* as a rejec-

tion of criticism of the book, vividly expressed a fundamental discontent of many Soviet writers when he said: "I think that we
might be allowed, like beginning swimmers, to try to swim on our
own, to take our own chances of drowning. But, alas, I always feel
a halter, like the harness that children are sometimes supported by.
And it keeps me from swimming." [10] Though press accounts of the
meeting are far from complete, the spirit of the proceedings is suggested by the complaint of *Literaturnaya gazeta* that the session
lacked a "truly businesslike . . . atmosphere" and that a "nonpro-
fessional, if literary-minded audience, which attended in sizable
numbers, created unhealthy disturbances." [11] A reference to the
meeting in an article published by *Pravda* contributed to the evidence of the recalcitrant writers' boldness and shed further light on
the situation within the Moscow writers' association, which, as one
writer later observed, was "badly split." [12] The article complained
that the editors of *Moskovsky literator* — the bulletin of the Moscow association, at that time circulated only among members —
reported the plenary session tendentiously, devoting far more space
to speeches by defenders of the anthology *Literaturnaya Moskva*
than to its critics and, adding insult to injury, printed verses "in
which the critics of the anthology were ridiculed in a tactless and
uncomradely fashion." [13]

The energy with which writers under attack defended their
views was an indication of the strength of the hopes aroused by the
events of 1956, just as it was a measure of writers' awareness of
how much was at stake in the early months of 1957. The comparative weakness of the campaign in literature at this point was perhaps a reflection of the uncertain situation in the Presidium of the
party, where a struggle for power was taking place; Khrushchev
was on the defensive until mid-February, and, though he consolidated his forces rapidly after that time, it was not until July that
he clearly emerged from the struggle as victor.[14] The course of
literary politics paralleled developments within the party. The
Third Plenum of the board of the Writers' Union in May furnished
evidence of the increasing strength of the campaign in literature.

The Third Plenum was notable first of all for the extraordinary
measures taken by high party officials to ensure that its outcome
would be the desired one. Both on the eve and at the close of the

plenary session, members of the Central Committee met with leading writers, and on each occasion Khrushchev delivered a speech;
in addition, two members of the Secretariat of the Central Committee, Shepilov and Pospelov, participated in the proceedings of
the plenum.[15] The collective report of the secretariat of the Writers' Union gave further evidence of carefully laid plans to heal the
breach in the ranks of Soviet writers. Relying upon tactics used by
official speakers at the Second Writers' Congress and at other times
of stress, the secretaries of the union adopted a restrained tone and
endeavored to delineate a middle way by criticizing both right and
left deviations. With this effort, the essential features of the new
orthodoxy, which would be elaborated by the Khrushchev regime
during the next two years, began to emerge. Having indicated that
the postwar decree on literature was still operative, the report
turned to the question of creative writing itself, commenting on
the danger both of "varnishing" reality and of representing it in a
"onesidedly negative" fashion. One passage on the sore subject of
depicting negative aspects of Soviet society is particularly significant, for it lays bare the core of post-1956 literary doctrine:

The new in our life [said the report] prevails over the old, the advanced
over that which lags behind. In our society as a whole, there are many more
genuine members of the new society than there are those who are ulcerated
with the diseases of the past. This does not mean, however, that literature
can only represent negative phenomena as lone instances or isolated occur-
rences, and negative characters as something equally unique and exceptional.
  By their very nature, belles-lettres render typical whatever they deal
with. And even though the positive principle prevails in our life, . . . literature, understandably, renders typical not only the positive, but the negative
as well.[16]

This statement was followed by a criticism of Aliger's poem "The
Most Important Thing," in which the poetess allegedly "took the
wrong course" in her attempt to typify Soviet man: "The generalized image of Soviet man is something quite different from what
she represents in her poem." The writer himself, the authors of the
report were thus careful to indicate, is not to be considered the
final authority on what is typical. But the larger intent of this
section of the report was to inform Soviet writers that they could
and should depict Soviet life more truthfully, and that they might

even delve into its darker sides, so long as they show that Soviet society is moving inexorably toward a cloudless future. The section of the report dealing with the administration of literary affairs similarly contained a note of promise. Though emphasizing the "fruitfulness of party guidance of literature," the report spoke of "the inadmissibility of petty tutelage, of overzealous bossing and of incompetent interference in the complex development of new literature and new art," and it suggested that the "immense possibilities" of the community of writers should be exploited more fully by placing greater control of literary affairs in the hands of writers themselves:

The union [of writers] has done too little to put into action such powerful means of democratic management of writers' affairs as collective editorial boards in the case of newspapers and magazines, collective editorial councils in the related arts, which would function collectively and be collectively responsible to the literary community as a whole.[17]

These remarks are reminiscent of proposals advanced by Nazarov and Gridneva in their much maligned article, which the report of the secretariat explicitly repudiated. But it is to be noted that the secretariat, characteristically, was proposing to solve through administrative devices problems which were in part created by administrative devices.

Writers attending the plenum reacted in a variety of ways to the position taken by the leadership of the Writers' Union. In view of the enthusiasm aroused by the liberalizing tendencies of 1956, it was hardly to be expected that the report of the secretariat, which marked an effort to check those tendencies, would be received joyously by writers who had encouraged liberalization. Ovechkin perhaps expressed the discontent of this group when, according to one account, he remarked that the report of the secretariat "does not arouse a desire to argue" [18] and, according to another, he "dismissed the secretariat's report out of hand with one sweeping phrase." [19] But there were few traces of active opposition to the official line at the Third Plenum, which was far more orderly than the meeting in March had been. One speaker, it is true, remarked that "frank drubbing of writers is of little use," and, rather surprisingly, Konstantin Fedin, then head of the Moscow branch of the Writers' Union, delivered a speech which was a partial defense of the activities of the Moscow group, a speech which, according to the official report of it, "did not . . . satisfy the participants of the plenum in all respects." [20] The intensification of the drive for orthodoxy was, however, reflected in the behavior of writers at bay, particularly in that of the group associated with *Literaturnaya Moskva:* having tried on earlier occasions to defend their views, they now fell into stubborn silence, refusing to recant, refusing to deny charges, refusing to reply to the often irrelevant remarks of their critics — refusing to speak at all. Highly placed literary officials were incensed by this development, and they exerted great effort to force a response from the delinquent writers. L. Sobolev, soon to become head of the writers' union of the RSFSR, denounced what he termed the "feat of silence"; A. Surkov called upon refractory writers to break their "vow of silence"; and both accused the editors of *Literaturnaya Moskva* of trying to make a "literary platform" out of the almanac.[21] Implying that "clique interests" were concealed behind "the resplendent banners of 'a stand on principle' and 'creative convictions,'" Sobolev stressed the obligation of writers whose books or views had caused confusion to explain themselves publicly. Though this is difficult, he said, "it is necessary for the cause that we serve," and he added:

It is well known that in music a pause sometimes expresses greater feeling and thought than a melody or a chord. Your silence is dangerous. It disorients readers. What does it mean? What does it indicate? A haughty disregard for the opinion of others? A disdainful conviction of one's own infallibility? An insulting "however could you hope to understand me"? The drama of sacrifice? What does this silence signify? [22]

In passing, Sobolev consoled writers with the thought: "We are adults and we must understand that penitent speeches and beating one's breast are not required here." In view of the general tenor of his speech — which the press account of the plenum approvingly described as "impassioned and principled" — the reader may wonder how convincing his reassurance was to the writers under attack.

Despite the pressure, none of the persons associated with *Literaturnaya Moskva* spoke out at the plenum. Of the writers who had committed serious mistakes in 1956, only one, Konstantin Simonov, recanted at this time. Simonov had erred not only by permitting such works as *Not by Bread Alone* to be published in *Novy mir*, but by writing a controversial essay on the party's policies in literature and by making a speech later described as a revision of certain formulations in the party's decrees on literature and the arts.[23] Simonov had already tried to make amends by publishing a staunch defense of socialist realism in the March 1957 issue of *Novy mir* and by expressing second thoughts about Dudintsev's novel at the meeting of Moscow writers in March. Now he announced his regrets more firmly and explicitly. But his repentance did not satisfy everyone: it should have contained "more self-criticism," said the account of the plenum published by *Literaturnaya gazeta*.[24]

With the Third Plenum, the drive for "fundamental consolidation," as Surkov characterized it in his opening speech, became the order of the day. Developing this theme in his closing remarks, Surkov cautioned that the plenum should not be considered a signal "to open fire on those who hold divergent views on literary creation," and he remarked that persuasion and re-education are the bases of genuine consolidation; but, he continued, "consolidation must be achieved on a clear ideological platform that unites all the living forces of our literature and rejects everything that impedes its development." [25] In brief, moderate attitudes would prevail, and the discontented need only confess their guilt, surrender their principles, and behave properly. "Consolidation," in the usage of Soviet officialdom, is scarcely distinguishable from "capitulation."

Not long after the close of the Third Plenum, the wall of resistance, such as it had been, began to crumble. At a joint meeting of the Moscow writers' party organization and the board of the USSR Writers' Union early in June — a meeting, it is worth noting, attended by Yekaterina Furtseva, a secretary of the Central Committee and of the Moscow party committee — there were signs of the impending disintegration.[26] According to one speaker, Semyon Kirsanov had already announced his intention to revise the poem "Seven Days of the Week," in official eyes one of the most objectionable works published in 1956. Two editors of *Literaturnaya Moskva*, Emmanuel Kazakevich and Margarita Aliger, at least broke their silence — Kazakevich in a speech defending the almanac and Aliger in a letter which, like Kazakevich's speech, "expressed no desire" to admit honestly the mistakes committed, according to the report of the meeting in *Literaturnaya gazeta*, which reproduced neither the speech nor the letter. Nothing was heard from the other editors of *Literaturnaya Moskva* or from the authors of condemned works, with the exception of Alexander Yashin, who was apparently still defending his story "Levers." That depression and disillusion were beginning to afflict those who had fought strenuously for more liberal policies was indirectly suggested by a defender of orthodoxy who remarked: "Some people are inclined to regard the justifiably sharp criticism leveled at the line taken by the editorial board of *Literaturnaya Moskva* as amounting almost to a retreat from the aims of the 20th Party Congress." [27] A few days later, at a general meeting of Moscow writers, three editors of *Literaturnaya Moskva* — Kazakevich, Aliger, and Bek — admitted their errors and promised to correct them through their work in the future.[28] At the same time, Fedin acknowledged the validity of criticism of the Moscow writers' organization, criticism which he had been reluctant to accept in May, and he declared that the editors of *Novy mir* had acknowledged the mistakes they committed in 1956.[29] Decisions made at the previous party meeting of writers probably played some role in inducing a change of heart, at least on the part of the editors of *Literaturnaya Moskva;* for at that meeting, L. Rudny, one of the editors, was expelled from the party committee,[30] and the committee was instructed "to take up the behavior" of the party members of the editorial board of *Literaturnaya Moskva.*[31]

In mid-summer, 1957, the drive for orthodoxy in the ideological realm entered its decisive and final phase. With the defeat of opponents in the party Presidium, Khrushchev perhaps found it possible to devote greater energy to outstanding problems in the cultural realm. However that may have been, the turning point was marked by an editorial published by *Kommunist* late in July which vigorously reaffirmed party control in the arts, attributing much responsibility for the spread of "unsound tendencies" to the "antiparty group," especially to Shepilov and Malenkov.[32] A month later, the Soviet press made public a major document on literature and the arts — purportedly a combined and condensed transcript of Khrushchev's speeches at three previous conferences of writers, artists, and party officials.[33] The effort made in one lengthy section of the document to refurbish Stalin's reputation was a symbol of the orthodoxy that Khrushchev was trying to impose on the arts. Attributing the "wavering" of certain figures of the literary and artistic world to an "incorrect" understanding of the party's criticism of Stalin, Khrushchev placed much emphasis on Stalin's "positive role" in Soviet history, though he did not forgo mentioning the late dictator's "errors and distortions." Khrushchev went to some pains to display a similar "balance" in delineating orthodoxy in the arts. He lashed out at the inventors of the term "embellisher," asserting that they pinned this label on everyone "who wrote truthfully about our reality," "who created positive images of Soviet people"; and in striking contrast to views expressed in 1954 by writers such as Sholokhov, he asserted that, with "rare exceptions," winners of Stalin Prizes had justly earned them. Khrushchev made his main point frankly: "We support writers who maintain the correct position in literature, who write about what is positive in life." At the same time, he tried to emphasize the essential moderation of his policies in literature and the arts. The truthful representation of reality, said Khrushchev, hardly bothering to rephrase familiar formulas, requires both the portrayal of the bright sides of Soviet life, which are its essential features, and negative phenomena that obstruct progress: those who search out only the negative aspects of Soviet life and those who present only "sugary" portrayals of it are to be equally repudiated. When he turned to the current situation in the community of writers, Khrushchev took up the theme of "consolidation," urging the "unity of all the forces of literature and art on the basis of principle," and he suggested, by referring to the cases of specific writers, that this should be achieved through the gentle techniques of persuasion and education. Khrushchev's remarks hinted that Tvardovsky and Panfyorov might be restored to unqualified favor, since they had drawn the necessary conclusions from criticism in 1954 (both lost their jobs as editors of literary journals for errors that seemed comparatively unimportant after the events of 1956); even Dudintsev, said Khrushchev, might, with the help of the party, find the correct path. Khrushchev's harshest remarks were reserved for Aliger, whom he twice criticized, observing at one point that the views of the nonparty writer Sobolev were much closer to his than those of Aliger, a party member who "holds a false position and responds incorrectly to criticism of her mistakes." About the prospects of Aliger's redemption Khrushchev expressed no opinion.

With the weight of Khrushchev's recently increased authority squarely behind the drive for consolidation, it was not surprising that significant advances were made in the fall of 1957. What is surprising is that the successes were not greater and that consolidation was apparently something not easily achieved. In September, Sobolev warned that it would be incorrect to believe that "passions have calmed down and quiet has descended," and he asserted that a survey of literary journals revealed that "the process of correcting certain mistakes is lagging." [34] The upshot of this discovery was that in the last months of 1957 and the early part of 1958 the editorial boards of literary journals were subjected to increasing pressure to heighten their ideological vigilance. But Sobolev's remarks referred to the period from May to September, and in any case they probably pointed less to the continuing strength of resistance than to the decreasing threshold of tolerance.

A meeting of writers early in October furnished dramatic evidence of the main trend of developments. Though the meeting apparently was not a complete success in official eyes — a press report several weeks later reproached Dudintsev and two of the editors of *Literaturnaya Moskva*, Kaverin and Paustovsky, for not using the occasion to acknowledge their mistakes[35] — one of the most ardent advocates of liberalization, Margarita Aliger, confessed her guilt. Aliger's statement, which recalls Babel's and Olesha's speeches at the First Writers' Congress, deserves to be quoted at length:

> I have had to live through several months of bitter thoughts, of deep reflections, of frank and merciless arguments with myself. It became clear to me long ago that I committed a series of outright mistakes in my public work, and, having recognized this fully, I remained for a long time in a state of mental depression and passivity. . . .
>
> As a Communist who accepts every party document as something wholly and unreservedly her very own, something unquestionable, I can now, without any evasion or qualification, without any false fear of losing my sense of personal worth, say frankly and firmly to my comrades that it is all true, that I really committed those mistakes about which Comrade Khrushchev speaks. I committed them, I persisted in them, but I have

comprehended and admitted them deliberately and consciously, and you know this. I spoke of this at a similar meeting more than three months ago. However, since that time . . . , it seems to me, I have succeeded in understanding more profoundly the causes of those mistakes, and even that some of the causes lie simply in my character as a human being, which perhaps somehow hinders me in my public work.

I am sometimes inclined to substitute moral and ethical categories for political categories. . . .

Obviously, I must now be much more exacting with myself, free myself of an inclination toward abstract thinking, more rigorously verify my views on the phenomena of life by life itself . . . , see with my own eyes those enormous changes that have taken place in the life of the people, especially since the Twentieth Party Congress — in short, do what Comrade Khrushchev teaches and urges in his speeches.

I think that I shall be able to tell fully of the profound conclusions which I have drawn for my future life only by doing worthy work, by always remembering that any work of a Soviet writer is political work, and that it is possible to perform it with honor only by steadfastly following the party line and party discipline.[36]

Soviet writers are adults, Sobolev had said a few months before, and "penitent speeches" are not required of them. Apparently in some cases this was true. Dudintsev, at least, appears to have emphasized a different theme when, later in the year, he acknowledged criticism of *Not by Bread Alone* to be correct: he said, according to the press account, that he was writing a novel in which positive characters would be portrayed "warmly and lovingly." [37] Two other writers whom Khrushchev mentioned by name in his pronouncement on literature and art evidently demonstrated that they had profited sufficiently from earlier criticism. In November, Panfyorov, having written a patriotic article for the October issue of *Kommunist*, was restored to his post as editor of the literary journal *Oktyabr*, and in mid-1958 Tvardovsky replaced Simonov as chief editor of *Novy mir* when the editorial board of that journal was reorganized.

By the end of 1957 it was evident that the supporters of orthodoxy had the better of the battle, though theirs was still not an unqualified victory. On the eve of the Fourth Plenum of the board of the Writers' Union, the editors of *Literaturnaya gazeta* revealed the incomplete success in a backhanded way by stressing that only a few persons stubbornly refused to give up their erroneous views, and one speaker at the plenum revealed that among these were some of the writers associated with *Literaturnaya Moskva*.[38] If the attacks on "revisionism" heard at the Fourth Plenum, which was intended as a celebration of the victory of orthodoxy, suggested that the requisite consolidation had not yet been achieved, they only emphasized the importance of the main task of 1958 — to reinforce the positions stormed in the previous year.

Organizing a writers' union in the RSFSR, which, unlike the other union republics, did not have its own writers' association, absorbed much of the energy of Soviet literary officialdom in 1958. The organization was evidently created as a device for securing the orthodox line in literature, as Khrushchev had defined it. True, writers in outlying areas had complained for years about problems created by the overcentralized administration of the Writers' Union, and it was undoubtedly hoped that the new organization would solve some of these problems. That other considerations were more important, however, is suggested by the very fact that even though complaints of provincial writers had been heard for years, it was only in May of 1957, on the eve of the Third Plenum, that Khrushchev himself — or so it was later claimed — first proposed that a writers' union of the RSFSR be created.[39] A major purpose underlying the founding of the Russian writers' union was to weaken the influence of the large urban organizations — especially of the Moscow organization, the main source of trouble in 1956 — on the work of the USSR Writers' Union and on the literary life of the country in general. This was to be accomplished in part by basing the largest writers' organization in the Soviet Union (just over half of all Soviet writers live in the RSFSR) on the younger and more malleable literary forces of the provinces, as yet comparatively free of the corrupting influence of the more sophisticated intellectual life of the capital. It is significant in this respect that in his pronouncement on the arts in 1957 Khrushchev discussed the need to create a Russian writers' union immediately after he had referred to the grave shortcomings of the Moscow organization, observing that "serious thought should be given to measures which would foster the growth of writers' forces in the localities." [40]

The importance of this trend in official thinking was disclosed by the frequent references during the Third Plenum, and in follow-ing months, to the unreliability of the Moscow organization and to the unhealthy atmosphere prevalent in some Moscow literary cir-cles. Indeed, Sobolev, in his speech at the first congress of the RSFSR writers' union, stressed the point that one task of the new organization was to shield younger writers from the unhealthy in-fluences of the confined literary circles of the capital by bringing them into closer contact with the "spacious and beneficial life of our Motherland." [41] The opinion that the leadership of the Russian writers' union intended to rely primarily on writers of the autono-mous republics, territories, and regions, leaving the Moscow or-ganization in a shadow, was widespread enough among writers themselves to evoke a denial of it in the press.[42] Finally, the mem-bership figures of the Writers' Union suggest that in recent years the admissions policy has favored writers from the "periphery": although the membership of the union increased by almost 30 per-cent between 1954 and 1959, with most of the increase occurring after 1956,[43] the proportion of the union's members who live in Moscow dropped by approximately 9 percent during that period. The creation of a new administrative tier also opened the possibility of tightening control over the Moscow organization — which, ac-cording to a press comment suggestive of the trends toward plural-ism in the Writers' Union, "has often opposed itself to the board of the union" [44] — and over writers of the "periphery," previously somewhat neglected by the overburdened apparatus of the all-union writers' organization.

The policies pursued in the arts throughout most of 1958 indi-cated that the Khrushchev regime was anxious to emphasize the essential moderation of the new orthodoxy. If "revisionists" were subjected to criticism, so were unregenerate extremists when they manifested tendencies toward the older, Zhdanovist methods of attack and defamation. The party's correction of certain "erroneous evaluations" contained in the 1948 decree on music and the series of meetings held to discuss the significance of this rectification of error dramatized the moderation of Khrushchev's cultural policies. Yet the violently abusive campaign against Boris Pasternak un-leashed in the fall of 1958 seemed to raise the threat of a full return to Zhdanovism.

The newspaper *Literaturnaya gazeta* opened the attack on Pasternak and his novel *Doctor Zhivago* on October 25, 1958, two days after Pasternak had been awarded a Nobel Prize. The events surrounding the attack cast interesting sidelights on the current situation in Soviet literary politics, though, because the most important developments were shrouded by secrecy and confused by rumor, the incident perhaps raised more questions than it furnished answers. A striking aspect of the initial attack was the difference in the tone of two documents published by *Literaturnaya gazeta*. One of these was a long letter signed by Fedin, Simonov, and other members of the editorial board of *Novy mir;* purportedly the letter sent to Pasternak when the journal rejected *Doctor Zhivago* for publication in 1956, it was comparatively moderate in tone, though its main point was that the novel expressed a hostile attitude toward the Soviet system. The other was a long editorial, much more abusive and defamatory in tone, which called Pasternak a "Judas" and an "ally of those who hate our country." The anti-Pasternak movement developed rapidly. On October 26, *Pravda* published an article, signed by the critic D. Zaslavsky, which surveyed Pasternak's career, demonstrating that the writer had always been basically hostile to the revolution and to socialism; the critic labeled *Doctor Zhivago* "reactionary journalism" and concluded that the least Pasternak could do would be to refuse the Nobel Prize. On the following day, the Writers' Union declared that Pasternak could not be considered a Soviet writer and expelled him from the union.[45] Two days later, in the presence of Khrushchev and other leading party figures, the secretary of the all-union Komsomol organization, addressing an audience of fourteen thousand, delivered an attack on Pasternak that could at best be called vile, even using the lowest level of Soviet defamatory rhetoric as a standard; this section of the speech and the secretary's suggestion that Pasternak leave the Soviet Union were greeted by applause, according to the press transcript of the event.[46] On October 31, at a meeting of Moscow writers, a resolution was adopted asking the Soviet government to deprive "the traitor B. Pasternak" of his citizenship.[47]

Though the denunciations were unusually virulent and the proposed sanctions unusually severe, up to this point the anti-Pasternak campaign had in general followed the pattern customary in the cases of writers guilty of serious errors. Normally in such cases, the press continues the campaign for months, and every speaker at a writers' conference observes the custom of adding his own denunciation of the guilty victim or the harmful book. But in this respect the Pasternak case was different. After Pasternak had sent a letter to Khrushchev, in which he announced his rejection of the Nobel Prize and begged not to be exiled,[48] and another letter to *Pravda*, in which he apologized for what had happened,[49] the public campaign virtually came to a stop and Pasternak's name figured only episodically in the press. When he was mentioned, it was always in the most derogatory terms; but these references were few in number, even at such an important occasion as the first congress of the RSFSR writers' union, held in December 1958.[50] Perhaps concern on the part of the Soviet government about public opinion abroad played the decisive role in determining the outcome of the Pasternak incident. But it may be that the uproar over Pasternak's novel arose out of, or was in some way related to, a struggle within the Writers' Union; though this can only be conjecture, later developments lend themselves to this interpretation. In 1958, *Literaturnaya gazeta*, which led the attack on Pasternak, was controlled by persons closely linked with the ultraorthodox literary line — V. Kochetov, who, it is true, was on leave from his post of chief editor at the time of the attack on Pasternak, and V. Druzin, the deputy editor. It is perhaps not accidental that both lost their jobs in the reorganization of the newspaper's editorial board in March 1959, at the time when the gentler "middle course" in literature was receiving renewed emphasis. It is conceivable that the attack on Pasternak was initiated or at least sharpened considerably by persons with a stake in the Stalinist system who were interested in reviving a more rigid orthodoxy in literature. Whether the attack on Pasternak was launched in defiance of a significant body of opinion among Soviet writers, whether it was initially approved by the highest party authorities, whether some of its features were unintended consequences of an increase in authority — perhaps in this case deliberately misused — which may have been granted to officials of the Writers' Union are questions that may never be answered.

Whatever the principal driving force behind the attack on

Pasternak was, the incident did not mark a return to an orthodoxy more severe than that outlined in official pronouncements of 1957. Writers' meetings held toward the end of 1958 and early in 1959 in preparation for the Third Writers' Congress, though they proceeded under the banner of defending socialist realism and combating revisionism, were comparatively moderate in their general tone, and quite uneventful. At the first congress of the RSFSR writers' union in December, for example, the torrent of familiar phrases concerning the tasks of Soviet literature was relieved by nothing more startling than one writer's subdued complaint about the stereotyped character of the discussions and the failure of the speakers to say what was really on their minds.[51] This congress was a foretaste of the all-union writers' congress which met several months later.

The Third Congress of Soviet Writers, held in May 1959, was in effect a celebration of the settlement which Khrushchev had achieved in literature. Of the three all-union congresses held, this was by far the dullest. Its proceedings were characterized by a show of unity not equaled by the earlier congresses. The silence of writers who in the recent past had been among the main sources of disturbance made possible the atmosphere of calm. None of the writers who were most forthright in expressing their views at the Second Congress — Sholokhov, Ehrenburg, Ovechkin, Aliger, Berggolts — spoke at the Third Congress, nor, with perhaps one exception, did those who were most deeply involved in the struggle for liberalization in 1956–1957. Semyon Kirsanov cast a pebble at the placid surface of the proceedings when he criticized authors of conventional, mediocre works and opponents of novelty in literature; but his criticisms — which were partly personal in character, though they seemed implicitly to disparage ultraorthodox views in general — provoked only a phrase or two of reproach from three later speakers. Whether dissident writers were discouraged or prevented from speaking, in order to preserve an appearance of unity, or whether they simply recognized the futility of trying to speak out at this time can only be matters for conjecture. In any case, most of the speeches at the congress were little more than reiterations of well-known literary clichés. The prime example of this was a long, tedious report read at the opening of the congress by Alexei

Surkov, the first secretary of the Writers' Union. Surkov's report, interestingly enough, was criticized by several speakers precisely because it was boring and sterile; but possibly these criticisms were made by persons who knew that Surkov would soon lose his post as chief of the union. A certain dissatisfaction about matters other than Surkov's speech did find expression at the congress. Several speakers attacked bureaucratism in the Writers' Union, and an even larger number displayed concern about the quality of current writing. Thus themes of criticism which had dominated the discussion in 1954, at the Second Congress, were revived; but references to them in 1959 were scattered, brief, and for the most part less sharp and penetrating than they had been even in 1954.

The few contributions to the congress which deviated significantly from the general tone of the proceedings recalled, though only indirectly and incompletely, some of the central issues of the literary debate of 1956. The noteworthy observations were made primarily in connection with the problem of improving the quality of Soviet literature, a subject that had received ever-increasing attention since 1951; and, because they took the form of a defense of experimentation and a warning against misuse of the term "formalism," they were reminiscent of remarks made by Selvinsky five years earlier, on the eve of the Second Congress, and even of Ehrenburg's caution about the use of "formalism" twenty-five years earlier, at the First Writers' Congress. Kirsanov turned his attention to the matter when, listing obstacles to the improvement of the artistic quality of Soviet literature, he cited the practice of attaching such labels as "naturalism" or "formalism" to works of writers and poets "who want to use colors of the spectrum other than gray": "Is this needed by Communism," he went on, "this intolerance of novelty, of the unexpected, of bold and bright descriptions?" [52] Vsevolod Ivanov was equally emphatic, declaring that young writers must be encouraged to experiment and that they should not have to run the risk of being called formalists, which, he asserted, is nonsense anyway: "There is no danger of formalism in our literature and there simply cannot be any, for this was a very brief and by-gone stage in the lives of certain writers, and it by no means embraced the whole of Soviet literature." [53] Some of the implications of attitudes such as those held by Ivanov and

Kirsanov were stated more boldly and fully in an article written by Konstantin Paustovsky and published in *Literaturnaya gazeta* while the congress was in session; since Paustovsky did not speak at the congress, his discordant views did little to mar the proceedings themselves. Two of the themes of the article, which touched on a number of sore points, were of special interest in light of what had been said in previous years and what was not being said at the congress. One of these was the defense of literary experimentation. Paustovsky's disparaging remarks about surrealism, dadaism, and other artistic isms were tempered by the assertion that younger writers' attraction to such experimental movements is a natural, harmless manifestation of youthful enthusiasm and that it is indirectly beneficial to older writers, since it prevents them from luxuriating in self-satisfied contentment and from regarding themselves as infallible.[54] Paustovsky's second theme was a criticism of virtually everything associated with the phrase "embellishing reality" — stereotypes, false optimism, and, above all, dishonesty and deceit. "Perhaps we shout so much and so loudly about truth in literature," he said boldly, "just because we are so deficient in it." That an article so similar in tendency to views expressed by rebellious writers in 1956 — and, indeed, written by one of them — could be published at this time was an indication that other currents were running behind the façade of conformism presented by the congress as a whole. Though Paustovsky's article was criticized by some speakers, it did not provoke an outburst of denunciation, as it might have had it been published in mid-1957. This, together with other curious developments at the congress, suggests that some highly placed officials may have been concerned about the effect the congress was having on the literary community and the Soviet public at large.

Because the congress did not come to grips with the problems that most agitated the literary community, and because writers who might have breathed some life into the congress did not participate in its public proceedings, the Third Congress was in danger of becoming a dismal failure. It seemed that the first all-union congress of the Khrushchev era might be memorable to writers and to Soviet citizens who follow literary developments — and they are many — only for its dreary parade of outworn clichés or, at most, for minor sensations connected with certain instances of backbiting criticism and deprecating innuendoes. In his article, Paustovsky in effect challenged the agents of orthodoxy by raising the question about the meaning of the congress that may well have been in the minds of many people:

The Writers' Congress is under way. Will it affirm for writers that free and bold scope of creative endeavor which alone will make Soviet literature the greatest literature of our age? Or will the congress occupy itself with petty tutelage over writers and with old reprisals? In the latter case, it will not be of benefit. It is time once and for all to stop calling friends enemies just because they speak the unpleasant truth, are not hypocritical, and, being utterly devoted to their people and country, do not demand a monopoly on that devotion or any reward for it.

As it turned out, the leadership of the party took some pains to provide reassurances. It was perhaps in an effort to demonstrate that the congress marked a significant development in a desirable direction that *Pravda* seized upon Tvardovsky's speech — the only speech of much interest or possible significance, other than Khrushchev's, made at the congress — for publication in its pages.[55] For Tvardovsky's speech was not only piquant and nicely balanced — liberal-minded and bold within the bounds of orthodoxy — but its purport, or at least the hope it held out, was that Soviet literature was entering a new and better stage, one sharply differentiated from the past. Tvardovsky suggested this most directly when he said: "We cannot go on living this way — this is what we must say to our literary yesterday and even to our today — and we will not go on living this way." But if the congress was in any sense redeemed in the eyes of those who longed for freer conditions, that could only have occurred when Khrushchev made a dramatic and unusual speech in which he attempted to delineate the new orthodoxy, prescribe the climate that should prevail within the literary community, and lay down the principles that should govern the relationship between Soviet writers and the ruling powers of the Soviet Union.

The chief task that Khrushchev set himself in his speech was to reassure writers of the essential moderation of the new orthodoxy. Even the manner of his address was calculated to demonstrate that the attitude of the ruling hierarchy toward writers was tolerant and friendly; for in his rambling, impromptu speech, which consisted of a skillful interlarding of conventional literary formulas and spicy asides, Khrushchev attempted to place himself on a level with his audience by adopting a conversational, bantering tone refreshingly different from the pedantic sermonizing of most official pronouncements on literary matters — different, indeed, from the tone of his own pronouncements in 1957. And Khrushchev made a point of emphasizing the spirit of moderation by commenting on the novel *Not by Bread Alone* and its author in a more tolerant manner than he had in the past. But a more tangible promise of an amelioration of conditions was to be found in his elaboration of the point that the recent ideological struggle — which, he observed, was of a "rather sharp character" — had come to an end with what he asserted was the total defeat of "bearers of revisionist views and attitudes": "The struggle is over, and 'the angels of reconciliation,' as the saying goes, are already on the wing." [56] A comradely atmosphere should prevail in the literary world, Khrushchev said, and writers who erred in the past should be treated with tact and understanding. Comforting as these remarks may have been, they had certain menacing features that could not have escaped the attention of the assembled writers. To his insistence that writers once guilty of mistakes should not be constantly reminded of their deviations, Khrushchev added an ominous caution:

It is not necessary to remind them of this, but neither should it be forgotten. In order to be on the safe side we should, as the saying goes, "tie a knot," so that if it is necessary we can look and recall how many knots there are and to whom these knots refer.[57]

Moreover, Khrushchev made it perfectly clear that he was rejecting neither the techniques by which the recent victories in the literary realm had been achieved nor any part of those victories themselves. The tact and tolerance that Khrushchev said should be exercised with respect to errant writers were to be reserved, he firmly stated, for those who had surrendered, admitted defeat, and expressed a readiness to take the correct position. Recantation, in short, was to remain a condition for the remission of sins. Khrushchev was simply saying, as he put it, that one should not "hit a man when he's down." [58] But he had, on the other hand, already emphasized another important strand of his argument with a quotation from Gorky: "If the enemy does not surrender, he must be destroyed." [59] Khrushchev in effect summarized his views on this whole subject when he said that he was advocating neither reconciliation — which would be surrender — nor the kindling of passions, but "the unity of forces on the basis of principle." [60] From the point of view of the rebels of 1956, this could mean only one thing: capitulation.

Though it was perhaps heartening to be told by a reliable authority that the acute phase of the "antirevisionist" struggle was a matter of the past, the most impassioned defenders of truthfulness and sincerity in literature could have found little comfort in Khrushchev's reflections on the traits that distinguish good writing from bad. For in characterizing the kind of literary works required by the regime, Khrushchev firmly aligned himself with writers who stress the positive, who show "the life-affirming power of the new and its triumph over the old" — writers to whom some persons have attempted to attach the label "embellisher." [61] True, Khrushchev had some harsh things to say about dull books, and he asserted that he was not defending works in which "life is so embellished that it does not correspond to reality"; but these reservations were vitiated by his tireless repetition of the old Zhdanovist formula that writers must illumine the path to the future by focusing on the inevitably triumphant new while condemning obstacles to progress. Khrushchev's remarks implied that there can be only two approaches to writing — the correct "positive" approach that he described and the approach of the "nonembellishers" who "search out all possible vices and deficiencies." Having made it plain that writers must be circumspect in dealing with "negative phenomena," Khrushchev seemed to claim for the party leadership the sole right to direct attention to serious problems when he said: "So listen, dear friends, if there is anyone who reveals and lays bare shortcomings and vices . . . it is the party and its Central Committee that do this." [62] As if to clinch the point, Khrushchev observed that the party had deprived writers not only of the right to write badly — as Sobolev had remarked at the First Writers' Congress — "but above all of the right to write wrongly." [63]

Twice in his rambling discourse Khrushchev commented provocatively, in passing, on writers' responsibility for governing their own affairs. The "sweet candies" of approval and the "bitter pill" of criticism should be distributed by writers themselves, he said at one point, and later, referring to the difficulty of deciding whether a work should be published, he observed:

you know that it is not easy to decide right off what to publish and what not to publish. The easiest thing would be to publish nothing—then there would be no mistakes. . . . But that would be stupidity.

Therefore, comrades, do not burden the government with the solution of such questions — decide them yourselves in a comradely fashion.[64]

Some commentators in the West have seen in these remarks the promise of a significant concession to writers or, as one observer put it rather more cautiously, "a certain abdication by the party of its exclusive prerogatives in the control of literature" and a "grant of relative autonomy" to writers.[65] While this may be so, it should be noted that Khrushchev, in touching upon this subject, added nothing to statements that had been made long before on high authority; and, even if he meant to say what his remarks implied, other evidence suggests that a greater devolution of responsibility for administering literary affairs would have little immediate impact on the main course of Soviet literary life.

During 1957, when the campaign against "revisionist" tendencies among writers was at its highest pitch, the party press from time to time stressed the party's willingness to place increasing reliance on writers and artists to solve their own problems. An editorial in *Kommunist* stated this point in a typical fashion:

The Central Committee of the party places full trust in the art intelligentsia to solve crucial ideological and creative questions itself, in its own organizations.

Experience shows that our creative organizations — the unions of writers, artists, composers, and others — have achieved a high level of ideological and political maturity and are able to find a principled party solution to the most complex of ideological and political problems.[66]

Although such statements were probably meant to be both a summons to duty and a salve for ruffled feelings, their emphasis on the existence within the professional unions of forces that could be relied upon to take a correct position unquestionably contained more than a grain of truth. Many of the party's policies in recent years seem to reflect the conviction that Soviet education and indoctrination have been effective, that a high degree of uniformity of outlook has been achieved, that, as Khrushchev put it at the Third Congress, it is not easy to distinguish a party member from a nonparty member — in short, that Soviet citizens can be trusted to a greater degree than Stalin realized or was willing to admit. There was certainly no reason that the same considerations should not affect Khrushchev's attitudes toward the Writers' Union as well, for the events of 1957–1958 demonstrated that the orthodox and the timid among the union's membership outnumbered the rebellious and that the leadership of the union was in reliable hands.

Nor has there been any evidence that the party is prepared to slacken supervision of writers; indeed, the evidence has been quite to the contrary. *Kommunist*, for example, characteristically coupled one of its testimonials to the reliability of the art intelligentsia organized in professional unions with the caution: "Party workers must associate more with writers and artists and explain to them the policies of the party in various spheres of economics and culture." [67] More significant in this respect was an article published in *Kommunist* a few months after Khrushchev delivered his address to the writers' congress. The article stressed the increasing role of the party in the arts, but at the same time it made much of the point that party guidance in the present era is assuming new forms. If at one time the party's "guiding influence" was realized through numerous official documents, decrees of the Central Committee, and organizational measures, now the methods have become more flexible, said the authors of the article, reducing primarily to "the explanation of tasks and comradely persuasion and criticism"; the party plays an expanding role in arts, the authors went on, not by interfering directly in creative activity, but by strengthening its "ideological influence" on writers and artists and by helping them "to determine the general direction of their creative work." [68] Statements such as these had been made frequently throughout the postwar period, and in themselves they suggested no essential change in the party's exercise of tutelage over writers, though one purpose of the article was to reassure writers that there would be no return to the excesses of the Zhdanov era. One passage in the article was particularly suggestive as to the scope of the "autonomy" that writers might be permitted to exercise:

"The party, strengthening its guiding role in the sphere of literature and art, is helping the art intelligentsia to overcome a tendency toward a concept of freedom of creative endeavor that is alien to us, a tendency that sometimes affects individual representatives of this intelligentsia." [69] But it was Khrushchev himself who revealed most vividly the essential character of the current official attitude toward the writer and the proper position of the writer vis-à-vis the party. Addressing a Central Committee conference on automation in July 1959, Khrushchev suddenly, apropos of nothing he had been saying, lashed out at nonconformist writers:

Among the writers in our country are individuals who say: How can there be party guidance of literature? . . . one writer or another may sit at his country house, hatching a sniveling book, yet want it to be recognized as an expression of the sentiments of the people of our times, of all the people. Is that not a real cult of one's own personality, which, you see, does not want to suffer the guidance of the party, expressing the will of millions. And such a man with his contrived book wants to rise above the party, above the people.[70]

This statement is, in addition, a revealing expression of Khrushchev's distrust of and even contempt for writers — and quite likely intellectuals in general. Khrushchev displayed similar feelings at the Third Congress both in the patronizing tone of his speech and in remarks which suggested that he regards writing at best as a lower form of work that a man should engage in during his leisure hours, after he has made a meaningful contribution to building the new society by laboring manfully in the fields, factories, or mines.

Khrushchev's address at the Third Congress — despite its dearth of new ideas, its ominous overtones, and a certain discordance between its dominant tone and its actual content — was meant to inspire a sense of relief in writers. He seemed concerned above all to create the impression that, while the party remains ever vigilant, its attitude toward writers is a friendly and relatively tolerant one. This marked the continuation of a policy that emerged in 1957, when it was apparently decided that results are best achieved by combining cajolery with threats. The policy has been manifested not only in the form of increasingly insistent assurances that party leaders take a deep interest in the problems of writers, but in the newly established tradition of informal annual meetings of party and government leaders with representatives of the art intelligentsia, which provide occasions both for impromptu speeches and intimate and cordial exchanges of opinion. By humoring writers to some extent, Soviet rulers may hope to win over those who are still sulking and to render others more pliable by giving them the flattering sense of being close to members of the ruling group, who find time to concern themselves with writers' problems and needs. Finally, while Khrushchev at the writers' congress vigorously reaffirmed the old clichés about the educative functions of literature and the civic responsibilities of the writer, he suggested indirectly — with his conciliatory remarks about Dudintsev, for example — that writers might presume to depict significant "negative phenomena" if they exercise sufficient restraint and take care to give a predominant place to the positive.

Revisions in the statutes of the Writers' Union adopted by the Third Congress and a change in the leadership of the union made at the same time were expressions of the triumph of orthodoxy that emerged from the literary struggles of 1957–1958 and reflections of the literary line promulgated by Khrushchev in his pronouncements of 1957 and 1959. The most important modifications of the statutes were made in the sections which outline the meaning of socialist realism and the tasks of the union. Two changes were made in the paragraph which defines socialist realism. The importance of socialist realism was stressed more heavily by the added assertion that it "has been, and remains, the tried and tested creative method of Soviet literature." [71] This change was one aspect of the victory which the congress marked. The speaker who reported to the congress on revision of the statutes directed attention to this when, referring to the new clause, he said: "After the struggle that we have conducted in recent years for the ideological and creative principles of our literature, we have every moral right to single out this side of the matter and to give it particular emphasis." [72] The other change restored to the definition the clause requiring that reality be represented in a "historically concrete" fashion. The motivation for this is suggested by the complaint of one literary critic that the elimination of the clause in 1954 had opened the door to "ideological subjectivism" and other alien forces that led to an incorrect representation of reality in certain of the "critical" literary works in the past few years.[73] The revised statutes also contain a provision to the effect that Soviet writers are guided by "Leninist partiinost, which constitutes the highest form of the narodnost of art." [74] This emphasis on the unity of narodnost, generally understood to mean the identification of art with the people, and partiinost was undoubtedly a response to the dangerous tendency manifested by some writers in 1956 to identify themselves with the "people," as distinguished from the party. In addition, the new statutes state that one of the tasks of the union is to wage a consistent struggle against "all types and forms of bourgeois influence, including revisionism as the chief danger to the development of literature and literary theory," as well as against "dogmatism, sectarianism, and vulgarization" [75] — an obvious effort to characterize, in abstract terms, Khrushchev's "middle course" in literature.

If the revisions of the statutes bore witness to the preponderant emphasis in 1959 on the return to orthodox positions, the change in the leadership of the Writers' Union betokened the spirit of temperance which would condition the interpretation of orthodoxy. Alexei Surkov, whose name is indissolubly linked with the harsher attitudes of the recent past, was demoted to the rank of an ordinary secretary of the Writers' Union, and the post of first secretary was given to Konstantin Fedin, who has managed to stand somewhat aloof from the most virulent literary polemics and who evidently views the newer tendencies in Soviet writing with a certain tolerance. It is noteworthy that as of 1959 the top posts in the two most important writers' associations — the writers' union of the RSFSR and that of the USSR — were filled by men who are not party members, Fedin and Sobolev. This may have been a calculated move, a symbol of the promised release of writers from "petty tutelage" and of the party's proclaimed trust in writers' ability to find the "correct" solutions to problems. Whether or not this was so, the nonparty character of the top leadership is rather more impressive as a symbol of the completion of that process marked by Vsevolod Ivanov in 1934 when he observed that party and nonparty writers were approaching a common ground — a symbol, more broadly, of the widespread uniformity of thinking on basic questions which has been an outstanding feature of the literary life of the Soviet Union in the postwar period. Divergencies of viewpoint and conflicts of opinion there have been, it is true, and evidences of them are so refreshing and encouraging that it is difficult to avoid the temptation to concentrate on them to such an extent that the limits within which they occur and the prevailing conformity which makes them so startling are obscured. It is always instructive, as a means of restoring the balance, to contemplate the variety of Soviet literary life in a bygone era — in the 1920s or the early 1930s.

Developments during the months immediately following the Third Writers' Congress indicated that Soviet literary life had entered a new period of stability. Spokesmen for the regime's literary line seemed intent upon making good Khrushchev's promise of cautious liberality within the limits of ideological conformity, and if the party's policy contained no hope of a return to the freedom of 1956, it also contained no threat of a return to the repression of 1949. The "middle course" seemed well established. This did not mean that there were no skirmishes on the literary front in 1959. Despite the frequent self-congratulatory protestations that unity had been achieved in the literary community, disagreement over the proper interpretation of the literary line enunciated by Khrushchev found expression in the press. On one occasion, Vsevolod Kochetov, the former editor of *Literaturnaya gazeta* and a leading defender of ultraorthodox views, even referred to a conflict between two opposing "sides," [76] only to be rebuked by the new editorial board of *Literaturnaya gazeta* for suggesting that such a division had occurred after the Third Congress.[77] Yet differences in attitude toward literary policies were revealed not only in this interchange, but in various articles written by critics who disagreed about the merits of particular literary works, as well as in articles which dealt more broadly with such topics as the meaning of "consolidation," the desirability of striving for greater variety in belles-lettres, or the necessity of improving the quality of current writing. It was notable, however, that the principal disagreement that emerged in the press after the Third Congress was one between the advocates of moderation, who appeared to have the weight of Khrushchev's authority behind them, and the diehard literary

Stalinists, such as Kochetov, who in the circumstances were on the defensive. Characteristically, each group was able to invoke the name of Khrushchev by citing that aspect of his far-from-consistent pronouncements which ostensibly supported the position it was pleading.

During the postcongress discussion, it became apparent that the editorial boards of the two most important literary newspapers, *Literaturnaya gazeta* and *Literatura i zhizn*, differed in certain respects over policies. *Literatura i zhizn*, the organ of the RSFSR writers' association, showed signs of becoming a forum for the more doctrinaire defenders of ideological firmness and conformity in literature, while *Literaturnaya gazeta*, the organ of the Writers' Union of the USSR, went out of its way to establish itself as a proponent of moderation. Indeed, the new chief editor of *Literaturnaya gazeta*, S. S. Smirnov, personally played a leading role in urging moderate policies. In August 1959, he opened the pages of his newspaper to a discussion of the state of literary criticism and the question of variety in belles-lettres with an article which, elaborating on Khrushchev's message that literary criticism should be carried out in a "comradely fashion," argued for more conciliatory attitudes on the part of writers, critics, and editors.[78] One of the more revealing interchanges between the two newspapers occurred after *Literatura i zhizn* published an article which urged the importance of ideological conformity even at the expense of artistic quality. The authors of the article — V. Druzin, formerly deputy editor of *Literaturnaya gazeta* under Kochetov, and B. Dyakov — complained that some editors had interpreted "the completely correct demands" for high quality in literary works as a call to reject manuscripts that, in the opinion of certain editors, are not "outstanding"; what is important, Druzin and Dyakov emphasized, is that the author "should occupy correct ideological and political positions in his work." [79] *Literaturnaya gazeta* countered with an article by Alexander Tvardovsky, who observed that, although it would be pointless to call Druzin and Dyakov "conscious opponents of the party's resolutions on questions of literature," the harmfulness and absurdity of "their brazen preaching of mediocrity and dullness in art" must be exposed.[80] *Literatura i zhizn* replied by publishing a letter by Druzin and Dyakov, who took issue with Tvardovsky's views, and another by V. Andreyev, who said bluntly, "I think Comrade Tvardovsky is wrong." [81] *Literaturnaya gazeta* answered this with an editorial which supported Tvardovsky by pointing out that Khrushchev had said at the Third Congress that "Tvardovsky is right in announcing in his speech at the congress that in literary creation quality is of first and foremost importance." [82]

The discord between the two newspapers — which was only one more expression of that conflict between demands for both high artistic quality and ideological purity which lies at the heart of Soviet literary policy — added to the evidence that the RSFSR writers' union and *Literatura i zhizn* were created to act as a brake on the liberalizing forces within the literary community. But it suggested, in addition, that the Khrushchev regime might be preparing to perfect and exploit a system of countervailing pressures as a way of preserving the middle course in literature. By allowing the defenders of ultraorthodoxy to fight their verbal battles with the advocates of moderation, party leaders might reasonably hope to avoid the threats latent in the positions of both groups and the fluctuations in policy that occur when such threats become manifest. The party could, that is, rely on the ultraorthodox to sound the alarm at the first sign of any tendency away from moderation toward liberalization; on the moderates to complain about unnecessarily narrow-minded and dogmatic attitudes among critics and editors; and on both groups to aim their fire at anyone who might dare to cast doubt on the fundamentals of literary doctrine and party controls. More extensive reliance on this technique of control might permit the officially approved practice of "criticism and self-criticism" in literature to fulfill better one of its intended functions — to expose malpractices and erroneous views so that they can be corrected and those guilty of perpetrating them subjected to "educational influence," "explanation," and "comradely persuasion." However, the conflict between the two newspapers was hardly more than a suggestion of a new emphasis in the control of literature. It may simply have been that the editors of *Literatura i zhizn* and some writers were unduly slow in adjusting to the orientation in literature that Khrushchev had attempted to establish at the Third Congress.

It would be misleading to concentrate on the divergencies that emerged during the postcongress discussions to the point of suggesting that the disputants were separated by a deep chasm. Though the arguments disclosed differing emphases in the interpretations of orthodoxy, they took place within the context of a far more significant agreement on fundamentals, and at times they assumed the aspect of meaningless hairsplitting. Even the line that seemed to separate *Literaturnaya gazeta* from those who wrote for *Literatura i zhizn* was nearly, if not completely, obliterated toward the end of 1959, when the editorial board of *Literaturnaya gazeta* attempted to clarify the position of the newspaper by commenting at length on a number of articles that had appeared on its own pages and in other literary publications during the postcongress literary discussions.[83] Though the editorial disclosed that *Literaturnaya gazeta* was still presenting itself as an exponent of the middle course, it obviously marked an effort to conciliate the more orthodox. While the editors criticized writers who were excessively impatient and intolerant in arguing for conformity in writing, they also reproached those who were lax in making ideological demands of literary works. Even the article that their chief editor, Smirnov, had written in August came in for criticism for its "faint notes of liberalism" and its failure to underscore sufficiently "the significance of the ideological position of the writer." Again and again the editors stressed the overriding importance of ideological purity, stating emphatically that "the ideological position of the author is decisive in the evaluation of a work of art." It was hardly conceivable that the most doctrinaire of the orthodox could have taken exception to these formulations. This did not, of course, preclude disagreements in the future over whether this or that writer had taken a sufficiently clear "ideological-political position." But the editorial composed by the editors of *Literaturnaya gazeta* made the postcongress discussion appear a somewhat artificial and strained exercise in the proper methods of "persuading and educating" writers.

Writers who in 1956 had actively agitated for a broader scope of freedom than that permitted by Khrushchev's policy of moderation failed to make significant contributions, in the form of essays on problems of literature, to the discussion of 1959. Since it was no longer possible for them, even had they thought it desirable, to elaborate their views in the outspoken manner that some had three years earlier, their failure to participate should hardly cause surprise. But perhaps for them — and for a new group of young writers — carrying on the struggle by direct argumentation had become less important; perhaps engaging in polemics couched in abstract doctrinal terms had become increasingly irrelevant. For the middle way in literature opened opportunities for revealing their attitudes concretely in imaginative writing, and it augmented the possibilities for attempting to expand the limits of orthodoxy gradually by means of literary works themselves. In two rather startling poems published in 1959, Margarita Aliger seemed to take this position and to urge it on other writers. In one of the poems, printed in the journal *Oktyabr*, Aliger entreated fellow writers to create honest, sincere works without worrying about whether or not they will be published.[84] If you write what you really live and feel, she said, if you are your own "honorable law," your own "strict judge," you will win support and words of approval. In another poem Aliger expressed her contempt for pretentious hack works written to serve immediate purposes — works "without conscience," "without shame" — and she advised her colleagues not to waste themselves polemicizing with such works but to save their energies for creative labor.[85]

A part of the post-1956 literary output suggested that moods similar to Aliger's infected a number of writers. Just as strikingly, Soviet writing throughout the period from 1957 to 1959 revealed that the urges which gave birth to the "critical" literature of 1956 were by no means exhausted. The humanistic impulse, the yearning for truthfulness and sincerity, and the critical attitudes engendered by such tendencies persisted and continued to find expression, though more guardedly and often indirectly, in a comparatively small but nonetheless significant number of literary works. One Soviet critic pointed to this in mid-1959 when he complained that "to this day something like echoes, even if distant, of the false assertions of comrades who made mistakes in the years 1956–1957 once in a while begin to resound in isolated works." [86]

A key feature of a considerable amount of post-1956 writing was a humanistic orientation which, in its literary embodiments, had many facets. Though the emphasis on humanism itself seemed consistent with the atmosphere which the Khrushchev regime was trying to establish, in the hands of some writers humanism acquired meanings sharply divergent from those traditionally associated with the official concept of Soviet or socialist humanism, which is distinguished rather more by severity and intolerance than by generosity. Some writers, pleading for an end to man's inhumanity to man, seemed to call for a revision of moral sentiments, for a revaluation of values. They argued for a more generous moral code, for a humane morality that would give high value to such qualities as honesty, kindness, and compassion, which, they suggested, had been ignored or extirpated during the long, dark years of Stalinism. Nina Ivanter, in her novel *It's August Again*,[87] treated the need for a modification of moral values in a way which must have struck responsive chords in other writers, particularly those younger authors who are critical of what they consider the warped values of the older generation. In a key passage Ivanter attributes to one character — a former political prisoner, amnestied after Stalin's death — views with which she is obviously in sympathy:

it turns out that kindness is the most valuable of human qualities and sometimes outweighs every other virtue. The thing is that in those years when a person engages most actively in molding himself, I considered it essential to cultivate in myself the firmness of iron, the staunchness of steel, and other such metallic qualities. As for kindness, sensitiveness, and tactfulness, all these I placed in the category of human attributes which, I thought, I could acquire any time I wanted to. . . . Both in myself and in other people I admired other things. And how many years had to pass before I suddenly understood that human kindness is a fine and most necessary thing in life.[88]

Ivanter manifestly regards the exaltation of "metallic" qualities as a source of moral insensitivity, and she longs for conditions which will permit human relationships to be open and warm. Sentiments somewhat similar to Ivanter's lay behind Sergei Voronin's much criticized story "On Native Ground." [89] The story depicts the encounter of a war veteran, Kasimov, with a friend of his youth who deserted to the Germans during World War II and fought against the Soviet Union. Years later the deserter, having returned quietly to his native village at the end of the war, remains unexposed and unpunished. Kasimov, recognizing that the man has suffered the worst of punishments — the torments of conscience — decides not to denounce him to the authorities, though the former comrade now seems "a stranger" to Kasimov.

The tendencies represented by Ivanter's novel and Voronin's story provoked objections from party-minded critics and writers, and the upshot was a discussion in the Soviet press about the meaning of humanism. One critic, taking the orthodox position, sounded a warning against "kindness" and "humanism" if they are set off against "political and ideological consistency," and he suggested that Ivanter had made this mistake in the section of the novel quoted above.[90] Voronin's story was subjected to severe criticism. The chief editor of *Literaturnaya gazeta*, Smirnov, reacted, in his own words, "in rage, indignation, and sharp protest" to the story, which he described as "an attempt to speak publicly in the saccharine tone of Christian all-forgiveness about the fortunes of an accomplice of the enemy," [91] and another prominent literary figure, D. Granin, stated firmly at a party meeting held to discuss the story: "It is too early for us to disarm. We cannot teach young people from stories like Voronin's. We must inculcate in the growing generation hatred for traitors." [92]

Those who were alarmed by some of the implications of the humanistic tendencies in current writing had to fight on many fronts, for the trend was widespread and strong. It was reflected in a revulsion against the inflated, pompous literary style that characterizes much of Soviet literature. It appeared in the form of a reaction against false heroics and oversized fictional characters intended by their creators to capture the essence of an epoch. It could be felt in the devotion of some writers to the task of writing believable, unvarnished works about the everyday lives of ordinary people. All this pointed to a spreading of attitudes which had revealed themselves even before the death of Stalin. Views which appeared to lie behind a portion of the works published during the period of the drive for consolidation were stated briefly by Grigory Medynsky in his novel *Honor*, written in 1959.[93] At one point Medynsky muses:

Of course, there are times, even whole epochs, when the individual is a grain of sand, lost in the overwhelming storm of inevitable events. But there comes a time when the fate of the individual person becomes the primary concern of a human and humane society, when society cannot consider itself happy if the members who constitute it are not happy. Behind the vastness of historical events, achievements, and epochal plans, one must look attentively at the little fate of the solitary man wandering along the paths of life, and perhaps this little thing will sometime, somehow respond with a great, loud echo — it cannot fail to respond, for the soul of man is resonant.[94]

Authors who were trying to write straightforward, down-to-earth works about the lives and loves of ordinary Soviet citizens, works without obvious political morals and doctrinal asides, were frequently subjected to sharp criticism, though they had their defenders as well. Critics and editors who opposed this trend in writing could easily find support for their point of view in pronouncements made on high levels. They could, for example, point to a volume of essays published by the USSR Academy of Sciences in 1959, on the occasion of the Twenty-First Party Congress. The volume, issued as an authoritative statement on problems involved in the transition to Communism, contained an essay on literature which, significantly enough, lashed out at "advocates of everydayness [*bytovizm*]" in literature, who, it said, "have even begun to regard the propensity of our literature for heroic images as the source of its shortcomings." The essay warned writers dealing with themes of everyday life about the dangers of "uninspired commonplaceness" and reminded them that "the only fruitful path to a genuinely artistic embodiment" of contemporary Soviet life is "the portrayal of our everyday affairs in their lofty, heroic essence." [95]

Themes of social criticism which had been articulated vigorously and vividly in 1956 continued to appear from time to time during the following years, though they were necessarily modified and attenuated in their literary manifestations. If the persistence of socially critical attitudes was evident in a number of published works depicting past and present conditions of Soviet life with a certain amount of candor, it was perhaps even more apparent in manuscripts which remained unpublished. At any rate, a complaint voiced late in 1958 by Yevgeny Popovkin, chief editor of the literary journal *Moskva*, lent itself to that interpretation. The editorial staff of the journal "experiences serious difficulties," said Popovkin, in its search for good works about "our people today,

the splendid toilers, the creators of a new world"; and he expressed
astonishment that the editors receive manuscripts which pretend to
be about contemporary life but which have as main characters
"bureaucrats, petty functionaries, scoundrels, and saboteurs." [96] The
critical tendency, coupled with a revulsion from drum-thumping
optimism, seemed especially strong among younger writers. One
critic pointed to a striking aspect of this tendency when he accused
those who focus on "negative phenomena" of copying from literature of the past rather than drawing from present-day reality. It
was this, in his view, which accounted for the occasional appearance
of "despondent" works by young authors, works which he described as "filled with a sluggish feeling not even of pessimism,
but of a kind of boredom, reminiscent of the literary manner of
the period of social stagnation at the beginning of the twentieth
century." [97] It was perhaps a significant indication of the mood of
the new generation of writers that some appeared to draw their
inspiration from such authors as Chekhov and Bunin, a development which more than one literary critic noted with evident dis-
comfort.

The drive for consolidation had the effect, on the whole, of
deflecting socially critical trends in Soviet literature from their
main course into more acceptable bypaths. During this period
there began to emerge, even more distinctly than in earlier years,
a literature of compromise, built upon a careful and calculated
amalgam of critical and conformist elements. Soviet readers had
perhaps become habituated in the post-Stalin era to the excitement
of critical themes in their reading matter; and authors of basically
orthodox works often tried to satisfy the need by introducing such
themes before leading readers on to comforting conclusions intended to reinforce loyalty to party and state. One Soviet critic,
V. Arkhipov, referred more or less openly to this kind of writing
in a review which was meant to expose the artificial and contrived
structure of Galina Nikolayeva's novel *Battle on the Way*. Arkhipov in effect accused Nikolayeva, along with other unnamed
authors, of writing with her eyes glued too firmly to a list of
permitted problems and the latest party decrees. Commenting on
her careful balancing of negative and positive elements, Arkhipov
asked sardonically about the novel: "And is there [shown in it]

a violation of socialist legality in the past? But without this novels are no longer written — of course there is." [98] Though the critic might have made his point more convincing had he vented his anger on writing of less interest and merit than Nikolayeva's, his remarks had the virtue of directing attention to a body of works which, though they contained ostentatiously critical passages, were profoundly conformist in their basic orientation.

The literary output of 1957–1959 revealed that, despite the hardening of the literary line during those years, Soviet writers found it possible to deal in one way or another with subjects and themes that were forbidden during the worst years of Zhdanovism. To some extent, this grew out of the efforts of the Khrushchev regime to overcome the paralysis and stagnation produced by Stalinist terrorism, reflecting the regime's more tolerant attitude toward discussion and criticism contributing to the elimination of officially recognized evils. It was a reflection, too, of the Khrushchev literary line, which permitted the portrayal of negative phenomena if sufficiently counterbalanced by an emphasis on the positive. But works which mirrored conditions of Soviet life and attitudes of Soviet people with greater accuracy than in the past also bore witness to some writers' skill in insinuating meanings through allegory and allusion or in working meaningful critical themes into what seemed an innocuous literary fabric. Such works could appear only on the sufferance of literary officialdom and, ultimately, of the party, for the scope of autonomy enjoyed by writers was as closely dependent as ever on the literary line adopted by party leaders. But some writers were apparently attempting in their works to explore, and perhaps to stretch, the limits of the new orthodoxy. The resistance that they provoked from critics, editors, and literary bureaucrats pointed to the risk that such efforts entail for Soviet writers: major breaches of orthodoxy might induce a reaction in the form of a sharp tightening of literary policies. From the standpoint of the party, the risk was of a rather different order. Post-1956 trends in writing raised the possibility that literary works might act as a stimulant to critical thinking by presenting Soviet society with a truer image of itself. The middle way in belles-lettres, as past experience has shown, is not an easy one to maintain.

VI ❖❖❖❖❖

Bureaucratic Controls and
Literary Production

❖❖

An outstanding feature of the Soviet literary scene is the vast
bureaucratic apparatus that exercises surveillance over the whole
range of activities involved in the production of literary works. As
in other realms of Soviet life, it has been necessary to employ
bureaucratic devices to translate the general precepts of the party's
literary policies into actual practice. And, as elsewhere, the bureaucratic system realizes only imperfectly the intentions of the party's
leaders. The shortcomings are in part the consequence of human
fallibility, conscious evasion, and resistance. But the bureaucratic
structure itself creates new problems, intensifies others, and gen-
erates forces which contravene the policies it was designed to im-
plement. Moreover, as the policies are being executed, the inconsistencies inherent in them are often revealed more starkly.

The following discussion is chiefly concerned with the contrary
forces that the controls system sets in motion and with weaknesses
in the operation of the system. Because the main responsibility for
day-to-day supervision of literary activities rests with the leadership of the Union of Soviet Writers, attention is focused on the
operation of the central organs of the union and the work of the
editorial boards of literary journals which are attached to the
union's central apparatus. The system of rewards and penalties and
other aspects of the less formalized but all-important pattern of
postpublication controls are also considered. The discussion does
not include the entire network of public agencies — the agencies
and subdivisions of the party, government, and semiofficial pro-

fessional groups — whose activities are related in some way to facets of literary production. Information about the activities and the interrelationships of these agencies is scanty, and a survey of it contributes little to the understanding of the basic techniques of bureaucratic control and their impact on Soviet literary life. The purpose here, then, is to characterize the devices used in the daily execution of the party's program by investigating the institutions most immediately and continuously concerned with belles-lettres and to examine the contradictory effects which these devices produce. Since the emphasis is more on shortcomings than achievements, the result may be a somewhat one-sided representation of the operation of the system; but the material presented in preceding chapters should in some measure compensate for this emphasis. It will be noted that many of the problems to be examined have been serious enough to provoke widespread and sometimes sharp debates among Soviet writers, and all of them have been disclosed in one way or another by reports in the central press. These reports in certain cases suggest that a single set of factors has given rise to trends of a quite contrary nature, and, although effects can sometimes be traced and their significance suggested, it is not always possible to determine which is the main current. The difficulty is especially great with respect to the post-Stalin period, for changes in the political climate of the Soviet Union in recent years have affected to some degree the operation of the system of controls in literature.

It was evidently intended that the vital center of Soviet literary life should be the Union of Soviet Writers, the single organization binding together those who wish, as the statutes of the union put it, "to participate through their creative work in the class struggle of the proletariat and in socialist construction" and whose aim is "the creation of artistic works worthy of the great epoch of socialism." [1] The union was to provide a forum for the interchange of ideas, a means whereby writers might aid and stimulate one another, and a channel through which the party, aided by the party groups in the union, could elucidate more fully the meaning of socialist realism and the tasks of Soviet literature. The union was also meant to be a means whereby the party could guide writers along the correct path, helping them to avoid the blunder of pro-

ducing works alien to the spirit of socialist society. A glance at
the operation of the central organs of the union will help to indicate in what respects and why the organization has not wholly
fulfilled the party's aspirations for it.

As with other Stalinist institutions, the actual power in the
Writers' Union became concentrated at the top of the union's
pyramidal structure; democratic processes atrophied; and the pro-
visions of the statutes were openly violated.[2] The all-union congress is formally the ultimate source of authority in the Writers'
Union; but it met only twice between 1934 and 1954 despite the
stipulation of the original statutes that it meet once every three
years. In 1954 the statutes were amended to require the congress
to meet once every four years, and, although the Third Congress
was delayed a few months, the present intention is evidently to
enforce this provision. The congress elects an executive board
which was required by the original statutes to hold plenary sessions
at least three times a year; in fact it met only fifteen times between
1934 and 1954. The statutes as amended in 1954 require the board
to meet at least once a year, a provision which has been observed
since the change was made. At the First Congress a bloc of one
hundred one writers was chosen unanimously by acclamation to
constitute the board, and later on additional members were co-
opted. At the Second Congress a board of one hundred thirty-five
members was chosen, this time by secret ballot, and the Third
Congress elected a board of one hundred forty-three members.
The large membership of the board itself suggests that the body
cannot fulfill executive functions. But, in addition to this, the
actual membership of the board has always constituted a minority
at the plenary sessions because of the large number of nonmembers
— writers and others — who have been allowed to attend: it has
been estimated that the percentage of board members among the
actual participants varied from 40 percent to 10 percent for the
fifteen sessions held between 1934 and 1954.[3] Until 1959 the board
elected from its members both a presidium and a secretariat,
though there has never been any indication that it did anything
more than confirm choices actually made by the existing presidium
and secretariat. The presidium of forty-two members selected at
the end of 1954 was the largest in the history of the union, the

size of the body having varied between that and fifteen members over a period of twenty years. In earlier years, the presidium was the dominant organ; but after the war it was eclipsed by the secretariat, though it still occasionally reviewed the work of literary journals and discussed the larger problems of Soviet belles-lettres and even individual literary works. As with the board, the meetings of the presidium were normally "expanded," its actual members in a minority, and its proceedings dominated by the first secretary. The presidium was supposedly a primary source of "directors of literary production" — that is, heads of literary commissions and personnel for the editorial boards of journals and publishing houses — although a relatively small portion of the members of the presidium participated actively in this work.[4] Because it performed poorly and fulfilled no essential functions, the presidium was abolished at the Third Writers' Congress in 1959.

After 1946, when Alexander Fadeyev again became first secretary, the secretariat was the central power in the union, and it continued to be so under Surkov, who took over Fadeyev's post in October 1953. During the postwar period, the secretariat has been composed of from six to, most recently, twenty-eight members, though a much smaller group controls its operations. Fadeyev more than once admitted, toward the end of his career, that the secretariat was directed by only two or three people.[5] Actually, Fadeyev himself played the leading role, and the vigor with which he asserted his authority apparently led to discord within the secretariat.[6] It is reasonable to suppose that since May 1959 — when the eleven-man secretariat set up in 1954 was expanded to twenty-eight — the power of decision and control has been wielded, if not by a single man, then by an "inner secretariat" of no more than thirteen members, probably headed by the new first secretary, Konstantin Fedin; for the expansion was chiefly the result of including in the membership of the secretariat the fifteen heads of the writers' organizations of the union republics, who do not normally live in Moscow. Evidence of the extent to which control had shifted from the presidium to the secretariat by 1954 was furnished by the report of the auditing commission at the Second Congress: the secretariat held thirty-four sessions and considered four hundred thirty-nine questions in 1954, whereas the presidium met only seven times to consider twenty-eight questions.[7] The concentration of power in the secretariat has provoked much critical comment in recent years, and at the Second Congress even Fadeyev echoed the party's call for collegial leadership, declaring that the secretariat must be subordinate to the larger elective bodies of the union. But he opposed those who would limit the secretariat's activities to routine administrative tasks — the role which the statutes seem to have envisaged for it — and asserted instead that it must be "a directing organ with full authority, but unconditionally accountable to the board and the presidium." [8] In 1959 the statutes were modified to require biannual election of the secretariat by the board. The announced purposes of this change were to enhance the significance of the board "as the collective leader" of Soviet literature and to augment "the responsibility and the role of the secretariat of the union in the whole of current literary life." [9] Fadeyev's conception of the role of the secretariat apparently has been adopted. In view of the large membership of the board and the abolition of the presidium, there can be little doubt that the secretariat will remain the seat of power within the Writers' Union.

The responsibilities of the secretariat are great: its sessions may be concerned with anything from broad questions of literary policy through organizational problems on the union, republic, district, or local level to individual petitions relating to personal problems. In practice, the central literary journals and the union's publishing house "Sovetsky pisatel" are accountable to the secretariat, which exercises the right to appoint and remove members of their editorial boards. The secretariat may also discuss individual literary works; though press reports of such discussions were very rare during the first decade after the war, they have appeared more frequently in recent years. These discussions usually deal with works of important authors or works that present special difficulties, and at least in the earlier period the fate of an individual work was sometimes determined by "the opinion of a few leaders," as Fadeyev said with reference to an incident involving Vasily Grossman's novel *For the Just Cause*, after a negative evaluation had been reversed.[10] Until the creation of a distinct Moscow writers' organization in 1955, the secretariat was also responsible for supervising the activities of the creative (genre) sections of Moscow writers. In addition, the secretariat is held accountable for the work of several commissions which deal with various aspects of Soviet literature and literary activities. There have been repeated complaints that the secretariat shows little interest in the creative work of these commissions and that their effectiveness has declined as a result: the commissions "go their bureaucratic way and literature goes its own way, and these ways almost nowhere meet," said one group of Moscow writers not long before the Second Congress opened.[11] In an apparent attempt to correct the situation, the writers' union of the Russian republic, founded in 1958, absorbed most of the commissions; but shortly thereafter the secretariat established a group of new councils and commissions under the jurisdiction of the all-union organization.[12] In view of the many duties which the secretariat attempts to fulfill, it is hardly surprising that it is often accused of inefficiency and failure to carry out its decisions. The records of the secretariat's sessions, *Literaturnaya gazeta* once observed, sometimes seem "a dismal graveyard of good intentions."[13] And the auditing commission's report at the Second Congress gave a generally unflattering impression of the secretariat's administrative efficiency. Even with respect to so important a matter as the functioning of the literary journals, the secretariat's activity is spasmodic. Fyodor Panfyorov, for many years the chief editor of *Oktyabr*, has thus described the secretariat's practices: "A misfortune occurs in this or that journal and a meeting of the secretariat is hurriedly called: at the secretariat they talk for a long time about the misfortune, violently criticize whoever is responsible for it, then create a commission to work out a resolution . . . and the whole business founders, like a brick dropped into the sea."[14]

Discontent over the inefficiency of the union's apparatus gave rise to various suggestions in 1954 that the auditing commission be revitalized and its power expanded. The commission is elected by the all-union congress; it is supposed to examine the financial and other activities of the union's governing organs and inspect the management of all operations. The commission does not appear to have been very active in past years, nor has its own efficiency been very high, as its report to the Second Congress indicated. But the activity of the commission apparently quickened in 1954, when it undertook a survey of the union's operations. Its report to the Second Congress contained numerous proposals for reform and strongly suggested that more order would be introduced into the administrative and financial practices of the union. Since that time reforms have taken place within the apparatus; although exact information about their effect is not available, it should be noted that the familiar criticisms continue to appear in the Soviet press.

The most superficial outline of the main organs of the Writers' Union would be incomplete without mention of the union's party organization, which seems to have an unlimited right to concern itself with every aspect of literary life. Party meetings of writers are normally held after a significant editorial or an authoritative article has appeared in the party press and, of course, after the Central Committee has issued a decree. Besides maintaining ideological vigilance, the party organization is evidently supposed to exercise daily surveillance over the union through its network of party groups in the various subdivisions and agencies of the union. An incident that occurred in 1951, when proposals were made to abolish the creative sections, illustrates some of the functions that the party organization performs or is expected to perform. According to B. Rodionov of the Central Committee's Propaganda and Agitation Department, the party committee of the Writers' Union "noticed this danger in time, formed party groups in the creative sections, strengthened the leadership of some sections, and revised the regulations relating to the sections." [15] The party organization has been active throughout the postwar period, and much importance is attributed to its work. It is significant that in 1954, when again there was talk of disbanding the creative sections, one objection to the proposal was that it "provides no place for the party organization" and ignores it "as an instrument of party influence on creative processes in literature." [16] Though the party organization is apparently unrestricted in the range of problems with which it may deal, it has not supplanted the secretariat as the source of authority within the Writers' Union. The main reason for this would seem to be that the line of communication between union leaders and higher party authorities does not pass through the party organization. Ranking union officials are themselves usually party members; whether or not they are, they may receive instructions from the top echelons of the party through the Propaganda and Agitation Department or through direct contact with leading party figures. It is worth noting, in addition, that although editorials in the party press and broad policy decisions made in the name of the Central Committee provide guides for the leaders of the union, the Central Committee has sometimes intervened directly in the administration of literary affairs. Thus the journal *Znamya*, having suffered a "misfortune" in 1948, had to report directly to the Central Committee, which then passed a resolution criticizing the publication.[17] Furthermore, the subdivisions of the party on lower administrative levels are expected to supervise the work of the corresponding subdivisions of the Writers' Union.[18]

The centralized control that characterizes the operation of the governing bodies of the all-union organization is also the dominant feature of the relationship between the central apparatus and branches of the writers' organization in republics, territories, and regions. The organizational structure of the branches is essentially the same as that of the parent body, though the apparatus of the smaller branches is understandably less elaborate. According to the statutes of the Writers' Union, the executive boards of the writers' organizations on lower administrative levels are accountable both to the writers' congresses of the corresponding levels and to the central executive board, and decisions of the governing bodies of the all-union organization are binding on all branches of the union. It appears that the all-union organization strives to maintain close supervision over its branches. The expanded meetings of the board and, since the abolition of the presidium, of the secretariat provide occasions for bringing local officials and writers into contact with the union's leaders and for familiarizing them with the current literary line, as do the ten-day festivals devoted to the literature and art of various nationality groups, held periodically in Moscow, which bring leading writers from outlying areas to the capital. The inclusion of the heads of the writers' organizations of the fifteen union republics in the all-union secretariat also serves to strengthen the control of Moscow over the branches. Moreover, members of the secretariat and the board often play a leading role at congresses and conferences in outlying areas. The central apparatus of the union also maintains contact with the republican and regional organizations through the commission on the literatures of the peoples of the USSR, and until 1959 the commission on Russian literature in republics, oblasts, and krais was also used for this purpose. The secretariat has more than once been accused of using arbitrary and bureaucratic techniques in directing the activities of the union's branch organizations. A protest from three Voronezh writers illustrates a common dissatisfaction and gives some indication of the methods of the secretariat:

Relations between the secretariat of the board of the Writers' Union and oblast branches are mainly of an administrative character. Mimeographed minutes of the secretariat's meetings, loaded with resolutions on minor organizational matters, and also extended resolutions on the celebration of various anniversaries are constantly being sent to the local branches.

The secretariat has fully entrusted guidance of local organizations to the commission on Russian literature in republics, krais, and oblasts. This commission, once a voluntary public organization maintaining creative ties between the writers of the capital and the periphery, has now become a bureaucratic literary office, often determining the fate of writers living in the krais and oblasts.[19]

The same writers objected to a resolution of the secretariat which abolished two local writers' organizations and warned others of a similar fate if their work failed to improve. The secretariat's decision was probably the outgrowth of questions that had recently been raised about the proliferation of small writers' groups, a tendency fostered by the secretariat's practice of approving the creation of a new branch upon the application of three members or candidate members of the union. One writer asserted that sometimes members filed such applications chiefly to gain access to the benefits of the Literary Fund, and he added that official funds had been diverted to personal use, that writers had found security in semiofficial posts and were able, by virtue of their positions, to publish mediocre works in the provincial press year after year, and that small organizations contributed little to creative writing.[20] As a remedy, it was proposed at the Second Congress that branches not be formed in krais or oblasts where there are fewer than ten writers.[21]

For many years there was neither a writers' union of the RSFSR nor, rather curiously, a Moscow writer's association. In 1954 there was much grumbling by Moscow writers that they were the victims of an undemocratic system and an overburdened apparatus, and in 1955 a Moscow branch was formed. The next logical step — the creation of a writers' union of the RSFSR — was accomplished in 1958. These changes, which entailed a degree of administrative decentralization, were part of an effort to remedy the ills caused by an excessively centralized system of control within the union, though, as it was noted in the preceding chapter, the founding of the Russian writers' organization had other purposes as well. The creation of the Moscow association did little to mitigate dissatisfaction among Moscow writers with the allegedly arbitrary methods of the leadership of the union. Whether this can be achieved through the new Russian writers' union remains to be seen. It may be suggested, however, that the method by which power is exercised within the Writers' Union will probably remain basically unchanged until the party itself discards the method of command from above.

The concentration of power in the hands of a few literary officials has affected writers' willingness to participate in the activities of the Writers' Union. Complaints that writers fail to take part in the work of the board and presidium have been frequent. The obvious reason for this indifference is that the board, like the recently abolished presidium, lacks real power to initiate policies or to resolve issues, a point that was made clearly enough at a writers' conference in 1954: to one speaker's observation that the board and presidium for the most part only confirm decisions already made by a few members of the secretariat, another added, "There is nothing surprising about the fact that most writers, absorbed in creative work, decline to participate in such meetings, which are of a purely formal character." [22] Perhaps more significant in terms of the party's broader interests in the Writers' Union is the effect this has had on the creative sections. For the sections were designed to be centers of literary activity, laboratories for creating a literature "worthy of the great epoch of socialism," and also to be the first stage of a process for screening new works; they were to take their place among the several instruments for securing a literature not only artistically but ideologically sound. But there has been much evidence in recent years to indicate that centralization of control has induced lethargy in the sections and that the groups contribute little to the creative efforts of a large number of writers.[23] In actuality, the sections have been denied effective means of influencing Soviet literary life either through administrative or creative work. The secretariat's practice of discussing individual literary works is one of the causes of the reduced importance of the sections. One writer's complaint about this points to the general nature of the problem: "The sections and commissions of the union are not now centers of creative intercourse between workers in this or that genre but, having no rights, are only transmission belts in the board's cumbersome apparatus. All questions pertaining to individual writers are decided by the board or the secretariat in those lengthy closed sessions whose proceedings are not disclosed to the majority of the union's members." [24] At times the secretariat has shown great sensitivity to any potential encroachment on its administrative duties; for example, Surkov on one occasion denied the prose section an opportunity to review the plans of the union's publishing house on the grounds that such action would be "superfluous" because the plans had already been approved by the secretariat.[25] Furthermore, the publishing houses and literary journals rely upon the services of their own reviewers, and editors are not inclined to take note of the recommendations of the sections. As a result, the bureaus of the sections are inactive, and even a writer who seeks help or criticism may have difficulty getting it. But for the most part writers avoid bringing their work to the sections, fail to attend meetings — sometimes even those devoted to their own works — and ignore advice given them when they do attend. Again and again writers have declared that section meetings are formal affairs which contribute little to literary creation. Even the new first secretary of the Writers' Union, Fedin, once remarked that the commissions and sections are not very active and that in some of them there is "hardly a glimmer" of life; efforts to stimulate their activity and to encourage participation by writers have too often been neither imaginative nor successful, he suggested, producing only paper results, "only protocols for the archives." [26] One consequence of all this is the reduction of the effectiveness of the sections as instruments of control.

Dissatisfaction with the sections has more than once provoked suggestions that they be abolished. When a proposal to this effect was made by a group of leading Moscow writers in 1954, a debate of some interest ensued, though the proposal was not accepted.[27] The Moscow organization was founded partly in response to these urges, as Simonov indicated at its opening when he said, with something less than complete candor, that "all the previous discussions about the need or lack of need for creative sections arose because of the absence of unified guidance of [the sections'] work."[28] But dissatisfaction with the sections persists, and as recently as 1958 the question of abolishing them was raised, this time by a writer who thought that at least the smaller writers' associations should disband their sections.[29] Actually, abolition of the sections would mark a significant change in the conception of the functions of the union, and it might be a first step in the direction of disbanding the union itself.

Proposals that the sections be discarded are only part of the evidence which indicates that writers are often more than merely apathetic toward the union. Many persons have displayed resentment over the division within the union between "those who serve and those who are served, the 'recognized' and the 'not-quite-recognized,' " as one writer put it.[30] By the end of 1954, to call the union's leaders "literary bureaucrats" was to be guilty of banality, and the organization itself was frequently referred to as an "administrative department of literary affairs." In an article criticizing "nihilistic" attitudes toward the union, Vasily Azhayev cited as remarks frequently heard before the Second Congress opened: "I don't expect anything from the Congress. We'll shoot the breeze and go home"; "The Writers' Union has outlived its purpose. No one needs it."[31] There can be no doubt that such attitudes persisted through the years following the Second Congress. Konstantin Fedin furnished authoritative proof of this late in 1959 when he spoke at a session of the secretariat devoted to the question of reorganizing the administrative apparatus of the Writers' Union.[32] Commenting on writers' failure to participate in union activities, Fedin suggested that the enlargement of the literary bureaucracy was among the causes of this shortcoming. The apparatus must not be allowed to grow into a "barrier between the writers and their union," he urged, adding the revealing comment: "Yet this barrier exists, and in recent years the building of the wall not only has not stopped, but, you may agree, continues to move at a rather fast pace." Another speaker reported that a survey of the union disclosed that "almost everywhere the administrative apparatus has grown and 'departmental' forms of work hinder the development of writers' initiative in public activities." But a prerequisite for inducing a change of attitude toward the union is a thoroughgoing revision of its methods of operation, and as yet there is no evidence that such a fundamental change has occurred, despite the reforms made after 1954. Indeed, it is apparent that the formation of the Moscow and Russian branches of the union only intensified existing problems in certain respects by increasing the size of the union's administrative staff. At the end of 1959, the secretariat was engaged, as so often in the past, in proposing new organizational techniques to solve problems created by organization itself, and it seemed unlikely that in the near future there would be an end to the recurrent complaining about the dead weight of bureaucratism, the inadequate realization of collegial leadership, and the unbearable dullness and sterility of the interminable meetings and conferences.

Although the sections of the Writers' Union are not highly effective as literary workshops or as instruments in the screening process, work done in the editorial offices of literary journals and publishing houses compensates for this to a considerable degree. But here, too, writers and editors find themselves caught in a web of conflicting demands and expectations. Writers sometimes complain because they are not informed about the work of the internal reviewing systems of publishing houses and journals, even though internal reviews may determine the fate of their books, and they have displayed resentment because recommendations of the creative sections are generally disregarded.[33] On the other hand, editors are under pressure to construct a fool-proof reviewing system. Thus, on one occasion, when the party press criticized the union's publishing house for distributing a harmful novel, the secretariat proposed that "no fewer than two members of the editorial council be instructed to familiarize themselves with each work accepted for publication" and urged the chief editor and director of the publishing house to "strengthen control over the work of reviewers and editors." [34] Such incidents have inevitably put editors and reviewers on their guard, and excessive caution is often blamed for long delays in the process of transforming a manuscript into a finished book.

Observing the party's injunction to help writers improve the quality of their work, editors often undertake revisions of manuscripts. Here editors and writers are plagued by tensions between the claim of ideological orthodoxy and the demand for artistic diversity, and what goes on in editorial offices explains much about the dullness and uniformity of books published. After Fyodor Panfyorov's outburst in 1946 against editors' rewriting of manuscripts,[35] several years lapsed before there appeared a spate of complaints about revisions, sometimes made without authors' knowledge or consent, that rendered all books as alike "as two drops of water." *Literaturnaya gazeta*'s report of a presidium session in mid-1956, one devoted largely to the work of the publishing house "Sovetsky pisatel," contains a trenchant summary of such complaints.[36] Although the editors are excellent, the system is bad, said N. Chukovsky, observing that it was something of an anachronism that after nearly forty years of Soviet rule a writer's manuscripts are corrected like a schoolboy's essay: "As a result, the books that appear are very much like soup through which everyone has trailed his fingers." And O. Chyorny remarked that the system is such that "it is more difficult for an original book to make its way through than for a mediocre, featureless book." Given these conditions, it is hardly surprising that writers display a sense of alienation even with regard to "their own" publishing house. Chyorny expressed this feeling with some force in asserting that the publishing establishment is so constructed that "the writer is only an awkward link in this complex chain." Undoubtedly such remarks are to some degree only instances of the friction that arises everywhere when writers and editors come into contact. But it is worth nothing in view of the current situation in the Soviet Union that literary bureaucrats in the publishing houses appear to be a major source of resistance to pressures for liberalization. In this connection, an interchange at the presidium meeting between writer A. Bek and N. Lesyuchevsky, chief editor of the union's publishing house, is of interest. Complaining that Pasternak's works had not been printed and that the publishing house rejected Dudintsev's novel *Not by Bread Alone* (which the journal *Novy mir* accepted), Bek asserted that "everything that is not alien to us should be published." According to *Literaturnaya gazeta*, Lesyuchevsky "correctly rejected" Bek's claim on the grounds that this would lead to "omnivorousness."

The process of controlling literature begins, of course, neither in the Writers' Union nor in editorial offices, but at the writer's desk, when the "internal censor" becomes operative. This is not the place to discuss the Soviet educational system or to analyze the numerous techniques of ideological indoctrination. But mention must be made of some special institutions whose purpose, at least in part, is to heighten the writer's ideological awareness.

Like other Soviet schools, the Literary Institute of the Writers' Union — an institution of higher learning which trains a carefully selected group of aspiring young writers, critics, and scholars — is expected to equip its students with a sound knowledge of Marxism-Leninism. A fair indication of the party's attitude toward the tasks of the institute is to be found in a letter published by *Pravda* in 1951 which reproached those who conduct literary seminars for concentrating "on literary details, technique, and craftsmanship, ignoring questions of content and the ideological intent of works." [37] Periodic complaints about the weakness of the institute's courses in Marxism, as well as about students' erratic attendance of classes devoted to ideological and political subjects, only emphasize the importance attached to indoctrination, though they suggest that in official eyes the performance of the institute leaves something to be desired. In response to criticisms of the institute voiced by Yekaterina Furtseva at the Twenty-First Party Congress,[38] the first secretary of the Writers' Union proposed in 1959 that the institute increasingly devote its resources to correspondence courses for working youth and require work experience of applicants for admission to full-time study, so that young writers could no longer move from the security of the secondary school through the institute to the security of membership in the Writers' Union, knowing nothing but "the bell glass of the little world of literary interests." [39] Although these proposals were perhaps inspired by the general educational reforms which Khrushchev announced in 1958, they are undoubtedly in some measure a reaction to the "apolitical," "decadent," "formalistic," and "modernistic" tendencies which were allegedly manifested by some students of the institute in 1956 and 1957.[40] In view of the insistent identification of ideological orthodoxy and literary quality in the Soviet Union, it is not unreasonable to suppose that other institutions organized for the benefit of young authors — literary circles attached to journals and publishing houses, conferences, and seminars — furnish ideological guidance as well as literary instruction. Even older writers, especially those who are members of the party, are expected to attend the lecture courses and seminars on Marxism held in writers' clubs or to commit themselves to individual plans of study. But these efforts appear to meet with less than complete success: many writers ignore the programs, and others enroll but remain inactive, sometimes evading criticism by submitting the same plan of study year after year.[41]

The restrictions institutionalized in the Writers' Union, publishing houses, and other agencies are complemented by a system of incentives which inevitably creates its own problems. The emoluments, prerequisites, and rewards available to Soviet writers, beyond furnishing protection from indigence, at once encourage writers to enlist their art in the party's service and provide them with material compensation for the compromises that must be made. The rewards available may, then, render more submissive to the regime's demands a group which, at least in other societies, appears to contain a high proportion of nonconformists. Furthermore, denial of access to material benefits is a penalty that can always be invoked. In terms of the advantages available to them, writers occupy a privileged position in Soviet society, though the manner in which rewards are distributed has produced stratification within the literary community itself. These and related phenomena have created conditions which are not wholly compatible with the party's own aims in belles-lettres, and they have intensified some of the evils which arise from centralized bureaucratic controls.

The most important source of aid for writers is the Literary

Fund of the Writers' Union. The Litfund is an all-union organization with branches on the republic, regional, and local levels; it is administered by a board which is held accountable to the governing organs of the central union. The Litfund engages in extensive and diverse operations: it builds and maintains sanatoriums, medical clinics, writers' clubs, retreats for creative work, apartment buildings to house writers, summer cottages which writers may rent, and even nurseries, kindergartens, and summer camps for the children and grandchildren of writers; it makes loans and grants to writers and to families of deceased writers; and it provides funds for so-called creative missions — journeys to collect material for literary works — and for sojourns at health resorts and writers' retreats. Dues paid by members and legally required payments made by publishing houses, literary journals, and theaters constitute the financial resources of the Litfund. Its facilities are available to all members of the Writers' Union, and even writers who have not been admitted to the union may be allowed to join the Litfund.[42]

The Litfund has not remained free from criticism; sharp complaints have been made from time to time about mis-management and misuse of funds. The report of the auditing commission to the Second Writers' Congress in 1954 indicated the magnitude of the problem in disclosing that between 1951 and 1954 "losses and wasteful expenditures" consumed more than ten million rubles of the funds of the Writers' Union and that of this total the Litfund was responsible for six and one-half million rubles.[43] More recently the newspaper *Izvestiya* published an article which accused the Litfund of indulging in lavish and imprudent expenditures in a whole range of its activities.[44] The article left no doubt that writers make extensive use of the direct financial aid available through the Litfund. Indeed, the implication of the article was that some writers regard loans as normal supplements to their incomes, for there are borrowers who repeatedly obtain advances without repaying them, and the total sum owed by writers to the Litfund is large. The article also criticized certain practices connected with the creative missions, complaining not only that writers receive almost twice the daily allowance granted to other persons traveling for official purposes, but that the missions sometimes become mere "tourist jaunts." Moreover, writers tend to be negligent in filing the required reports about their trips. The article devoted much attention to the question of writers' retreats; but the information it presented is in some respects inconsistent with statements made by writers at various times in the past. According to *Izvestiya*, administrators of writers' retreats are unable to keep accommodations filled, partly because demand is low, perhaps more importantly because the retreats can accommodate more persons per year than there are members of the Litfund; consequently, the retreats are subsidized at great expense, and "the majority" of them have been converted into ordinary rest homes. Despite the abundance of unused facilities revealed by *Izvestiya*, writers sometimes grumble about the difficulties they meet in gaining access to the retreats. It is perhaps not surprising that some of these complaints originate among writers from outlying areas, who are at a disadvantage with respect to enjoyment of the facilities provided by the Litfund. Writers from Siberia and the Soviet Far East, in particular, have pointed out that the cost of transportation prevents them from utilizing the writers' retreats in Central Russia and the Crimea, and they have urged the Litfund both to pay transportation costs to existing retreats and to establish new retreats near Lake Baikal.[45] On the other hand, even Moscow writers have complained that they meet difficulties in gaining admittance to retreats because of administrative malpractices, such as the granting of accommodations to persons — often acquaintances and distant relatives of writers — who are not members of the Litfund and have no connection with literature.[46] But whatever its shortcomings, the Litfund, with the many benefits it dispenses, contributes much to the preservation of the privileged position enjoyed by writers in Soviet society. Despite its critical intent, *Izvestiya*, by publishing a detailed account of sums expended on the various functions of the Litfund, only emphasized this, and the assurance given in the article that "there is no leveling in our society" may well have seemed superfluous to some readers.

For many years the highest awards for writers were Stalin Prizes, conferred annually in three categories paying one-hundred thousand, fifty thousand, or twenty-five thousand rubles. No doubt the prizes served as strong incentives, but their impact was not wholly a positive one. At the Second Writers' Congress, both

Surkov and Simonov took note of some of the less desirable effects
of the awards, and Sholokhov and Ovechkin there and elsewhere
decried the evils with vigor.[47] Ovechkin voiced the opinion that
the prizes were among the major causes of the decline in Soviet
letters: many writers, he said, "began to write very quickly indeed,
as if frying pancakes, and sent to press unfinished, imperfect works
— anything not to miss the date of nomination for prizes." [48] Both
Sholokhov and Ovechkin charged — as they could in the post-
Stalin period of literary re-evaluation — that in many cases prizes
had been awarded to poor books and that this not only encouraged
the authors of prize-winning works to remain content with slight
achievements but disoriented other writers. To avoid these evils,
Ovechkin urged that books first be submitted to a test of time,
that prizes be awarded only at three- or five-year intervals; presumably artistic quality would then be accorded greater weight,
and topicality less. Although the prizes fell into disuse after Stalin's
death, they were revived in 1956 as Lenin Prizes, to be conferred
annually in uniform grants of seventy-five thousand rubles. The
procedure for awarding the prizes was changed to meet some of the
criticisms of practices used in awarding Stalin Prizes. These criticisms were summarized at the Second Congress by Ovechkin, who
complained that the method of awarding prizes was not a democratic one, that readers' opinions were not taken into account, that
appraisal of books was superficial, and that the leadership of the
Writers' Union behaved with excessive caution, hence irresponsi-
bly, in nominating for an award virtually every work that had
received some degree of public notice.[49] Since 1957, a modified
system of awarding prizes has been employed. In order to draw
the creative sections and the public at large into the process of discussion and selection, lists of works nominated by various public
organizations for prizes have been published some time before the
prizes were actually conferred. According to new regulations
promulgated early in 1960, the committee on Lenin Prizes, having
considered works proposed by the board of the Writers' Union,
must publish a list of the remaining contenders at least two months
before the awarding of prizes.[50] The result of these reforms has
been that fewer works are considered for prizes and fewer prizes
awarded. Indeed, in 1958 the committee conferred only four of the

eight Lenin Prizes allotted to the area of literature and the arts, and it was unable to find a single literary work deserving of the honor. This slight annoyed some writers; but the committee clearly hoped in this way to stimulate greater concern among writers about the literary quality of their work.[51]

In addition to literary awards, the Soviet government has established a complex royalties system calculated to provide authors with substantial material incentives to produce the kind of books required by the regime. But if the royalties arrangements serve the regime well in certain respects, they are partly responsible for some of the ills that afflict Soviet literature and the literary community. The categories and scales fixed by legislation dealing with royalties are structured to reward writers for the public utilization of their works, measured by the size and number of editions, and for quality, understood to mean not simply the level of literary craftsmanship but also the "timeliness and importance" of the topic and the "ideological purposefulness" of the works.[52] Governmental decrees have established three categories of payment: the first category is for outstanding works, the second for good works, and the third for satisfactory works and works of beginning writers. Prose writers receive four thousand, three thousand, or fifteen hundred rubles per "printer's sheet" of forty thousand typographical units, and poets, twenty, fourteen, or seven rubles per line.[53] For "mass editions" — defined as no fewer than seventy-five thousand copies for prose and twenty-five thousand for poetry — publishing houses must calculate royalties on the basis of one of the two highest categories of payment.[54] Payments for successive editions of a work are reduced according to a sliding scale: for a second and third edition the rate is reduced to 60 percent of that of the first; for editions through the seventh, to 50 percent; and for the eighth and subsequent editions, to 40 percent.[55] Although editions often run to one hundred thousand copies and more, the established norm for a first edition is fifteen thousand copies for prose works and ten thousand copies for poetry;[56] the copies in excess of the norm are counted as new editions. Hence a book may go through several editions in a single printing, and royalties are paid accordingly.

It is unlikely that Russian literary traditions or peculiarities of the Russian character alone account for the verbosity — an outstanding feature of much Soviet writing — which some critics in the USSR decry as the bane of Soviet literature: the Soviet royalties system has made its own contribution to this. As several directors of publishing houses observed — though they were not referring primarily to belles-lettres — the compensation based partly on the length of a manuscript does not encourage brevity but, on the contrary, promotes the writing of "bulky, bloated books whose dimensions frighten readers away." [57]

The royalties system not only contributes to the maintenance of writers' favored position in Soviet society, but it fosters stratification within the literary community. The graded schedules of rates obviously favor those who are successful in the eyes of the party. Winners of Lenin Prizes, in addition to their initial monetary awards, profit substantially from the large editions of their works published by the central and provincial presses, as do other authors of books deemed worthy of multiple editions or writers whose influence and "connections" — apparently factors of considerable importance in the Soviet publishing industry[58] — are such that the publication of their books in large-scale editions is assured. Given this situation, statements such as the one made by the poet and playwright Sergei Mikhalkov, who reportedly boasted while visiting the United States that he was a "millionaire from the Soviet Union," [59] are not in the least incredible. But Soviet critics of these methods of dispensing royalties argue that the effects on the writer are undesirable in themselves and indirectly harmful for Soviet literature. Valentin Ovechkin, for example, once said about the system that

it results in such emoluments that one must speak of this as something absolutely unnatural, something alien to the whole tenor of Soviet life and harmful in every sense — both in the sense of the uneconomical expenditure of state funds and in the sense of the encouragement of the writer himself. Such "encouragement" spoils talents, spoils people. The author of one more or less successful work may also finish with that and "rest on his securities." He builds an estate, buys antique furniture and rare tableware — and for all these cares he simply doesn't have time to think of new themes.[60]

Ovechkin suggested that either a steeply progressive income tax or a maximum annual income be imposed on writers and that fees be sharply reduced somewhere between the twentieth and thirtieth edition of a book. Ovechkin may have overstated his point, and what his remarks suggest may apply only to a comparatively small number of persons; but these forces tend to affect precisely those writers who have shown themselves to be most willing and able to serve the party.

Geographical factors, too, have influenced the distribution of benefits and sharpened divisions within the literary community. Almost any article in the Soviet press which contains the assertion that the distinction between "provincial" writers and writers of the capital has become outmoded also contains complaints indicating that the distinction is still a real one. For one thing, until 1957, when the discrepancy was eliminated, royalties paid by publishing houses in the territories, regions, and autonomous republics were 25 to 30 percent lower than those paid by central publishing houses.[61] And writers in outlying areas continually complain that editions published in the so-called periphery are smaller than those published in the capital, that it is difficult for them to get their work published in the central press, that literary critics ignore them, and that officials of the Writers' Union are unresponsive to their appeals for aid. The reports of the auditing commission at the Second and Third Congresses indicated, in addition, that the benefits of the Litfund flow less freely to writers of the periphery than to others.[62] It is not particularly surprising that writers find it easier or suppose it to be easier to advance their careers when living in Moscow, and undoubtedly this is one of the considerations leading them to congregate there.[63] Both Sholokhov and Ovechkin have strongly urged writers to leave Moscow in order to renew their contact with the people and, as their remarks hint, to escape the pressures and petty surveillance that is a part of life in the capital; more recently, persons particularly concerned about orthodoxy have suggested that writers should free themselves from the inbred and, in some cases, ideologically contaminated literary circles of Moscow. But for most writers the advantages of such a move would seem to be outweighed by the disadvantages, and at least in the near future these admonitions will probably pass unheeded — even though the newly founded Russian branch of the Writers' Union may induce a gradual improvement in the lot of the provincial writer.

It appears that the material benefits which are intended "to secure writers in their creative work," in the words of the auditing commission's report at the Second Congress, have provided some writers with security from creative work and to a certain extent from the party's demands in literature. In this respect, too, the system of payments and rewards has created its own antitheses. Sholokhov commented tartly on the problem at the Twentieth Party Congress when, after referring to the large membership of the Writers' Union, he warned his audience not to be awed or gladdened by these figures since they only "appear to be" and "in fact a significant portion of the writers' register consists of 'dead souls.' " He went on:

The trouble is that not a few, but very many writers long ago lost contact with life; they did not "tear themselves from it" but merely withdrew quietly to one side, where they peacefully exist in a state of dreamy and incomprehensibly contemplative inactivity. However paradoxical it may seem, they have nothing to write about. . . . And they have nothing to write about because they do not know life, they do not mingle with the people as writers should.[64]

Both Sholokhov and Ovechkin have expressed great concern about "premature retirement" and "separation from life," and it is not inconceivable that they have been guilty of polemical exaggeration in their treatment of these themes. But the widespread attention given to these matters and the manner in which others have discussed them suggest that the problems are real, even though the stress on the need for close contact between writers and the masses is by no means novel.

The use and misuse of Litfund benefits have some bearing on chronic complaints about writers' failure to produce, for the services provided by the Litfund, together with royalties from re-editions of earlier works, may permit some writers to live for years without publishing new works. When the newspaper *Izvestiya* discussed this problem, it suggested that the Litfund rid itself of persons "who have not created anything of value for decades" and help them find socially useful employment.[65] In this connection it is of some interest that in recent years the Writers' Union has expelled members for failure to create, undoubtedly depriving such persons of access to Litfund benefits.[66]

It is inevitable that the system, by transforming writers into a privileged group, tends to weaken writers' ties with the everyday life of ordinary Soviet citizens. Men of letters are inclined to move in higher social circles, to live within what Sholokhov called "the magic triangle: Moscow — summer cottage — health resort," and even in the capital to congregate in special areas, on Lavrushinsky street or in the writers' colony at Peredelkin. It was for such reasons and for fear of creating a "caste" of writers that Gorky opposed the establishment of Peredelkin, as Ovechkin disclosed at the Second Congress by reading from one of Gorky's unpublished letters.[67] From the writer's point of view, of course, the advantages afforded by comfortable living conditions and the reduction of pressures to produce for economic reasons may be great precisely in terms of literary creativity. Reports of visitors to the Soviet Union and manuscripts that have made their way to the West suggest that some writers use their leisure to pursue their own literary interests and to produce works that may or may not be circulated in the Soviet Union in manuscript form. And enough remarks have been made in the press about persons who consciously shun the gloomier aspects of Soviet life to suggest that writers may find it easier to give literary embodiment to the party's conception of reality when they are not too much absorbed by the actual conditions of life. Nonetheless, this may ultimately be incompatible with the party's utilitarian interests in belles-lettres, with its insistence that works find an audience in the masses and speak to the people in their own terms. For a real separation from this audience would make it only more difficult for writers to convey in an appealing and convincing manner the ideas which the party expects them to embody in their works.

The very bureaucratization of literary life has contributed to a problem frequently discussed in the Soviet press — the low literary productivity of some writers. The necessity of establishing an administrative structure to carry out the party's program in literature has unavoidably made literary bureaucrats of some of the persons most willing and able to serve the party, and this in turn has had a detrimental effect on the primary instrument with which they are expected to render service, their writing. In recent years there has been much criticism of authors whose assumption of heavy administrative responsibilities has reduced the quantity and quality of their literary output. One writer observed that, the question of justice aside, democratization and wider distribution of duties in the Writers' Union would have the beneficial effect of making genuine "public responsibilities" of the "highly paid official posts" which make it possible for some writers "to postpone work on their next book 'temporarily' — sometimes for months and even years." [68] Sholokhov's speech at the Twentieth Congress focused on these problems, principally blaming writers for allowing such conditions to establish themselves. But in asking how writers "who know nothing at all about collective farmers and workers" could be expected to produce new books, Sholokhov at least stated the point that needed to be made: "There are no high-quality, first-rate books and there will be none unless the situation in literature changes radically, and only the party can change it." There has been no indication since the Twentieth Congress, however, that the party contemplates undertaking the basic reform necessary to eliminate the incongruities of Soviet literary life.

The character and circumstances of the younger generation of writers are obviously matters of utmost importance for the future of Soviet letters. Ovechkin said at the Second Congress, while discussing the problem of writers' retreat from reality, that young writers now entering literature are "firmly linked with life," that they often follow a second profession, and he seemed to look to them as a means of revitalizing the literary community — as "new and fresher cartridges" for the "literary ammunition belt," to use Sholokhov's metaphor.[69] It is not easy to determine what the impact of the control system on young writers has been, although there are indications that all is not well within this group. During the postwar period there have been countless complaints about the failure of the Writers' Union, editorial boards, and leading authors to trouble themselves about the apprenticeship of young writers, and, of the many persons who have expressed concern about the increasing average age level of the membership of the Writers' Union, some have voiced what appears to be genuine alarm over the allegedly inadequate numbers of qualified writers who have made debuts in recent years. Though comprehensive information on the age of the union's membership is not available, published data indicate that the membership as a whole has aged significantly. The reports on the ages of delegates to the all-union writers' congresses are suggestive of the trend, though they cannot be taken as exact descriptions of what has occurred, since older writers of some reputation are more likely to be selected as delegates than younger, comparatively unknown authors. The reports leave no doubt, however, about the aging of the most influential group within the union. In 1934, at the First Congress, about 75 percent of the delegates were under forty-one years of age; but at the Second Congress, in 1954, 79.3 percent were older than forty, and at the Third Congress, in 1959, 86.1 percent were in this age group. Moreover, at the Third Congress writers over fifty years of age were more heavily represented than they were at the Second Congress: the over-fifty group constituted 50.7 percent of the delegates in 1959, as compared with 31.7 percent in 1954. As older writers have become increasingly prominent at congresses, representation of the youngest age group has decreased. Thus, in 1934 a little more than 9 percent of the delegates were under twenty-six; but in 1954 only 1.8 percent were under thirty; and in 1959 a mere 0.6 percent were in this age group.[70] In connection with the recurring statements about the need to inject fresh blood into the literary organism, it is of interest that in March 1954 Surkov reported that only 10 percent of the members admitted to the Writers' Union during the postwar years were under thirty years of age.[71] Two years later, a somewhat different set of figures was given by Azhayev, who considered excessive much of the alarm over the age of new members: he said that half of the more than fifteen hundred members admitted during the past ten years had been under thirty-five years of age.[72] Azhayev pointed to another factor, beyond the natural effects of time, that had contributed to the increase in the average age of the union's members; he observed, as others commenting on this matter have, that, whereas in the 1920s or '30s, it was not unusual for persons to begin their professional writing careers while very young, now it is common for writers to spend a longer time in school, find jobs, and acquire experience before beginning to produce finished works.

Other forces have evidently contributed to the aging of the membership of the Writers' Union. Commentary in the press suggests that the admissions policies of the union have been highly restrictive and that the age level of the membership gives a distorted impression of the actual availability of qualified young writers. Since the Writers' Union does not release information about the number and character of applications received and rejected, it is impossible to speak of the nature of these policies with any certainty. But reports from local organizations indicate that applications of young authors are treated with considerable circumspection, suggesting that a certain closing of ranks has taken place. One writer complained about the commission on admissions of the Leningrad organization in this way:

How afraid it is to open the door wider to young people! . . . And talented young people there are: young writers produce books and publish in journals and have a public. But [the commission's members] do not find it possible to admit them to the Writers' Union even as candidate members. They continue to await a "following" book having independent "literary-artistic significance" and are undisturbed by the fact that in the Writers' Union there are people who for decades haven't had even a small book to their name, except for the Union's membership booklet, and have produced no literary work at all, except for internal reviews for publishing houses and petitions to the Litfund.[73]

Centralized control over admissions creates further difficulties. After an application for membership has been made through a creative section of a local organization and has been accepted by the admissions commission and local secretariat, it must be sent to the Writers' Union headquarters in the appropriate republic, where it enters another bureaucratic hopper. The statutes as amended in 1954 decentralized control to a certain extent by permitting branches of the union with no fewer than forty persons to admit new members; at the same time, some additional modifications were made in the statutes to maintain suitable standards of qualification for new members.

Though grumblings about the reluctance of the Writers' Union to admit young authors are still heard periodically, scattered press reports indicate that the situation improved sometime after 1956. During this period there was a general increase in the rate of influx of new members. The available data indicate that, throughout the postwar period ending in 1954, from 150 to 160 new members were admitted annually.[74] Figures cited by Sholokhov at the Twentieth Party Congress reveal that during 1955 the union's membership increased by only 78 persons, though it may be surmised that actual admissions were somewhat greater, since figures on deaths and expulsions of members were not reported. But between December 1954 and February 1959, the membership of the union increased by almost 30 percent — from 3695 to 4800 — or at an average annual increase of approximately 276 persons.[75] Yet the percentage of young writers among the new members was reported to be small.[76]

Opinions in the Soviet Union about the adequacy of the material aid available to beginning writers vary considerably, leaving the outsider with rather contradictory impressions. That younger, lesser-known writers in particular have difficulty in gaining access to the benefits which accompany membership in the Writers' Union suggests that even in the USSR, where much is made of budding literary talent, a writer may suffer material deprivations during the early stages of his career. And the position of the newcomer to literature may be even more unenviable, despite the sizable sums that the Litfund sets aside for aid to beginning authors who are not members of the Litfund. Sholokhov, touching upon this subject at the Twentieth Party Congress, urged that greater material assistance be made available to young writers: "Hardly any of them live on literary earnings, and having left their regular profession in order to write their first big book or a series of stories, they find themselves helpless with respect to their material circumstances." [77] Others have expressed the view, however, that the Litfund, wholly aside from such imprudent expenditures as grants to students who already receive state stipends, is too lavish in aiding young writers.[78] Moreover, it has often been asserted that young writers who achieve quick success become victims of "early professionalization," at the same time submitting themselves to a variety of forces whose impact on more experienced writers is widely decried. Ilya Ehrenburg's comments on the matter are typical of those made by many others:

We have frequently seen a young author's star fall after the appearance of a first brilliant and talented novel. . . . A tragedy like this is usually connected with the author's life. A young person who is active, an engineer or geologist, a worker or student, has experienced and seen something; being talented, he used his experience in a book which brought him success. But then he became a professional writer and abandoned his former life. The flood of observations of life and experiences was shut off. The second and third books did not succeed because they were written not on the basis of experience, but with the help of guessing, book-knowledge, and ready-made outlines.[79]

Interestingly enough, Ehrenburg also pointed out that the difficulty of living by writing in the West forces authors, before they have attained fame, to work at other jobs and thus increase their experience and knowledge of people, all of which helps them when they "write novels showing the dark sides of capitalist society." Young authors in the Soviet Union are continually urged to maintain a second profession and to overcome their distaste for newspaper work, which is recommended as a sure way of establishing contact with the masses. Thus, even though Ovechkin looked hopefully toward the younger generations, it is not self-evident that those who are successful, or some of them, will not be caught up by that life which Ovechkin himself characterized as the fate of the group of writers midway between older Soviet authors and beginners — by that involvement in "duties, conferences, receptions, banquets" which keeps writers from productive literary activity.[80]

Scrutinizing works after publication constitutes an important part of the control system in belles-lettres. It provides occasions for ideological indoctrination and for exploring the meaning of the party's literary line in its particular applications. At this stage, latent powers of penalization may be activated. Because much has been said in preceding chapters about this facet of the system, only certain of its effects on the processes of literary production need be considered here. It must be noted that in recent years, particularly since the Twentieth Party Congress, Soviet literary life has been undergoing change and that some of the practices described below apparently are being modified, perhaps certain of them already outmoded.

A large part of the responsibility for determining whether works meet the party's standards is supposed to devolve on members of the literary community themselves, particularly on literary critics. Besides acting as propagandists of Marxist-Leninist ideology, critics are expected to ferret out error, to promote the development of literature along lines indicated by the party, and to contribute to the qualitative growth of belles-lettres. In order to fulfill adequately their functions as guardians and goads, critics must exercise a certain amount of initiative; but the authoritarian principle at the basis of Soviet literary life has engendered conditions which considerably reduce critics' effectiveness. The insistence that critics adhere to a single "ideological position" and the effort to predetermine the course of literary discussions only too frequently render "exchanges of opinion" pointless and sterile. Real disputes may arise, but at least in the past those of significance were usually cut short by articles in the party press which either set matters straight or declared the debates themselves a mistake. This has been generally less characteristic of the period since Stalin's death, particularly with respect to literary discussions on specialized questions. But the principles behind these practices have not been jettisoned — they have only been applied more leniently. It is not unfair to take Fadeyev's justification of such practices in 1954 as a representation of attitudes that prevail today. Replying to Aliger's assertion that discussion should mean an elucidation of different viewpoints on a controversial question, not an administrative summary which "labels these different viewpoints 'errors,' " Fadeyev said:

there is no sense in a discussion which only elucidates different viewpoints. Not all different viewpoints can be correct. There is an old joke: "If it is necessary to choose between two evils, then one incorrect viewpoint is better than two correct ones."

After all, we stand on the Marxist-Leninist science of society, according to which there exists an objective truth which can be known. Broad, free, creative discussion is necessary precisely in order to find the objective truth by comparing different viewpoints, to put it into the possession of as many writers as possible, and, holding to the truth thus discovered, to move forward to new achievements.[81]

As the tenor of Fadeyev's remark suggests, making the truth widely accessible takes precedence over the initial stage of the process described. This has engendered attitudes which are hardly conducive to a fruitful interchange of ideas, as G. Georgiyevsky, director of a provincial theater, pointed out in a remarkably frank consideration of usages common in the arts: "Before investigating the content of this or that article on artistic questions, we looked for the signature under it, took account of the publication in which it appeared, and on the basis of that decided whether or not it merited consideration." [82]

The party's monopoly on truth, its power to declare any opinion indisputably right or wrong, has paradoxically produced both extreme timidity and excessive zeal. And both have hindered criticism in the fulfillment of its tasks and retarded the development of Soviet writing, as it has been more openly admitted since the Twentieth Party Congress. Because higher authorities render vague standards precise in certain cases, subject even then to revision, it is not surprising that critics have often displayed an unwillingness to express their opinions before the party press reviewed a book or before literary prizes were awarded, or that many have manifested a preference for pure scholarship or writing nonpublic "internal reviews" for publishing houses. [83] One of the ways this impaired the therapeutic value of discussion is illustrated by an observation that could have been applied more broadly than to the theater, the immediate subject of the remark: "We usually only touch upon the most crucial problems of our work and in fact avoid a frank, straightforward discussion of the essence of the matter. More exactly, we talk a little, but we shun writing." [84] The hierarchical order in the literary community both increased this reticence and fostered extremism. It became customary before criticizing a writer's work or opinions to consider whether or not he had entered the ranks of those who, by virtue of their position, rarely commit serious errors; similarly, some writers acquired such authority that their views on questions of literature and literary politics inevitably came to be regarded as "instructions from above." [85] These practices were a part of the mechanism which so quickly turned any trend in criticism into a virtual campaign, with everyone moving in the same direction at the same time. The ultimate source of this lay elsewhere, of course; the basic principle was once expressed by Stalin in the exhortation, "the slogans of such a party [a ruling party] are not mere (agitational) slogans, but something much more, for they have the force of *practical decision*, the *force of law*, and must be carried out immediately." [86] Once the line was made clear, a decision taken in a specific instance, a slogan provided by the party — as in the case of the anticosmopolitan campaign — those who function as critics and guardians became relentless in their criticism and unstinting in their praise. As a result, the various drives against formalism, objectivism, aestheticism, and such, reached such extremes that people valuable to the party were put out of action. While ostensibly approving the purpose of such drives, Georgiyevsky thus criticized the manner in which they were carried out:

there invariably turned up people who love to transform a useful, important cause into a "campaign," to consider it a signal for severely "punishing" people, for openly discrediting erring but honest artists. And this was done without the requisite discrimination, with an excess of caution which is especially dangerous in such cases and which led many professional organizations to consider it a duty to have "their own formalist," "their own aesthete" — someone to "unmask" sensationally and ostentatiously. . . .

Over a long period of time we often confused artistic mistakes with political error. Not infrequently we discredited erring artists, looked upon them as a hostile people, treated persons who had made mistakes in the past with unremitting caution, stigmatized them with every conceivable kind of label.[87]

That being right could also provoke such treatment was admitted late in 1956 by Simonov, who disclosed what has been apparent to the outsider for some time — that the rout of the "antipatriotic" drama critics in 1948–1949 was in fact a punishment of those who had dared to expose the shortcomings of Soviet dramaturgy.[88] There have been numerous indications in the press that, beyond zeal in fulfilling the party's will and fear of reprisal for failure to do so, personal ambitions and rivalries contributed to excesses committed during literary campaigns. Thus in an article on Pavel Antokolsky, after his vindication from charges of cosmopolitanism, Vladimir Lugovsky remarked pointedly that poets in the 1920s, despite professional disagreements, respected one another's personality and did not know such things as "material favors and backstage plots."[89]

The penalties built into the control system for the most part become effective automatically, and this apparently makes formal imposition of them a comparatively infrequent occurrence. Instances of expulsion from the Writers' Union disclosed by the mass press were few during the postwar years, and, with the possible exception of the unique case of Boris Pasternak, these were evidently publicized as object lessons for other writers. On the other hand, expulsions, when publicized at all, are less likely to be reported by newspapers intended for mass circulation than by bulletins or publications such as *Moskovsky literator* which are circulated almost exclusively among members of the Writers' Union; hence it is likely that writers are excluded from the union more frequently than it has appeared.[90] Furthermore, writers who have erred may be deprived of editorial posts or whatever jobs they hold in literary production, and in any case public recantation is a normal prerequisite for remission of sins. In many instances, of course, revision of works criticized has been required. Simonov's comment on the Fadeyev affair may be taken as an illustration of the waste involved:

and what if the criticism of *Young Guard* had limited itself to uttering a series of correct or incorrect, disputable or indisputable remarks, but had not had implicit in it a demand for a revision of the novel? Perhaps, in this case, readers would have on their bookshelves not only the first version of *Young Guard* (which satisfied readers, as every readers' conference down to the very last testified) but would have beside it, instead of a second version of the very same *Young Guard*, a completed *The Last of the Udege*, on the concluding part of which Fadeyev began to work in 1947 and could have finished completely during those four years that he spent rewriting *Young Guard*? [91]

Whatever the merits of this case, much the same thing can be said not only of authors who were obliged to rewrite their postwar books but of authors who carefully revised books written before and during the war. Another common penalty, unspectacular but effective, is imposed by the natural course of events: cautious editors simply refuse to publish the work of authors in disgrace. In recent years there has been a reaction against such practices. Georgiyevsky was particularly outspoken in his criticism of the system whereby talented artists were deprived of "the right to creative work and public confidence," and he demanded recognition of the artist's right to make mistakes — a right explicitly denied throughout the postwar period. "Every artist takes risks," Georgiyevsky said, "but an honest artist must know for certain that he does not risk his reputation as a citizen, that he will not be placed under political suspicion, that he will not lose the opportunity to work in art even after the most serious failure." [92]

Even if the specific question of penalties is set aside, it must be said that the structure of controls is hardly one that inspires boldness in artistic endeavor. The effects which Georgiyevsky attributed to harsh measures of reprisal are actually products of the structure as a whole:

Experiment, originality of artistic conception, and daring innovations have disappeared from creative practice with increasing rapidity. Thus we have ourselves created a cautious, timid, spineless art. Only too vivid have been the examples of an uneconomical and shortsighted attitude toward artists who are "heretical" in one sense or another.[93]

Soviet literary doctrines are themselves severely limiting in this respect, and the party's success in putting them into practice has not only produced a high degree of uniformity but revealed the fundamental contradiction between demands for a literature consciously subordinated to specific political purposes and for one that is rich and diverse. But the bureaucratization of literature has made its own peculiar contributions to the intensification of this contradiction. "The greatest misfortune of Russian art," Viktor Shklovsky once wrote, "is that it is not allowed to move organically, as the heart beats in the breast of man, but is regulated like the movement of trains." [94] The bureaucratic structure has incapacitated talents, confined artistic creativeness within administrative categories, and even interfered with exercise of the initiative requisite for producing works convincing enough to be effective as propaganda. Reproaching the leaders of the Writers' Union for their intolerant attitudes and habit of "sentencing" literary works, Ilya Ehrenburg said at the Second Writers' Congress: "One can only smile bitterly when one imagines how the young Mayakovsky would have been treated if in 1954 he had brought his first verses to Vorovsky Street [the location of the union's headquarters]." [95] But the conditions of Russian literary life had changed radically since the days of Mayakovsky's youth, and it would have been difficult in 1954 to imagine how, except by remaining silent, any writer could have escaped Vorovsky Street or what it represents. During recent years the party has manifested greater concern about the contradictory effects of its policies and practices in literature, and it continues to call for creative boldness and the elimination of bureaucratic methods in art. But the task is a formidable one, and, even if the same energy were to be devoted to corrective endeavors as has been expended in literary "campaigns," the goal would not be attained easily. For the Soviet literary bureaucracy, like bureaucracies everywhere, has developed its own routines, attitudes, and interests, and neither these nor the pattern of reflexes ingrained by many years of Stalinism can be abolished overnight. Perhaps evils which the party acknowledges can be mitigated to some extent by tinkering with the system; but they can be eliminated only by a basic reform, one that would release writers from the unrelenting surveillance to which they have been subjected for so long. This would imply a repudiation of doctrines which are the foundation and justification of the control system, something that is hardly conceivable unless the whole Soviet power structure is fundamentally revised. Even tinkering with controls in belles-lettres may give scope to forces which tend to undermine the system, as the events of 1956 so vividly demonstrate.

VII ◇◇◇◇◇

Perspectives and Prospects

◇◇

In its transient integument called man, the song flows on like the waters of eternity, washing all away, giving birth to all.

Isaac Babel

During the postwar years the application of controls in Soviet literature followed a remarkably regular pattern of oscillation. The pattern grew out of contradictions within the structure of controls, and it reflected efforts to preserve an equilibrium among forces which pressed in contrary directions. The experience of the period demonstrates that it is necessary to speak of Soviet literary "politics," rather than of "policies" alone; for the incompatibilities among the exactions made of writers and the divergencies of purpose among those concerned with belles-lettres give rise to genuine conflicts between those who formulate or administer policies and those upon whom the policies are imposed. The contradictions are translated into discontent and pressure for change which produce the "inner dialectic" that characterizes the operation of the control system. Expressions of discontent direct attention to consequences of the party's policy which the party itself regards as undesirable — not the least of which is the tendency toward resistance among those whose talents the party needs for its own purposes — and the result is an adjustment which takes the form of a more generous interpretation of literary doctrine and a more lenient application of controls. Yet each time this occurred during the postwar period, there arose threats to some fundamental tenet of literary doctrine or to an essential element of the control system, and as a consequence limits to the liberalization were established — in 1952, in 1954, and again in 1957. Although the party is forced to take cognizance of the difficulties created by its policies, it endeavors to cope with these difficulties without modifying the policies themselves. If there is something "artificial" about the dialectics of the control system, it is that the party seeks to turn the currents of discontent to its own advantage and to prevent them from corrupting the fundamentals of the system.

The oscillations in the exercise of literary controls have followed a regular pattern even though they occurred within a larger political framework conditioned by international developments and changes in the internal Soviet scene. It may be that changes in Soviet life which have taken place since Stalin's death will ultimately bring about basic alterations in the structure of Soviet society and, at the same time, radical modifications in the pattern of literary politics. It is not possible to foresee whether this will occur or what new pattern might emerge. But one thing is clear: a "return" to true Leninist principles, acclaimed by the Khrushchev regime as the panacea for evils deriving from Stalin's personality cult, in itself offers hope, at best, of an amelioration of conditions, not an eradication of the fundamental problems. The ultimate source of the problems is the principle of partiinost, which is the core of Leninism and the defining feature of the Soviet system. It is hardly to be expected that the party will renounce its claim to final authority in belles-lettres any more than in other spheres of Soviet life. There is scarcely more reason to believe that the basic pattern of literary politics which characterized the past will alter significantly in the near future.

Since 1953, however, the party has been less successful than before in predetermining the impact of its literary policies and in suppressing manifestations of discontent among writers. Despite periodic setbacks, an advance has been made toward a more liberal interpretation of literary dogmas and a more moderate application of controls. Undoubtedly this was made possible by the general relaxation of tensions after Stalin's death. But writers themselves have pressed more firmly and successfully for recognition of their needs and demands, and ultraorthodoxy in belles-lettres appears to be more on the defensive than it was during the years immediately following the war. This suggests that gradual changes may be taking place in the delicate equilibrium which has been maintained between the pressure of the regime's demands and the resistance of those subjected to control, though it is not at all certain that this is so. Should such a tendency arise, should solutions more favorable to writers' interests be granted over a period of time, extensive modifications might ultimately occur in the control system, and even more widely in Soviet society; for this could conceivably contribute to pluralistic urges in the realm of ideology and to changes in the existing configuration of social forces. A policy of moderation in belles-lettres is conducive to this, since it may permit the emergence of trends which are inherently, if unobtrusively, incompatible with official literary theory and orthodox practice in writing. Postwar experience indicates that the views of many Soviet writers on questions of art are much more generous than those stated or implied by the official theory of art. Writers' own views may not issue forth in fully developed theories or take the form of open or even conscious rejection of official doctrine; but such rejection and the rudiments of a contrary theory of art are often implicit in writers' declarations of dissatisfaction and in their discussion of the functions of literature. The developments of recent years also reveal irrepressible urges within the literary community to carry debate beyond officially prescribed limits and to widen gaps in the ideological front. Policies of moderation multiply the opportunities for this and give rise to the possibility that changes in attitude and practice might undermine the party's theories and its justification of controls, even if this were to be an unintended and very protracted development. The familiar clichés could persist, even while losing their meaning; then the specific manner of their interpretation and application would become much more significant than the frequency or insistence of their affirmation. In the years since Stalin's death, it has become ever more important to attend to the details of literary politics as well as to the specific content of published literary works. Perhaps in the future, even more than in the past, it will be characteristic of Soviet literary politics that *la verité reste dans les nuances.*

More significant in broad social terms is the possibility that the public functions of literature will undergo some modification — that literature's "subversive" potentialities will manifest themselves with greater forcefulness. Even the literary produce of the Zhdanov era was not wholly devoid of such potentialities. The party has not as yet made literature into a thoroughly reliable instrument of social integration. In order to determine the degree of the party's success, it would be necessary not only to analyze a vast quantity of Soviet literature, but to devise means for measuring readers' responses to books they read. Yet postwar literary politics itself indicates that the party did not fully realize its purpose of eliminating from belles-lettres everything which it regarded as harmful to the party cause. The recurring criticism of works for apolitical, individualistic, and subjectivistic tendencies, the chronic complaint that negative characters were made to seem more appealing than positive heroes and that excessive attention was devoted to the darker sides of Soviet life were sufficient evidence of this. Less doctrinaire interpretations of literary policies may provide belles-lettres with greater scope for "subversion" in the broad sense, even if direct social criticism in literary works is held within the limits of suitable self-criticism. Although dull, orthodox works continued to flood the Soviet book market after 1956, some honest and bold works appeared. Soviet readers of current fiction were no longer so deprived of imaginative experiences as they had been, and this made it possible to hope that a literary renascence might occur at some point in the future.

Though there were grounds for a cautious optimism even after the literary campaign of 1957–1959, the events of those years lend themselves equally well to less encouraging interpretations. The adoption by the Khrushchev regime of relatively temperate literary policies was perhaps only evidence of the growing strength of the party and the increasing totalitarianization of Soviet society. The achievements of the Soviet Union in the international arena, the rising level of well-being at home, and the tangible indications of a more prosperous and secure future for the Soviet people undoubtedly served to reduce discontent and to strengthen loyalty to the regime. Moreover, the Soviet rulers had perhaps become convinced that their aims in education and indoctrination had in the main been realized, that the masses of the people accepted, actively or passively, the values of the regime, that a broad conformity of thinking and outlook had been created, and, most important, that the imaginative and critical capacities of most Soviet citizens had been stunted or had atrophied. The regime could then afford the luxury of a moderate cultural relaxation; it could permit its subjects access to previously forbidden ideas and imaginative experiences, since the likelihood of undesirable and unpredictable reactions by a significant number of people would be slight. If such reasoning lay behind the behavior of the Khrushchev regime, and if it were well founded, the future of Soviet letters might be bleak indeed.

Though the positions of political power in the USSR will eventually be filled by a new generation, by a group of men who may be less fanatic and paranoic than their Stalinist forerunners, it does not follow that the Soviet writer will necessarily benefit from this in terms of increased scope for creative activity. It is likely that the new generation of rulers will be conformist and loyal to traditional values precisely because its members will be products of the Soviet educational system and because their aspirations for power, prestige, and material comfort will have been largely satisfied, leaving them with little desire for dramatic changes in the status quo. It is significant, too, that members of this group in particular, members of the upper strata of Soviet society, have been represented in the Soviet fiction of recent years as philistine and bourgeois — materialistic, self-seeking, vulgar, lacking in humanism, insensitive to aesthetic values. They live "narrow, complacent, and uninspired lives," wrote Zorin in *The Guests* of the social stratum which Paustovsky described as "a new petty-bourgeois caste"; it was of such people that a character in Pogodin's play *Petrarch's Sonnet* said, "They even want to see Communism as a bourgeois paradise — peace and quiet, plenty to eat, and no thoughts." It seems unlikely that the new Soviet rulers will, any more than their predecessors, be concerned about, or even understand, the aspirations of the Soviet writers who place a high value on truthfulness, sincerity, dedication to art, and freedom to create. Yet, given the realities of the Soviet political system and the probable inertia or indifference of the masses, there is no one other than those who hold the reins of power to whom the Soviet writer can direct his appeal for a measure of tolerance and understanding.

Chronic anxiety about the precariousness of their position and about the uncertain future is undoubtedly among the factors which have led writers again and again to plead for a grant of trust from higher authorities. One source of this anxiety, and the deeply felt need which lay behind writers' impassioned appeals in 1956 and 1957, was described forthrightly by a drama critic, Inna Solovyova, who wrote in 1956:

The personality cult . . . weakened a person's sense of responsibility for his own judgments. A habit developed of sincerely distrusting one's own point of view if it did not coincide with some opinion coming from above.

It is difficult to work if you are not trusted. But it is impossible to create if you have stopped trusting yourself. Without integrity and inner persuasion, creative freedom is unthinkable.[1]

But trust and confidence were not granted in the years after 1956, and the old yearnings continued to find occasional expression. In 1959, an unknown young poet, Leonid Tyomin, made his debut in the Soviet press with poems which gave voice to these longings. Tyomin's most striking poem began with the line, "Believe, please, believe in me!" and went on to caution that this was not a request "to forgive and understand" or "to remit punishments," but simply a request for a calm and firm trust. The poem closed hopefully with a reiteration of the appeal:

> I am all beginnings,
> Still at the starting point:
> All my words
> Are not yet the Word,
> All my truths
> Are only approaches to Truth
> (Even today
> I feel cramped in them) ——
>
> Believe in me ——
> I will only be beginning tomorrow!
> Thus out of melody
> A song is born.[2]

Tyomin's poem seemed to echo a poem written exactly two decades earlier by Olga Berggolts, who was then in her twenty-ninth year. Addressing the Motherland, Berggolts declared her willingness to suffer all tests, all deprivations, but one: "Do not withdraw trust and compassion," she implored, suggesting anxiously that this might result in apathy and spiritual death.[3] Trust from above, as Solovyova's remark suggested, has manifold consequences — it evokes reciprocal trust from below, creates an inner sense of confidence, and permits fruitful creative efforts. Perhaps over the years Berggolts maintained her own faith and sense of belonging; but it was symbolic of the denial of trust which her generation experienced that her poem, written in 1939 at the close of the Great Purge, was published for the first time only in 1956. Whether the generation to which Tyomin belongs will have a different experience is a question which only the future can answer.

Although "revisionism" in literature was vanquished shortly after it broke out, the Khrushchev regime was evidently unable to check completely the underlying forces which contributed to the emergence of the heresy. In the literary produce of the Khrushchev era the tendencies continued to appear, though in modified and less virulent forms. An outstanding feature of a portion of the literary output during this period was not only its low level of political fervor, but the sense of openness revealed in it, the awareness that the party ideology had not yet provided answers to all the questions that disturb people. This suggested that Soviet literature might yet have a role to play in eating away at ideological orthodoxy, breaking through old shibboleths, and fostering discontent with familiar formulas. The burden of the struggle which Soviet writers have carried on for many years has begun to pass to the rising generation of authors, some of whom appear willing, even eager, to accept the legacy. Whether they will find or create a responsive and sympathetic audience remains to be seen. There are grounds for hoping that Soviet literature will place itself in the service of those who are seeking, however few in number they may be. Though literary works cannot themselves furnish answers, they may at least stimulate questioning and help to keep the spirit of inquiry alive.

Developments in the years after Stalin's death revealed with increasing clarity the paradoxical character of the Soviet regime's program in belles-lettres. Fully aware of the potentialities of literature as an instrument of social control, the party has expended much energy to create a literature useful to the party and to provide a place for it at the center of Soviet life; equally aware of the threats inherent in imaginative writing, the party has attempted to eradicate its capacity for producing effects that contravene its goals. Fulfillment of both tasks is essential if literature is to play the role in

Soviet life that the party envisages for it. In this connection it is
appropriate to recall lines written by Boris Pasternak more than
thirty years ago:

> The great Soviet gives to the highest passions
> In these brave days each one its rightful place,
> Yet vainly leaves one vacant for the poet.
> When that's not empty, look for danger's face.[4]

The Soviet regime has not banished the poet from the state. On
the contrary, it has striven not only to fill his place but to make it
one of great social importance. At the same time it has sought to
fetter the poet's muse. Failure to succeed in this negative part of
the dual task would become the final irony of the party's whole
effort in belles-lettres.

NOTES
INDEX

Notes

Chapter I. The Theoretical Foundations of Literary Controls

1. Karl Marx and Frederick Engels, *The German Ideology, Parts I & III*, ed. R. Pascal (New York: International Publishers, 1947), p. 69.
2. *The Communist Manifesto.*
3. *Ludwig Feuerbach and the Outcome of Classical German Philosophy* (New York: International Publishers, 1935), pp. 32–33.
4. Marx and Engels, *Literature and Art: Selections from Their Writings* (New York: International Publishers, 1947), pp. 17, 61.
5. *Ibid.*, p. 76.
6. Quoted in Benedetto Croce, *Aesthetic*, trans. Douglas Ainslie (New York, Noonday Press, 1956), p. 302.
7. The contrast is emphasized in Burton Rubin, "Plekhanov and Soviet Literary Criticism," *American Slavic and East European Review*, XV (December 1956), 527–542, to which the following discussion is partly indebted.
8. Quoted in Rubin, p. 533.
9. G. V. Plekhanov, *Sochineniya*, ed. D. Ryazanov (Moscow, 1923–1927), X, 192, as trans. by Rubin, pp. 533–534.
10. See *Soch.*, X, 193–197.
11. *Soch.*, XIV, 137.
12. G. V. Plekhanov, *iskusstvo i literatura*, ed. N. F. Belchikov (Moscow, 1948), pp. 207–208.
13. Leon Trotsky, *Literature and Revolution*, trans. Rose Strunsky (New York: International Publishers, 1925), p. 178.
14. *Soch.*, XIV, 119.
15. "Iskusstvo i obshchestvennaya zhizn," *Soch.*, XIV, 120–182.
16. *Ibid.*, p. 131.
17. *Ibid.*, p. 137.
18. *Ibid.*, p. 138.
19. *Ibid.*, p. 150.
20. *Literaturnoye naslediye G. V. Plekhanova*, ed. P. F. Yudin and others (Moscow, 1934–1939), III, 201.
21. *Lenin o kulture i iskusstve*, ed. M. Lifshits (Moscow, 1938), p. 112.
22. *Ibid.*, p. 113.
23. *Ibid.*
24. *Ibid.*, pp. 114–115.
25. *Ibid.*, p. 298.
26. *Pravda*, Dec. 1, 1920; reprinted in *O partiinoi i sovetskoi pechati, Sbornik dokumentov* (Moscow, 1954), p. 220.

27. Quoted in P. S. Kogan, *Proletarskaya literatura* (Ivanovo-Voznesensk, 1926), p. 109.

28. According to Klara Zetkin, Lenin declared that he did not like and could not understand the art of "expressionism, futurism, cubism, and other such 'isms.'" *Lenin o kulture i iskusstve*, p. 299.

29. *Ibid.*

30. B. Yakovlev, "Veliky printsip," *Novy mir*, no. 2, 1947, p. 26.

31. "Diskussiya o predmete marksistsko-leninskoi estetiki," *Voprosy filosofii*, no. 3, 1956, p. 186.

32. Even Soviet writers whose works are held up as outstanding examples of socialist realism have not found it easy to explain what the doctrine means. When Mikhail Sholokhov was asked, during his trip abroad in 1958, to define socialist realism, he at first replied by citing a remark that his friend and colleague, the late Alexander Fadeyev, made shortly before his suicide in 1956: "If any one should ask me what Socialist realism is, I should have to answer that the devil alone knows." Sholokhov went on to say that his own answer would be that "Socialist realism is that which is written for the Soviet Government in simple, comprehensive [*sic*], artistic language." *New York Times*, May 11, 1958.

33. L. Plotkin, "Vazhneishy vklad V. I. Lenina v nauky o literature," *Oktyabr*, no. 11, 1955, p. 162.

34. *Vtoroi vsesoyuzny syezd sovetskikh pisatelei, Stenografichesky otchyot* (Moscow, 1956), p. 506.

35. A. Tarasenkov, "Zametki kritika," *Znamya*, no. 10, 1949, p. 176.

36. "Vyshe znamya ideinosti v literature," *Znamya*, no. 10, 1946, p. 30.

37. *Pervy vsesoyuzny syezd sovetskikh pisatelei. Stenografichesky otchyot* (Moscow, 1934), p. 312.

38. Quoted in William Edgerton, "The Serapion Brothers: An Early Controversy," *American Slavic and East European Review*, VIII (February 1949), 57.

39. "Za dalneishy podyom sovetskoi literatury," *Kommunist*, no. 9, 1954, p. 24.

40. *Literaturnaya gazeta* (hereafter cited as *Lit. gaz.*), May 5, 1955, p. 3.

41. *The Frogs*, line 1055.

42. P. Trofimov, "Yedinstvo eticheskikh i esteticheskikh printsipov v iskusstve," *Bolshevik*, no. 18, 1950, p. 36.

43. G. Lenobl, "Sovetsky chitatel i khudozhestvennaya literatura," *Novy mir*, no. 6, 1950, p. 215.

44. "Zametki pisatelya," *Novy mir*, no. 1, 1947, p. 172.

45. M. Rozental, "Voprosy sovetskoi esteticheskoi nauki," *Bolshevik*, no. 13, 1948, p. 56.

46. "O diskussionnom i nediskussionnom," *Znamya*, no. 7, 1954, p. 169.

47. "O lirike," *Lit. gaz.*, May 24, 1947.

48. Simonov, "O diskussionnom i nediskussionnom," p. 169.

49. An incident involving the poetry of V. Shefner is one of several which might be cited as evidence that this statement is by no means an exaggeration. In 1947, at a party meeting of Leningrad writers called to discuss his work, Shefner vowed to overcome the weakness of his poetry, which was said to be "gloomy" and to reveal the poet's inability "to feel

the times" ("O tvorchestve V. Shefnera," *Lit. gaz.*, August 9, 1947). Four years later it was said that, although in Shefner's recent poems there was an evident "effort to march in step with the times," the poet now treated approved themes "in such an abstract manner, with such didactic aridity, that a valid idea is willy-nilly discredited, and the verses can be taken only as declarations, formal pronouncements, and nothing more." L. Mikhailova, "Gruz starykh oshibok," *Lit. gaz.*, July 31, 1951.

50. Mikhailova, *ibid.*

51. A. Fadeyev, "Zadachi literaturnoi kritiki," *Oktyabr*, no. 7, 1947, p. 150.

52. "Nasushchnye zadachi sovetskoi literatury," *Kommunist*, no. 21, 1952, pp. 15–16.

53. "V dolgu pered narodom," *Lit. gaz.*, April 8, 1952.

54. *The Rambler*, no. 4, in *The Works of Samuel Johnson*, ed. Arthur Murphey (London, 1820), IV, 26.

55. Ilya Ehrenburg, "O rabote pisatelya," *Znamya*, no. 10, 1953, as trans. in *The Current Digest of the Soviet Press* (hereafter cited as *CDSP*), V, no. 52 (February 10, 1954), 12.

56. *Lit. gaz.*, January 15, 1957, p. 3.

57. Letter to George and Thomas Keats, December 21, 1817, in *Letters of John Keats*, ed. M. B. Forman (Oxford University Press, 1935), p. 72.

58. Ehrenburg, "O rabote pisatelya."

59. *The Politics of the Unpolitical* (London: Rutledge, 1943), p. 105.

60. Jean-Paul Sartre, *What Is Literature?* trans. B. Frechtman (New York: Philosophical Library, 1949), p. 81.

61. *Art as Experience* (New York: Minton, Balch, 1934), p. 346.

Chapter II. The Heyday of Zhdanovism, 1946–1952

1. O. Utis, "Generalissimo Stalin and the Art of Government," *Foreign Affairs*, XXX (January 1952), 197–214.

2. *Ibid.*, p. 204.

3. *Ibid.*

4. *Pravda*, July 3, 1941.

5. See Alexander Anikst, "Nasha literatura," *Znamya*, no. 4, 1945, p. 123.

6. N. Tikhonov, "Sovetskaya literatura v dni Otechestvennoi voiny," *Literatura i iskusstvo*, February 12, 1944.

7. "Pered voskhodom solntsa," *Oktyabr*, no. 6–7, 1943, pp. 58–92, and no. 8–9, 1943, pp. 103–133.

8. *Bolshevik*, no. 2, 1944, pp. 56–58.

9. "Dnevnik plenuma," *Literatura i iskusstvo*, February 12, 1944.

10. Yu. Lukin, "Lozhnaya moral i iskazhonnaya perspektiva," *Pravda*, July 24, 1944.

11. L. Dmitriyev, "Vopreki istorii," *Literatura i iskusstvo*, August 5, 1944.

12. "Yeshchyo o knige Fedina," *Literatura i iskusstvo*, September 9, 1944.

13. M. Rozental, "Ob ideinosti i tendentsioznosti iskusstva," *Oktyabr*, no. 1–2, 1945, p. 152.

14. "Mirovoye znacheniye russkoi kultury," *Literaturnaya gazeta*, April 20, 1946.

15. "O cherepkakh i cherepushkakh," *Oktaybr*, no. 5, 1946, pp. 151–162.

16. *Ibid.*, pp. 152–153.

17. O. Kyrganov and A. Koloskov, "Ob 'ispovedyakh' i 'propovedyakh' v zhurnale 'Oktyabr,' " *Pravda*, June 24, 1946.

18. Ye. Ryss, "Nevidyashchiye glaza," *Lit. gaz.*, April 27, 1946.

19. "Vecher," *Novy mir*, no. 1–2, 1946, p. 49.

20. "Ideino-vospitatelnaya rabota sredi pisatelei," *Lit. gaz.*, July 27, 1946.

21. "Razborchivaya krysa," *Oktyabr*, no. 5–6, 1945, pp. 78–79; "Svinya," *Oktyabr*, no. 8, 1945, p. 45.

22. "Vozvrashcheniye mira," *Znamya*, no. 9, 1945, p. 84.

23. See the speeches of A. Tvardovsky and V. Inber, *Lit. gaz.*, May 22, 1945, p. 1.

24. *Lit. gaz.*, April 27, 1956, p. 4.

25. A condensed version of the speeches appeared in *Lit. gaz.*, September 21, 1946; in Andrei A. Zhdanov, *Essays on Literature, Philosophy and Music* (New York: International Publishers, 1950), pp. 15–44.

26. "O zhurnalakh 'Zvezda' i 'Leningrad,' " *Kultura i zhizn*, August 14, 1946, as trans. in George S. Counts and Nucia Lodge, *The Country of the Blind* (Cambridge: Houghton, Mifflin, 1949), pp. 81–82.

27. Zhdanov, *Essays*, p. 33.

28. *Ibid.*, p. 35.

29. *Ibid.*, p. 27.

30. "Vyshe znamya ideinosti v literature," *Znamya*, no. 10, 1946, p. 37.

31. *Essays*, p. 44.

32. *Lit. gaz.*, September 21, 1946, p. 3.

33. A. M. Egolin [Yegolin], "The Ideological Content of Soviet Literature," trans. M. Kriger (Washington: Public Affairs Press, 1948), p. 21.

34. *Essays*, pp. 42–43.

35. *Ibid.*, pp. 27, 42.

36. *Ibid.*, p. 41.

37. Counts and Lodge, p. 82.

38. *Lit. gaz.*, September 7, 1946; trans. in Counts and Lodge, pp. 109–117.

39. *Lit. gaz.*, September 7, 1946.

40. "Za vysokuyu ideinost sovetskoi literatury," *Lit. gaz.*, June 21, 1947.

41. *Lit. gaz.*, June 29, 1947, p. 1.

42. "Protiv burzhuaznovo liberalizma v literaturovedenii," *Kultura i zhizn*, March 11, 1948.

43. For a detailed account of the Veselovsky controversy, see Robert M. Hankin, "Postwar Soviet Ideology and Literary Scholarship," *Through the Glass of Soviet Liteurature: Views of Russian Society*, ed. Ernest J. Simmons (Columbia University Press, 1953), pp. 265–279.

44. "Molodaya gvardiya," *Znamya*, nos. 2–6 and nos. 9–12, 1945.

45. "Dym otechestva," *Novy mir*, no. 11, 1947, pp. 1–123.

46. See S. V. Berezner, "Bolshevistskiye vskhody," *Literatura v shkole*, no. 2, 1946, pp. 43–50, and Z. Paperny, "Nevezhestvo i politicheskaya bezotvetstvennost," *Lit. gaz.*, May 24, 1947.

47. V. Yermilov, "Sovetskaya literatura — samaya demokraticheskaya literatura mira," *Lit. gaz.*, December 7, 1946 (italics added).

48. " 'Molodaya gvardiya' na stsene nashikh teatrov," *Kultura i zhizn*, November 30, 1947; " 'Molodaya gvardiya' v romane i na stsene," *Pravda*, December 3, 1947; "Roman 'Molodaya gvardiya' i yevo instsenirovki," *Lit. gaz.*, December 7, 1947.

49. "Nachalo diskussii," *Sovetskaya muzyka*, no. 10, 1949, p. 22.

50. "O 'byvalykh lyudyakh' i ikh kritikakh," *Zvezda*, no. 6, 1948, p. 106.

51. "Zametki o proze 1947 goda," *Novy mir*, no. 2, 1948, p. 109.

52. "V izuchenii zhizni — zalog uspekha," *Teatr*, no. 9, 1946, pp. 33–34.

53. See "Alexander Fadeyev," *Novy mir*, no. 2, 1947, pp. 189–190.

54. *Ibid.*, p. 190.

55. N. Maslin, "Zhizn vopreki . . ." *Kultura i zhizn*, November 30, 1947.

56. *Lit. gaz.*, February 8, 1950, p. 3.

57. "Kritikovat smelo i otkryto," *Lit. gaz.*, December 7, 1947.

58. See *Pravda*, December 23, 1951, p. 3, and K. Fedin, "Dukh molodosti," *Lit. gaz.*, December 25, 1951

59. See Konstantin Simonov, "Literaturnye zametki," *Novy mir*, no. 12, 1956, pp. 243–248.

60. Margarita Aliger, "Novye stikhi," *Znamya*, no. 8–9, 1946, pp. 83–87; Kornely Zelinsky, "O lirike," *ibid.*, pp. 179–199.

61. " 'Novye stikhi' Margarity Aliger," *Lit. gaz.*, October 26, 1946.

62. "Zametki pisatelya," *Novy mir*, no. 1, 1947, p. 167.

63. "O partiinosti v literature i ob otvetstvennosti kritiki," *Lit. gaz.*, April 19, 1947.

64. Semyon Tregub, "Pisatelyu Konstantinu Simonovu," *Novy mir*, no. 6, 1947, pp. 252–260.

65. "Nad polem medlenno i sonno," *Znamya*, no. 8–9, 1946, p. 84.

66. *Lit. gaz.*, October 26, 1946.

67. *Znamya*, no. 8–9, 1946, p. 84.

68. *Novy mir*, no. 1, 1947, p. 166.

69. *Lirika* (Moscow, 1955), p. 265.

70. *Znamya*, no. 8–9, 1946, p. 85.

71. *Lit. gaz.*, October 26, 1946.

72. *Novy mir*, no. 1, 1947, p. 167.

73. *Lirika*, p. 259.

74. *Novy mir*, no. 1, 1947, p. 167.

75. *Znamya*, no. 8–9, 1946, p. 194.

76. *Ibid.*, p. 195.

77. "O putanoi statye K. Zelinskovo v zhurnale 'Znamya,' " *Kultura i zhizn*, September 30, 1946.

78. "O literaturno-khudozhestvennykh zhurnalakh," *Pravda*, February 2, 1947.

79. "Russkaya sovetskaya literatura 1946 goda," *Lit. gaz.*, February 24, 1947.

80. See p. 18.

81. See "Zhit po-novomu," *Teatr*, no. 4, 1948, pp. 7–8.

82. "Za vysokoye kachestvo repertuara dramaticheskikh teatrov," *Kultura i zhizn*, March 11, 1948.

83. *Oktyabr*, no. 2, 1949, p. 148 and p. 153.

84. "Vyshe ideiny i khudozhestvenny uroven repertuara," *Teatr*, no. 6, 1948, p. 5.

85. *Ibid.*, p. 6.

86. *Lit. gaz.*, January 15, 1949, p. 2.

87. *Oktyabr*, no. 2, 1949, p. 152.

88. "Nekotorye voprosy raboty Soyuza pisatelei," *Lit. gaz.*, March 28, 1953.

89. "Ob odnoi antipatrioticheskoi gruppe teatralnykh kritikov," *Pravda*, January 28, 1949.

90. "Za patrioticheskuyu sovetskuyu dramaturgiyu," *Lit. gaz.*, February 26, 1949.

91. See *Lit. gaz.*, December 5, 1948, p. 2.

92. "Do kontsa razoblachit kritikov-kosmopolitov," *Lit. gaz.*, February 9, 1949.

93. *Pravda*, February 26, 1949, p. 3.

94. *Oktyabr*, no. 2, 1949, p. 154.

95. *Pravda*, January 28, 1949, p. 3.

96. *Oktyabr*, no. 2, 1949, p. 166.

97. *Pravda*, January 28, 1949, p. 3.

98. Quoted in Fadeyev, *Oktyabr*, no. 2, 1949, p. 149.

99. *Ibid.*, p. 144.

100. "My khotim videt yevo litso," *Lit. gaz.*, December 27, 1947.

101. "Za ideinuyu boyevuyu dramaturgiyu," *Lit. gaz.*, December 25, 1948.

102. *Oktyabr*, no. 2, 1949, p. 164.

103. *Ibid.*, pp. 164–165.

104. *Ibid.*, p. 154.

105. "Zadachi sovetskoi dramaturgii i teatralnoi kritiki," *Pravda*, February 28, 1949.

106. Daniil Granin, "Iskateli," *Zvezda*, no. 7, 1954, p. 46.

107. *Lit. gaz.*, January 15, 1949, p. 2.

108. "Sovetskaya poeziya v 1948 godu," *Lit. gaz.*, March 19, 1949.

109. See Y. Gilboa, "Jewish Literature in the Soviet Union," *Soviet Survey*, no. 18 (August 1957), pp. 5–13.

110. *Lit. gaz.*, January 12, 1949, p. 3.

111. *Lit. gaz.*, March 29, 1949, p. 3.

112. "Za sovetsky patriotizm v literature i kritike," *Znamya*, no. 2, 1949, p. 169.

113. *Lit. gaz.*, March 12, 1949, p. 3.

114. A. Sofronov, "Karyera Beketova," *Novy mir*, no. 4, 1949, pp. 44–89; V. Kozhevnikov, "Ognennaya reka," *Novy mir*, no. 3, 1949, pp. 15–60.

115. On Sofronov, see M. Tyurin, "Shag nazad," *Kultura i zhizn,* May 31, 1949, and D. Zaslavsky, "Plody nebrezhnosti i speshki," *Pravda,* July 14, 1949; on Kozhevnikov, see "Za vysokoye khudozhestvennoye masterstvo i printsipalnuyu kritiku v literature," *Kultura i zhizn,* July 21, 1949, and N. Losinov, "O posredstvennoi pyese i priyatelskikh retsenziyakh," *Pravda,* July 26, 1949.

116. "Za vysokuyu ideinost i khudozhestvennost literatury," *Izvestiya,* August 7, 1949.

117. "O literature i literaturnoi kritike," *Pravda,* August 7, 1949.

118. *Lit. gaz.,* August 6, 1949, p. 1.

119. "O zadachakh literaturnoi kritiki," *Lit. gaz.,* February 4, 1950.

120. "Za masterstvo dramaturga," *Lit. gaz.,* August 26, 1950.

121. "Zaklyuchitelnoye slovo A. Fadeyeva," *Lit. gaz.,* February 11, 1950.

122. "O nekotorykh oshibkakh v literaturovedenii," *Oktyabr,* no. 2, 1950, pp. 150–165.

123. *Ibid.,* pp. 160, 162.

124. *Ibid.,* p. 163.

125. "Protiv oposhleniya literaturnoi kritiki," *Pravda,* March 30, 1950.

126. "Protiv vulgarizatsii v literaturnoi kritike," *Lit. gaz.,* March 29, 1950.

127. Gleb Struve, *Soviet Russian Literature, 1917–1950* (University of Oklahoma Press, 1951), p. 370.

128. See G. Lukanov and A. Belik, "O tvorcheskom metode sotsialisticheskoi literatury," *Oktyabr,* no. 7, 1948, pp. 177–191, and A. Belik and N. Parsadanov, "Ob oshibkakh i izvrashcheniyakh v estetike i literaturovedenii," *Oktyabr,* no. 4, 1949, pp. 166–173.

129. Ye. Kovalchik, "Zhivaya literatura i myortvaya skhema," *Novy mir,* no. 5, 1950, p. 203.

130. *The Soviet Linguistics Controversy,* trans. John V. Murra and others (New York: King's Crown Press, 1951), p. 76.

131. A. Surkov, "Nekotorye voprosy razvitiya sovetskoi literatury," *Bolshevik,* no. 9, 1952, p. 33.

132. "Chelovek na stsene," *Novy mir,* no. 10, 1952, pp. 221–222.

133. N. Pogodin, "Perechityvaya Gorkovo," *Lit. gaz.,* June 16, 1951.

134. *Pravda,* April 19, 1951, pp. 2–3; trans. in *CDSP,* III, no. 12 (May 5, 1951), 13–16.

135. See "Dramaturg i teatr," *Lit. gaz.,* May 15, 1951.

136. "K itogam poeticheskovo goda," *Lit. gaz.,* January 10, 1953.

137. *Voprosy filosofii,* no. 2, 1950, pp. 361–362.

138. *Soviet Linguistics Controversy,* p. 70.

139. See "Teoreticheskaya konferentsiya v sektore estetiki," *Voprosy filosofii,* no. 1, 1951, pp. 236–241; P. S. Trofimov, "Ob otnoshenii iskusstva k bazisu i nadstroike," *Voprosy filosofii,* no. 2, 1951, pp. 167–178; I. A. Maseyev, "O sotsialnoi prirode iskusstva i khudozhestvennykh vzglyadov obshchestva," *Voprosy filosofii,* no. 2, 1952, pp. 217–230.

140. *Izvestiya Akademii nauk, Otdeleniye literatury i yazyka,* X, no. 3 (1951), 311.

141. "Nekotorye voprosy sovetskovo literaturovedeniya," *Lit. gaz.,* May 19, 1951.

142. *Soviet Linguistics Controversy*, p. 86.
143. "Nekotorye voprosy teorii sotsialisticheskovo realizma," *Lit. gaz.*, June 9, 1951.
144. "O meste i roli iskusstva v obshchestvennoi zhizni," *Voprosy filosofii*, no. 6, 1952, pp. 155–170.
145. "K voprosu o traditsii i ideinykh vliyaniyakh," *Izv. Akad. nauk, Otdel. lit. i yazika*, X, no. 5 (1951), 437–438.
146. B. Ryurikov, "Starye oshibki v novom oblichii," *Lit. gaz.*, December 20, 1951, and "Tuman, kotory nado rasseyat," *Lit. gaz.*, May 24, 1951.
147. "Protiv ideologicheskikh izvrashchenii v literature," *Pravda*, July 2, 1951.
148. "Sovetskaya literatura na podyome," *Bolshevik*, no. 14, 1951, p. 6.
149. "Sila polozhitelnovo primera," *Novy mir*, no. 9, 1951, pp. 151–216.
150. See *Lit. gaz.*, November 27, 1951, p. 3, and *Lit. gaz.*, March 28, 1953, p. 2.
151. "Protiv antipartrioticheskikh vzglyadov v literaturnoi kritike," *Pravda*, October 28, 1951.
152. "Pereodolet otstavaniye dramaturgii," *Lit. gaz.*, March 26, 1952.
153. Italics added.
154. See A. Surov, "Zametki dramaturgii," *Sovetskoye iskusstvo*, March 12, 1952, trans. and condensed in *CDSP*, IV, no. 8 (April 5, 1952), 9–10.
155. "Let Us Speak Frankly," *CDSP*, IV, no. 11 (April 26, 1952), 6–7; trans. in full from *Sovetskoye iskusstvo*, March 29, 1952, p. 2.
156. *Ibid.* (*CDSP*), p. 6.
157. "Poeziya prosit slova!" *Sov. iskusstvo*, April 5, 1952, as trans. in *CDSP*, IV, no. 13 (May 10, 1952), 16.
158. "Preodolet otstavaniye dramaturgii," *Pravda*, April 7, 1952; trans. in *CDSP*, IV, no. 11 (April 26, 1952), 3–5.
159. "V dolgu pered narodom," *Lit. gaz.*, April 8, 1952, as trans. in *CDSP*, IV, no. 13 (May 10, 1952), 16.
160. As trans. in *CDSP*, IV, no. 11 (April 26, 1952), 4.
161. "Nasushchnye zadachi sovetskoi literatury," *Kommunist*, no. 21, 1951, p. 19.
162. "Za pravdu zhizni!" as trans. in *CDSP*, IV, no. 21 (June 5, 1952), 3.
163. *Current Soviet Policies*, ed. Leo Gruliow (New York: Praeger, 1953), p. 115.
164. *Ibid.*, p. 155.

Chapter III. The Quest for a Middle Way, 1953–1955

1. A. Tvardovsky, "Za dalyu — dal," *Novy mir*, no. 6, 1953, p. 76.
2. "Problemy razvitiya sovetskoi dramaturgii," *Literaturnaya gazeta*, October 22, 1953.
3. "O rabote pisatelya," *Znamya*, no. 10, 1953, pp. 160–183.
4. *Ibid.*, as trans. in *CDSP*, V, no. 52 (Fabruary 10, 1954), 6.
5. *Ibid.*, p. 8.
6. V. Pomerantsev, "Ob iskrennosti v literature," *Novy mir*, no. 12, 1953, pp. 218–245.
7. *Ibid.*, p. 231

8. *Ibid.*, p. 219.
9. *Ibid.*, p. 235.
10. *Ibid.*, p. 231.
11. "Ottepel," *Znamya*, no. 5, 1954, pp. 14–87.
12. "O tvorcheskoi smelosti i vdokhnovenii," *Sovetskaya muzyka*, no. 11, 1953, as trans. in *CDSP*, V, no. 46 (December 30, 1953), 4.
13. "S nevernykh pozitsii," *Lit. gaz.*, January 30, 1954.
14. *Komsomolskaya pravda*, March 17, 1954, p. 3, as trans. in *CDSP*, VI, no. 7 (March 31, 1954), 3.
15. B. Ryurikov, "O bogatstve iskusstva," *Lit. gaz.*, March 20, 1954.
16. "Molodomu chitatelyu — bolshuyu talantlivuyu literaturu," *Lit. gaz.*, March 27, 1954.
17. "Pod znamenem sotsialisticheskovo realizma," *Pravda*, May 25, 1954; trans. in *CDSP*, VI, no. 19 (June 23, 1954), 3–5.
18. *Lit. gaz.*, June 5, 1954, p. 1.
19. *Lit. gaz.*, June 19, 1954, p. 2.
20. *Lit. gaz.*, June 17, 1954, p. 3.
21. *Pravda*, June 3, 1954, pp. 4–5.
22. See n. 24 below.
23. *Komsomolskaya pravda*, June 6, 1954, p. 2; trans. in *CDSP*, VI, no. 20 (June 30, 1954), 5–6.
24. "Uluchshit ideino-vospitatelnuyu raboty sredi pisatelei," *Lit. gaz.*, June 15, 1954.
25. "Novaya povest Ili Ehrenburga," *Lit. gaz.*, July 17 and July 20, 1954.
26. "O statye K. Simonova," *Lit. gaz.*, August 3, 1954.
27. See n. 24 above.
28. "Slovo pisatelya," *Oktyabr*, no. 7, 1954, p. 142.
29. *Lit. gaz.*, June 3, 1954, p. 2.
30. "Za dalneishy podyom sovetskoi literatury," *Kommunist*, no. 9, 1954, pp. 12–27.
31. *Ibid.*, p. 26.
32. "Za vysokuyu ideinost nashei literatury," *Lit. gaz.*, August 17, 1954.
33. "Lyudi kolkhoznoi derevni v poslevoyennoi proze," *Novy mir*, no. 4, 1954, pp. 210–231.
34. *Ibid.*, p. 220.
35. *Ibid.*, p. 217.
36. *Lit. gaz.*, August 17, 1954.
37. *Novy mir*, no. 12, 1953, p. 234.
38. "Raionnye budni," *Novy mir*, no. 9, 1952, pp. 204–221.
39. *Ibid.*, p. 212.
40. *Ibid.*, p. 220.
41. *Ibid.*, p. 217.
42. Mikhail Lifshits, "Dnevnik Marietty Shaginyan," *Novy mir*, no. 2, 1954, p. 230.
43. *Lit. gaz.*, June 15, 1954.
44. " 'Russky les' Leonida Leonova," *Novy mir*, no. 5, 1954, pp. 220–241.
45. *Oktyabr*, no. 7, 1954, pp. 139–140.
46. "Gosti," *Teatr*, no. 2, 1954, p. 42.
47. *Ibid.*, p. 43.

48. *Ibid.*, p. 19.

49. "Vremena goda," *Novy mir*, no. 11, 1953, pp. 3–101, and no. 12, 1953, pp. 62–158.

50. *Pravda*, May 27, 1954, p. 2, as trans. in *CDSP*, VI, no. 20 (June 30, 1954), 3.

51. *The Thaw*, trans. Manya Harari (London: Harvill Press, 1955), p. 153.

52. *Ibid.*, pp. 44, 52.

53. *Ibid.*, p. 38.

54. *Komsomolskaya pravda*, June 6, 1954, p. 2, as trans. in *CDSP*, VI, no. 20, 6.

55. *Znamya*, no. 4, 1954, p. 95, as trans. in *CDSP*, VI, no. 21 (July 7, 1954), 22.

56. *Pravda*, June 2, 1954, pp. 4–5, as trans. in *CDSP*, *ibid.*, p. 22.

57. Ernest J. Simmons, "Soviet Literature, 1950–1955," *Russia Since Stalin: Old Trends and New Problems*, ed. Philip E. Mosley, *The Annals of the American Academy of Political and Social Science*, vol. 303 (January 1956), 102.

58. "Y literatorov Leningrada," *Lit. gaz.*, April 16, 1953.

59. "Razgovor o lirike," *Lit. gaz.*, April 16, 1953.

60. "Protiv likvidatsii liriki," *Lit. gaz.*, October 28, 1954.

61. "Nabolevshy vopros," *Lit. gaz.*, October 19, 1954.

62. *Lit. gaz.*, November 29, 1954, p. 1.

63. Selvinsky, "Nabolevshy vopros."

64. "Pered Syezdom," *Lit. gaz.*, August 21, 1954.

65. *Vtoroi vsesoyuzny syezd sovetskikh pisatelei. Stenografichesky otchyot* (Moscow, 1956), p. 249; hereafter cited as *Vtoroi syezd*.

66. *Ibid.*, p. 32.

67. *Ibid.*

68. *Ibid.*

69. *Ibid.*, p. 34.

70. *Ibid.*, p. 31.

71. *Ibid.*, p. 68.

72. *Ibid.*, p. 36.

73. *Ibid.*, p. 33.

74. G. Sholokhov-Sinyavsky, "Nereshonnye voprosy," *Lit. gaz.*, October 5, 1954.

75. *Vtoroi syezd*, pp. 486, 569.

76. *Ibid.*, p. 248.

77. *Ibid.*, p. 374.

78. As reported in *Lit. gaz.*, December 24, 1954. The wording in the stenographic report diverges from this, and the tone, though not the substance, of the remark is somewhat different (see *Vtoroi syezd*, p. 346). What purports to be the complete stenographic record of the congress in several instances omits passages which originally appeared in the condensed reports published in *Lit. gaz.*; therefore, it is not certain that the former is always the more faithful record of what was actually said. One of Ovechkin's remarks suggests that both accounts may deviate in some details from words uttered in polemical outbursts. See *Vtoroi syezd*, p. 485.

79. *Vtoroi syezd*, pp. 291–292.

80. *Ibid.*, p. 136.

81. *Ibid.*, pp. 361–362.

82. *Ibid.*, p. 508.

83. *Ibid.*, p. 507.

84. *Ibid.*, p. 591.

85. *Pervy vsesoyuzny syezd sovetskikh pisatelei. Stenografichesky otchyot* (Moscow, 1934), p. 716; hereafter cited as *Pervy syezd*.

86. *Vtoroi syezd*, p. 93.

87. *Ustav soyuza pisatelei SSSR* (n.d.), p. 4.

88. *Vtoroi syezd*, pp. 513–521.

89. *Ibid.*, p. 36.

90. *Ibid.*, pp. 95–96.

91. See Chapter 6, pp. 248–249.

92. See Edward J. Brown, *The Proletarian Episode in Russian Literature, 1928–1932* (Columbia University Press, 1953), p. 217.

93. See J. Stalin, *Leninism: Selected Writings* (New York: International Publishers, 1942), p. 219.

94. *Pervy syezd*, pp. 574, 614.

95. *Ibid.*, p. 483.

96. *Ibid.*, p. 502.

97. *Ibid.*, pp. 490, 492.

98. *Ibid.*, p. 573.

99. *Ibid.*, p. 512.

100. *Vtoroi syezd*, p. 13.

101. *Pervy syezd*, pp. 573–578. But in a statement read by the presiding officer at the closing session of the congress, Bukharin apologized for his "polemical harshness" and noted that his evaluations of individual writers were not binding on delegates. *Ibid.*, p. 671.

102. *Ibid.*, p. 576.

103. *Ibid.*, p. 499.

104. *Ibid.*, p. 235.

105. *Ibid.*, p. 236.

106. *K voprosu o politike RKP(b) v khudozhestvennoi literature* (Moscow, 1924), p. 65.

107. *Pervy syezd*, p. 236.

108. See Gleb Struve, *Soviet Russian Literature, 1917–1950* (University of Oklahoma Press, 1951), p. 249.

109. *Vtoroi syezd*, p. 67.

110. See Max Eastman, *Artists in Uniform: A Study of Literature and Bureaucratism* (New York: Knopf, 1934), chaps. 8, 11.

111. See Philip E. Mosley, "Freedom of Artistic Expression and Scientific Inquiry in Russia," *The Annals of the American Academy of Political and Social Science*, vol. 200 (November 1938), 254–274.

112. *Vtoroi syezd*, p. 79.

113. *Pervy syezd*, p. 230.

114. *Ibid.*, p. 676.

115. *Ibid.*, p. 387.

116. *Ibid.*, pp. 247, 392, 230.

117. *Ibid.*, pp. 172–173, and *Vtoroi syezd*, p. 539.
118. As quoted in Brown, *Proletarian Episode*, p. 200.
119. *Pervy syezd*, p. 454.
120. *Ibid.*, pp. 279–280.
121. *Ibid.*, p. 538.
122. Alexander Blok, "O naznachenii poeta," *Sochineniya v dvukh tomakh*, ed. V. Orlov (Moscow, 1955), II, 354.
123. *Pervy syezd*, p. 185.
124. Ye. Zamyatin, *Litsa* (New York: Chekhov Publishing House, 1955), p. 208.
125. *Ibid.*, p. 189.
126. D. Shterenberg, quoted in Juri Jelagin, *Tyomny genii* (New York: Chekhov Publishing House, 1955), pp. 214–215.
127. "Tvorchestvo molodykh sovetskikh poetov," *Lit. gaz.*, January 12, 1956.
128. "Molodye sily sovetskoi prozy" *Novy mir*, no. 3, 1956, p. 272.
129. "V rodnom gorode," *Novy mir*, no. 10, 1954, pp. 3–65, and no. 11, pp. 97–178.
130. "Yelena," *God tridtsat vosmoi*, no. 19, 1955, pp. 70–235.
131. See the following issues of *Lit. gaz.* for 1955: March 22, March 26, April 19, June 7, August 25.
132. "Zametki pisatelya," *Lit. gaz.*, September 29, 1955.
133. S. Babenysheva, *Lit. gaz.*, April 26, 1955, p. 2.
134. T. Smolyanskaya, "Poetizatsiya poshlosti," *Komsomolskaya pravda*, April 10, 1955.
135. *Lit. gaz.*, April 26, p. 3.
136. "O psikhologicheskom analize v poslevoyennoi proze," *Zvezda*, no. 2, 1955, pp. 160–173.
137. *Ibid.*, p. 160.
138. *Ibid.*, p. 161.
139. "O dogmatizme v kritike," *Znamya*, no. 8, 1955, p. 189.
140. *Lit. gaz.*, April 26, 1955, p. 3.
141. "K novym vysotam," *Teatr*, no. 2, 1955, p. 53.
142. "Vysoko derzhat znamya ideinosti," *Lit. gaz.*, April 26, 1955.
143. *Lit. gaz.*, May 5, 1955, p. 3.
144. "O zadachakh marksistsko-leninskoi estetiki," *Voprosy filosofii*, no. 4, 1955, pp. 66–80.
145. *Ibid.*, p. 74.
146. A. Lebedev, "V otryve ot khudozhestvennoi praktiki," *Lit. gaz.*, December 11, 1954.
147. *Voprosy filosofii*, no. 4, 1955, p. 70.
148. "V plenu tvorcheskoi putanitsy," *Lit. gaz.*, July 14, 1955.
149. "Bez ponimaniya iskusstva," *Lit. gaz.*, November 20, 1955.
150. *Lit. gaz.*, November 1, 1955.
151. "K voprosu o tipicheskom v literature i iskusstve," *Kommunist*, no. 18, 1955, pp. 12–27; trans. in *CDSP*, VIII, no. 3 (February 29, 1956), 11–15. The translations used for this *Kommunist* editorial are taken from *CDSP*, though some changes in wording have been made.
152. *Kommunist*, no. 18, 1955, p. 13.

153. *Ibid.*
154. *Ibid.*, pp. 12, 16.
155. *Ibid.*, pp. 14–15.
156. *Ibid.*, p. 15.
157. N. Maslin, "Zhizn vopreki . . . ," *Kultura i zhizn*, November 30, 1947.
158. *Kommunist*, no. 18, 1955, p. 16.
159. *Ibid.*, p. 20.
160. *Ibid.*, p. 21.
161. *Ibid.*, p. 12.
162. See A. Fadeyev, "Zametki o literature," *Lit. gaz.*, September 20, 1955.
163. "V plenu yubileinovo slavosloviya," *Lit. gaz.*, July 16, 1949.
164. *Kommunist*, no. 18, 1955, p. 18.
165. *Ibid.*, p. 19.
166. *Ibid.*
167. *Ibid.*
168. *Lit. gaz.*, January 5, 1956, p. 3.
169. "My vtroyom poyekhali na tselinu," *Novy mir*, no. 12, 1955, p. 45.
170. *Ibid.*, pp. 47–48.
171. *Ibid.*, p. 62.
172. *Pravda*, January 5, 1956, p. 2, as trans. in *CDSP*, VII, no. 52 (February 8, 1956), 23.
173. V. Kadrin, "Tselina i knigi," *Novy mir*, no. 1, 1956, pp. 245–252.
174. *Ibid.*, p. 253.
175. "Kustanaiskiye vstrechi," *Znamya*, no. 9, 1955, p. 160.

Chapter IV. The Challenge of 1956

1. For Khrushchev's speech, see *New York Times*, June 5, 1956; for the Central Committee's resolution, see *Pravda*, July 2, 1956.
2. "Napisat by takuyu knigu!" *Literaturnaya gazeta*, April 21, 1956.
3. *Pravda*, October 18, 1957, p. 3.
4. "Zhizn i literatura," *Lit. gaz.*, May 8, 1956.
5. "Za leninskuyu printsipalnost v voprosakh literatury i iskusstva," *Kommunist*, no. 10, 1957, p. 15.
6. B. A. Nazarov and O. B. Gridneva, "K voprosu ob otstavanii dramaturgii i teatra," *Voprosy filosofii*, no. 10, 1956, pp. 85–94.
7. *Ibid.*, pp. 92–93.
8. *Ibid.*, p. 92.
9. *Ibid.*, p. 94.
10. M. Gorky, *O literature, Stati i rechi, 1928–1935* (Moscow, 1935), p. 49.
11. *Voprosy filosofii*, no. 10, 1956, p. 93.
12. *Pravda* and *Izvestiya*, November 25, 1956; *Voprosy filosofii*, no. 6, 1956, pp. 3–10.
13. "Lenin i sotsialisticheskaya kultura," *Kommunist*, no. 17, 1956, p. 56.
14. See *Lit. gaz.*, May 28, 1955.
15. "Pamyati A. A. Fadeyeva," *Novy mir*, no. 6, 1956, p. 5.

16. *Pravda*, August 29, 1956, as trans. in *CDSP*, VIII, no. 35 (October 10, 1956), 35.

17. "Literaturnye zametki," *Novy mir*, no. 12, 1956, pp. 239–257.

18. "Vyshe znamya marskistsko-leninskoi ideologii," *Kommunist*, no. 1, 1957, pp. 12–13.

19. "Ideinost — dusha sovetskoi literatury," *Lit. gaz.*, January 8, 1957.

20. *Lit. gaz.*, Nov. 17, 1956, p. 3; *Sovetskaya kultura*, Nov. 17, 1956, p. 3.

21. *Pravda*, August 31, 1956, p. 3, as trans. in *CDSP*, VIII, no. 34 (October 3, 1956), 8.

22. M. Kuznetsov and Yu. Lukin, "O svobode khudozhestvennovo tvorchestva," *Kommunist*, no. 15, 1956, p. 88. See also *Kommunist*, no. 12, 1956, p. 88.

23. *Novy mir*, no. 12, 1956, pp. 255–256.

24. Ya. Strochkov, "Neissyakayemy istochnik," *Lit. gaz.*, January 10, 1957.

25. For a discussion of the literary rehabilitations, see Gleb Struve, "Dead Souls and Living Reputations," *Soviet Survey*, no. 23 (January–March 1958), pp. 10–17.

26. A. Metchenko, A. Dementyev, and G. Lomidze, "Za glubokuyu razrabotku istorii sovetskoi literatury," *Kommunist*, no. 12, 1956, pp. 83–100.

27. *Ibid.*, as trans. in *CDSP*, VIII, no. 35 (October 10, 1956), 8.

28. Kuznetsov and Lukin, *Kommunist*, no. 15, 1956, p. 88.

29. See Igor Grabar, "Zametki o zhivopisi," *Lit. gaz.*, September 27, 1956; *Izvestiya*, October 13, 1956, trans. and condensed in *CDSP*, VIII, no. 42 (November 28, 1956), 11–12; and *Sovetskaya kultura*, January 3, 1957, trans. in part in *CDSP*, IX, no. 1 (February 13, 1957), 33–34.

30. V. Ivanov, "Leninsky printsip partiinosti literatury," *Kommunist*, no. 5, 1956, p. 70.

31. "Zametki o literature," *Lit. gaz.*, September 29, 1955.

32. A. Metchenko, "Istorizm i dogma," *Novy mir*, no. 12, 1956, pp. 236–237.

33. See *Komsomolskaya pravda*, December 4, 1956, p. 2, December 28, 1956, p. 2, and April 28, 1957, p. 4; *Lit. gaz.*, January 8, 1957, p. 2; *Izvestiya*, September 6, 1959, p. 4.

34. *Vestnik vyshei shkoly*, no. 8, 1956, as trans. in *CDSP*, VIII, no. 35 (October 10, 1956), 5.

35. *Sovetskaya kultura*, March 27, 1956, p. 4, as trans. in *CDSP*, VII, no. 13 (May 9, 1956), 11.

36. Alla Kireyeva "O kritike, poete i chitatele," *Den poezii* (Moscow, 1956), pp. 186–187.

37. In this context, it will be recalled that Pogodin, in his prepublication defense of what became the play *We Three Went to the Virgin Lands*, seemed concerned about the anticipated reaction of a broader group of readers to literary representation of the seamier sides of life, rather than about a possible violation of the official party viewpoint. But what the playwright had in mind when he wrote the lines can only be a matter for conjecture (see text above, p. 140).

38. "Novye gorizonty," *Teatr*, no. 8. 1956, p. 53.

39. *Ibid.*, p. 54.

40. Nazarov and Gridneva, p. 92.

41. *Voprosy filosofii*, no. 6, 1956, p. 8.

42. "Diskussiya o predmete marksistsko-leninskoi estetiki," *Voprosy filosofii*, no. 3, 1956, pp. 173–189.

43. *Ibid.*, p. 188.

44. *Ibid.*, p. 186.

45. L. N. Stolovich, "Ob esteticheskikh svoistvakh deistvitelnosti," *Voprosy filosofii*, no. 4, 1956, pp. 73–82.

46. "Y karty nashei literatury," *Novy mir*, no. 9, 1956, pp. 248-249.

47. "Initsiativa pisatelya," *Lit. gaz.*, July 26, 1956.

48. "Zolotaya roza," *Oktyabr*, no. 9, 1955, pp. 49–107, and no. 10, 1955, pp. 61–111.

49. Quoted in V. Sokolov "Mesto pisatelya v zhizni," *Novy mir*, no. 3, 1956, p. 288.

50. *Oktyabr*, no. 9, 1955, p. 56.

51. *Ibid.*, p. 58.

52. "Proza v 1955 godu," *Neva*, no. 1, 1957, p. 164.

53. *Ibid.*, p. 165.

54. For a more extensive treatment of Soviet literature during the post-Stalin period dealing with some of the works discussed in this chapter, see George Gibian, *Interval of Freedom: Soviet Literature During the Thaw, 1954–1957* (Minneapolis: University of Minnesota, 1960). See also the insightful analysis of Soviet writing in 1956 in Tom Scriven, "The 'Literary Opposition,'" *Problems of Communism*, VII, no. 1 (January–February 1958), 28–34.

55. "Ottepel," *Znamya*, no. 4, 1956, pp. 23–90.

56. "Sobstvennoye mneniye," *Novy mir*, no. 8, 1956, pp. 129-136.

57. "Ne khlebom yedinym," *Novy mir*, no. 8, 1956, pp. 31–118; no. 9, 1956, pp. 37–118; and no. 10, 1956, pp. 21–98.

58. "Gosti," *Teatr*, no. 2, 1954, pp. 24–25.

59. "Sobstvennoye mneniye," pp. 134–135.

60. *Ibid.*, p. 135.

61. *Partiinaya zhizn*, no. 24, 1956, as trans. in *CDSP*, IX, no. 3 (February 27, 1957), 10.

62. "Iskateli" *Zvezda*, no. 7, 1954, pp. 3–99, and no. 8, 1954, pp. 7–119.

63. *Lit. gaz.*, November 10, 1955, p. 2.

64. B. Platonov, "Realnye geroi i literaturnye skhemy," *Lit. gaz.*, November 24, 1956.

65. "Gosti," pp. 30, 43.

66. Platonov, "Realnye."

67. *Trud*, October 31, 1956, p. 3, as trans. in *CDSP*, VIII, no. 49 (January 16, 1957), 3.

68. *Lit. gaz.*, October 27, 1956, p. 3.

69. N. Akimov, "Teatr i zpritel," *Teatr*, no. 4, 1956, p. 72.

70. *Lit. gaz.*, October 27, 1956, p. 3.

71. *Novoye russkoye slovo*, May 17, 1957, p. 4; *L'Express*, March 29, 1957, p. 30.

72. *Lit. gaz.*, October 27, 1956, p. 4.

73. P. V. Annenkov, *Literaturnye vospominaniya* (Leningrad, 1928), p. 546.

74. N. Kryuchkova, "O romane 'Ne khlebom yedinym,'" *Isvestiya*, December 2, 1956.

75. "Sem dnei nedeli," *Novy mir*, no. 9, 1956, pp. 16–32.

76. *Ibid.*, p. 25.

77. *Ibid.*, p. 26.

78. *Ibid.*, pp. 31–32.

79. *Ibid.*, p. 16.

80. *Ibid.*, p. 17.

81. "Samoye glavnoye," *Oktyabr*, no. 11, 1956, pp. 3–5.

82. "Rychagi," *Literaturnaya Moskva*, no. 2 (Moscow, 1956), pp. 502–513.

83. "Svet v okne," *ibid.*, pp. 396–403.

84. "Sonet Petrarki," *ibid.*, p. 314.

85. A. Elyashevich, "Poeziya i realizm," *Zvezda*, no. 8, 1956, p. 160.

86. *Literaturnaya Moskva*, no. 2, p. 325.

87. "Odna," *Teatr*, no. 8, 1956, pp. 3–45.

88. *Ibid.*, p. 13.

89. *Ibid.*, p. 45.

90. See A. Anastasyev, "Teatralnye zametki," *Teatr*, no. 3, 1957, pp. 44–45.

91. "Stantsiya Zima," *Oktyabr*, no. 10, 1956, pp. 26–47.

92. *Ibid.*, p. 30.

93. *Ibid.*, p. 42.

94. *Ibid.*, pp. 43–44.

95. *Ibid.*, p. 44.

96. *Ibid.*

97. *Ibid.*, p. 47. For an interesting discussion of Yevtushenko, see Michael Futtrell, "Evgeny Evtushenko," *Soviet Survey*, no. 25 (July–September 1958), pp. 75–80.

98. "V trudnom pokhode," *Novy mir*, no. 11, 1956, pp. 105–206, and no. 12, 1956, pp. 82–189.

99. *Novy mir*, no. 12, 1956, p. 137.

100. *Novy mir*, no. 11, 1956, p. 145.

101. *Ibid.*, p. 204.

102. *Ibid.*, p. 202.

103. Inna Solovyova, "Dorogu osilit idushchii," *Teatr*, no. 9, 1956, p. 144.

104. B. Runin, "V zashchitu liricheskoi individualnosti," *Den poezii* (Moscow, 1956), p. 166.

Chapter V. The Drive for "Consolidation," 1957–1959

1. *Pravda*, November 10, 1956, pp. 1–2, and *Sovetskaya kultura*, November 20, 1956, p. 2.

2. *Kommunist*, no. 10, 1957, p. 21.

3. *Kommunist*, no. 1, 1957, p. 13.

4. See *Komsomolskaya pravda*, January 25, 1957, p. 1.

5. *Literaturnaya gazeta*, January 15, 1957, p. 3.

6. *Lit. gaz.*, January 31, 1957, p. 1.

7. *Lit. gaz.*, January 26, 1957, p. 3.

8. "Partiya i voprosy razvitiya sovetskoi literatury i iskusstva," *Kommunist*, no. 3, 1957, pp. 12–25.

9. *Lit. gaz.*, March 19, 1957, p. 3, as trans. in *CDSP*, IX, no. 13 (May 8, 1957), 22.

10. *CDSP, ibid.*, p. 23.

11. *Ibid.*, p. 24.

12. *Lit. gaz.*, May 22, 1957, p. 3.

13. *CDSP*, IX, no. 13 (May 8, 1957), 25.

14. See Merle Fainsod, "What Happened to 'Collective Leadership'?" *Problems of Communism*, VIII, no. 4 (July–August 1959), 1–10.

15. *Lit. gaz.*, May 18, 1957, p. 1.

16. *Lit. gaz.*, May 16, 1957, p. 2, as trans. in *CDSP*, IX, no. 21 (July 3, 1957), 14.

17. *CDSP, ibid.*, p. 13.

18. *Lit. gaz.*, May 21, 1957, p. 2, as trans. in *CDSP*, IX, no. 22 (July 10, 1957), 4.

19. *Lit. gaz.*, May 22, 1957, p. 3, as trans. in *CDSP, ibid.*, p. 10.

20. *Lit. gaz.*, May 22, 1957, p. 2, as trans. in *CDSP, ibid.*, pp. 7, 9.

21. *Lit. gaz.*, May 22, 1957, pp. 2–3; *CDSP, ibid.*, pp. 9–10.

22. *CDSP, ibid.*, p. 9.

23. *Lit. gaz.*, January 8, 1957, p. 1.

24. *Lit. gaz.*, May 21, 1957, p. 3.

25. *Lit. gaz.*, May 22, 1957, as trans. in *CDSP*, July 10, 1957, p. 10.

26. See *Lit. gaz.*, June 6, 1957, p. 3.

27. *Lit. gaz., ibid.*, as trans. in *CDSP*, IX, no. 23 (July 17, 1957), 19.

28. *Lit. gaz.*, June 13, 1957, p. 1.

29. *Pravda*, June 12, 1957, p. 4, and June 16, pp. 3–4.

30. *Lit. gaz.*, May 21, p. 4.

31. *Vechernaya Moskva*, June 6, 1957, p. 3; *CDSP*, July 17, 1957, p. 20.

32. "Za leninskuyu printsipalnost v voprosakh literatury i iskusstva," *Kommunist*, no. 10, 1957, pp. 13–22.

33. "Za tesnuyu svyaz literatury i iskusstva s zhiznyu naroda," *Lit. gaz.*, August 28, 1957, pp. 1–3.

34. *Pravda*, September 26, 1957; *CDSP*, IX, no. 39 (November 6, 1957), 31.

35. *Lit. gaz.*, December 26, 1957, p. 2.

36. *Lit. gaz.*, October 8, 1957, p. 2.

37. *Vechernaya Moskva*, December 6, 1957, p. 2; *CDSP*, X, no. 5 (March 12, 1958), 39.

38. *Lit. gaz.*, February 11, 1958, p. 1, and February 15, 1958, p. 1.

39. See *Pervy uchreditelny syezd pisatelei Rossiiskoi Federatsii. Stenografichesky otchyot* (Moscow, 1959), p. 187.

40. *Lit. gaz.*, August 28, 1957, p. 3.

41. *Pervy uchreditelny syezd pisatelei Rossiiskoi Federatsii*, p. 38.

42. *Lit. gaz.*, October 1, 1957, p. 1.

43. See p. 251.

44. *Izvestiya*, May 19, 1957, p. 2.

45. *Lit. gaz.*, October 28, p. 3. But Pasternak was apparently not expelled from the Litfund (see the notice of his death in *Lit. gaz.*, June 2, 1960, p. 4).

46. *Komsomolskaya pravda*, October 30, 1958, p. 3.

47. *Lit. gaz.*, November 1, 1958, p. 3.

48. *Pravda*, November 2, 1958, p. 2.

49. *Pravda*, November 6, 1958, p. 4.

50. The virtual cessation of the campaign in the public press did not necessarily imply an improvement in Pasternak's fortunes. As late as August 1959, in one of the moving letters which he wrote to Stephen Spender, Pasternak said: "It continues in all its strictness. My situation is worse, more unbearable and endangered than I can say or you can think of." *Encounter*, XV, no. 2 (August 1960), 4.

51. *Pervy uchreditelny syezd pisatelei Rossiiskoi Federatsii*, p. 392.

52. *Trety syezd pisatelei SSSR. Stenografichesky otchyot* (Moscow, 1959), p. 98; hereafter cited as *Trety syezd*.

53. *Ibid.*, p. 163.

54. "Besspornye i spornye mysli," *Lit. gaz.*, May 20, 1959.

55. *Pravda*, May 22, 1959, pp. 2–3.

56. *Trety syezd*, p. 223.

57. *Ibid.*

58. *Ibid.*, p. 224.

59. *Ibid.*, p. 223.

60. *Ibid.*

61. *Ibid.*, p. 221.

62. *Ibid.*

63. *Ibid.*, pp. 228.

64. *Ibid.*

65. Max Hayward, "Soviet Literature in the Doldrums," *Problems of Communism*, VIII, no. 4 (July–August 1959), 15–16.

66. "Za leninskuyu printsipalnost v voprosakh literatury i iskusstva," *Kommunist*, no. 10, 1957, p. 13. For a similar statement, see *Kommunist*, no. 3, 1957, p. 24.

67. *Kommunist*, no. 3, 1957, p. 25.

68. V. Ivanov, V. Pchelin, and M. Sakov, "Vozrastaniye roli partii v stroitelstve kommunizma," *Kommunist*, no. 17, 1959, pp. 19–20.

69. *Ibid.*, p. 20.

70. *Pravda* and *Izvestiya*, July 2, 1959, as trans. in *CDSP*, XI, no. 28 (August 12, 1959), 8, 35.

71. *Trety syezd* p. 248.

72. *Ibid.*, p. 156.

73. D. Yeremin, "Vazhneishy printsip sotsialisticheskovo realizma," *Lit. gaz.*, May 27, 1958, p. 3.

74. *Trety syezd*, p. 248.

75. *Ibid.*

76. "Puti boitsov," *Literatura i zhizn*, September 20, 1959.

77. *Lit. gaz.*, November 21, 1959, p. 3.

78. "Zametki o kritike," *Lit. gaz.*, August 8, 1959.

79. "Zhit i rabotat dlya partii i naroda," *Literatura i zhizn,* September 6, 1959.

80. "Propoved serosti i posredstvennosti," *Lit. gaz.,* September 10, 1959.

81. *Literatura i zhizn,* September 18, 1959.

82. *Lit. gaz.,* September 22, 1959, p. 3.

83. "Ideinaya pozitsiya pisatelya," *Lit. gaz.,* November 21, 1959.

84. "Pishi!" *Oktyabr,* no. 7, 1959, pp. 109–110.

85. "Stroitelyam," *Izvestiya,* July 31, 1959.

86. V. Sytin, "Zhizn pisatelei Moskvy," *Moskva,* no. 6, 1959, p. 184.

87. "Snova avgust," *Novy mir,* no. 8, 1959, pp. 7–82, and no. 9, 1959, pp. 3–72.

88. *Novy mir,* no. 8, 1959, pp. 73–74.

89. "V rodnykh mestakh," *Neva,* no. 9, 1959, pp. 15–22; trans. in *CDSP,* XI, no. 49 (January 6, 1960), 6–8.

90. Ya. Elsberg, "O politike i chelovechnosti," *Znamya,* no. 10, 1959, pp. 204–205.

91. *Lit. gaz.,* October 27, 1959, p. 3, as trans. in *CDSP,* XI, no. 49 (January 6, 1960), 8.

92. *Literatura i zhizn,* October 18, 1959, p. 1, as trans. in *CDSP, ibid.,* p. 9.

93. "Chest," *Moskva,* no. 4, 1959, pp. 17–74; no. 5, 1959, pp. 74–149; no. 10, 1959, pp. 7–74; no. 11, 1959, pp. 90–165.

94. *Moskva,* no. 4, 1959, p. 60.

95. V. R. Shcherbina, "Sovetskaya literatura v borbe za stroiteltsvo kommunizma," *Voprosy stroitelstva kommunizma v SSSR* (Moscow, 1959), p. 187.

96. *Lit. gaz.,* November 13, 1958, p. 1.

97. L. Fomenko, "Molodye prozaiki," *Zvezda,* no. 8, 1959, p. 203.

98. "Ot problemy," *Neva,* no. 1, 1958, p. 177.

Chapter VI. Bureaucratic Controls and Literary Production

1. *Pervy vsesoyuzny syezd sovetskikh pisatelei* (Moscow, 1934), pp. 716, 717; hereafter cited as *Pervy syezd.*

2. The following discussion of the central organs of the Writers' Union draws on Jack F. Matlock, Jr., "The 'Governing Organs' of the Union of Soviet Writers," *American Slavic and East European Review,* XV (October 1956), 382–399.

3. *Ibid.,* p. 385.

4. See V. Azhayev, "Uvazhat svoi literaturny tsekh," *Literaturnaya gazeta,* November 11, 1954, trans. in *CDSP,* VI, no. 50 (January 26, 1955), 3–4; and E. Kazakevich and others, "Replika tov. Azhayevu" *Lit. gaz.,* November 23, 1954, trans. in *CDSP, ibid.,* p. 6.

5. See A. Fadeyev, "Nekotorye voprosy raboty Soyuza pisatelei," *Lit. gaz.,* March 28, 1953, and "O rabote soyuza pisatelei," *Lit. gaz.,* October 29, 1954.

6. See Mikhail Sholokhov's speech at the Twentieth Party Congress, *Lit. gaz.,* February 21, 1956, p. 3.

7. *Vtoroi vsesoyuzny syezd sovetskikh pisatelei* (Moscow, 1956), p. 514; hereafter cited as *Vtoroi syezd*.

8. *Ibid.*, p. 510.

9. *Trety syezd pisatelei SSSR. Stenografichesky otchyot* (Moscow, 1959), p. 157; hereafter cited as *Trety syezd*.

10. *Lit. gaz.*, March 28, 1953, p. 2.

11. V. Kaverin and others, "Tovarishcham po rabote," *Lit. gaz.*, October 26, 1954, as trans. in *CDSP*, VI, no. 44 (December 15, 1954), 13.

12. *Lit. gaz.*, March 17, 1960, p. 2.

13. "Proverka ispolneniya," *Lit. gaz.*, August 18, 1951.

14. "Nash grazhdansky dolg," *Lit. gaz.*, March 1, 1951.

15. "O rabote partiinoi organizatsii Soyuza pisatelei," *Lit. gaz.*, January 19, 1952.

16. A. Bezymensky and Yu. Korolkov, "Za podlinnuyu demokratiyu v Soyuze pisatelei," *Lit. gaz.*, November 13, 1954, as trans. in *CDSP*, VI, no. 50 (January 26, 1955), 6.

17. "O zhurnale 'Znamya,'" *Kultura i zhizn*, January 11, 1949. This resolution is reprinted in *O partiinoi i sovetskoi pechati. Sbornik dokumentov* (Moscow, 1954), pp. 604–609, as are other Central Committee resolutions on literary matters; for resolutions of the postwar period, see especially pp. 599–602, 621–622, and 627–629.

18. See, for example, "Pomogat rostu sovetskoi literatury," *Partiinaya zhizn*, no. 4, 1955, pp. 30–35; *Literatura i zhizn*, October 18, 1958, p. 1; and *Lit. gaz.*, November 24, 1959, p. 1.

19. M. Sergeyenko and others, "Ob odnoi pisatelskoi konferentsii," *Izvestiya*, July 17, 1954.

20. Mikhail Lukonin, "Tvorcheskaya rabota — glavnaya," *Lit. gaz.*, October 13, 1953.

21. *Vtoroi syezd*, p. 479.

22. *Lit. gaz.*, December 9, 1954, p. 1.

23. See the following articles in *Lit. gaz.*: Vizbul Bertse, "Kakiye dolzhny byt tvorcheskiye sektsii?" May 8, 1954; A. Fadeyev, "O zabvenii obshchestvennykh form tvorcheskoi raboty v Soyuze pisatelei," June 30, 1951; V. Kavalevsky, "Zhizn tvorcheskikh sektsii," June 28, 1951; V. Kaverin and others, "Tovarishcham po rabote," October 26, 1954; G. Medynsky, "Tvorcheskim voprosam — glavnoye vnimaniye," October 12, 1954; N. Panov, "Tvorchesky soyuz dolzhen byt tvorcheskim," October 28, 1954; S. Zlobin, "O rabote tvorcheskikh sektsii," November 12, 1953.

24. Panov, *Lit. gaz.*, October 28, 1954.

25. Zlobin, *Lit. gaz.*, November 12, 1953.

26. *Lit. gaz.*, November 17, 1959, p. 1.

27. See Kaverin, *Lit. gaz.* and the articles trans. in *CDSP*, VI, no. 50 (January 26, 1955), 3–8.

28. *Lit. gaz.*, May 5, 1956, p. 3.

29. Berdy Kerbabayev, "Pogovorim ob organizatsionnykh voprosakh," *Lit. gaz.*, September 11, 1958.

30. Panov, *Lit. gaz.*

31. *Lit. gaz.*, November 11, 1954, as trans. in *CDSP*, January 26, 1955, p. 3.

32. Reported in *Lit. gaz.*, November 17, 1959, p. 1.

33. See Zlobin, *Lit. gaz.*; M. Slonimsky and D. Granin, "O molodykh," *Lit. gaz.*, September 25, 1954; and Ivan Antonov, "Vnimaniye knigam," *Lit. gaz.*, November 18, 1958.

34. *Lit. gaz.*, March 15, 1947, p. 4.

35. "O cherepkakh i cherepushkakh," *Oktyabr*, no. 5, 1946, pp. 151–162.

36. *Lit. gaz.*, July 24, 1956, p. 3.

37. Yu. Zubkov and A. Sinitsyn, "O rabote literaturnovo instituta," *Pravda*, December 17, 1954.

38. *Vneocherednoi XXI syezd Kommunisticheskoi partii Sovetskovo Soyuza. Stenografichesky otchyot* (Moscow, 1959), I, 271.

39. *Trety syezd*, p. 25.

40. See *Komsomolskaya pravda*, April 28, 1957, p. 4; *Literatura i zhizn*, November 2, 1958, p. 4; and *Pervy uchreditelny syezd pisatelei Rossiiskoi Federatsii. Stenografichesky otchyot* (Moscow, 1959), pp. 37–38, 483–487.

41. See "Ideinoye oruzhiye pisatelei," *Lit. gaz.*, November 29, 1952.

42. The membership of the Litfund exceeds that of the Writers' Union by approximately four hundred persons.

43. *Vtoroi syezd*, p. 521.

44. *Izvestiya*, December 2, 1959, p. 3; trans. in *CDSP*, XI, no. 48 (December 30, 1959), 14, 34.

45. *Pervy uchreditelny syezd pisatelei Rossiskoi Federatsii*, pp. 97, 210.

46. For such complaints, see *Moskovsky literator*, October 12, 1958, p. 4, and October 18, 1958, p. 4.

47. See *Vtoroi syezd*, pp. 107, 249, 376, and 574; V. Ovechkin, "Pogovorim o nasushchnykh nuzhdakh literatury," *Lit. gaz.*, July 31, 1954, and Ovechkin, "Pismo v redaktsiyu," *Lit. gaz.*, October 2, 1954.

48. *Lit. gaz.*, July 31, 1954.

49. *Vtoroi syezd*, p. 249.

50. *Lit. gaz.*, February 4, 1960, p. 1.

51. See *Lit. gaz.*, April 24, 1958, p. 2, and May 15, 1959, p. 3.

52. V. I. Serebrovsky, *Voprosy sovetskovo avtorskovo prava* (Moscow, 1956), p. 139.

53. *Ibid.*, pp. 140–141. That this method of payment may be used to discourage excessive "creative experimentation" by poets is revealed by a letter to the editor published in *Lit. gaz.*, December 15, 1959, p. 2.

54. B. S. Antimonov and Ye. A. Fleishchits, *Avtorskoye pravo* (Moscow, 1957), p. 207.

55. *Ibid.*, p. 209, and *Soviet Literature*, no. 7, 1954, p. 214.

56. Antimonov and Fleishchits, p. 208. Actually, the norm for a first edition varies from republic to republic. The RSFSR and three other union republics have established the largest norm for first editions of prose works — fifteen thousand copies. In the other republics the norm ranges from five to twelve thousand copies (see Serebrovsky, p. 149n2).

57. P. Burlaka and others, "Nasushchnye voprosy knigoizdatelskovo dela," *Izvestiya*, February 8, 1956.

58. See *Lit. gaz.*, July 31, 1954, p. 3, and *Trety syezd*, pp. 83, 97, 150.

59. Norman Cousins, "Of Rubles and Royalties," *Saturday Review*, XLII, no. 36 (September 5, 1959), 28.

60. *Lit. gaz.*, July 31, 1954. For a similar statement, see Serebrovsky, p. 150.

61. Antimonov and Fleishchits, pp. 204–205.

62. *Vtoroi syezd*, p. 519; *Trety syezd*, p. 31.

63. As of December 1958, just over one quarter of the writers of the USSR and about one half of those of the RSFSR were living in Moscow.

64. *Lit. gaz.*, February 21, 1956, p. 3.

65. *Izvestiya*, December 2, 1959, p. 3.

66. See *Moskovsky literator*, September 27, 1958, p. 3.

67. *Vtoroi syezd*, pp. 85–86.

68. Panov, *Lit. gaz.*, October 28, 1954.

69. *Vtoroi syezd*, pp. 250, 376.

70. Derived from data in *Pervy syezd*, p. 710, *Vtoroi syezd*, p. 79, and *Trety syezd*, p. 64.

71. *Lit. gaz.*, March 27, 1954.

72. *Novy mir*, no. 3, 1956, p. 256.

73. Yelena Katerli, "Tvorchesky soyuz ili 'literaturny departament,'" *Lit. gaz.*, October 30, 1954. For a similar comment, see A. Olenich-Gnenenko, "Pryamoi razgovor," *Lit. gaz.*, February 4, 1958. See also, "Na partiinoi, printsipalnoi osnove," *Lit. gaz.*, February 11, 1958.

74. *Novy mir*, no. 3, 1956, p. 256, and *Lit. gaz.*, March 15, 1951, p. 1.

75. *Trety syezd*, p. 64.

76. *Ibid.*, p. 24.

77. *Lit. gaz.*, February 21, 1956, p. 3.

78. *Izvestiya*, December 2, 1959, p. 3.

79. "O rabote pisatelya," *Znamya*, no. 10, 1953, as trans. in *CDSP*, V, no. 52 (February 10, 1954), 8.

80. *Vtoroi syezd*, p. 250.

81. *Ibid.*, p. 510.

82. "Novye gorizonty," *Teatr*, no. 8, 1956, p. 52.

83. For typical complaints about such phenomena, see *Lit. gaz.*, August 17, 1950, p. 1, and *Lit. gaz.*, April 23, 1953, p. 1.

84. A. Volgin, "Ne sluzhba, a privyazannost," *Teatr*, no. 11, 1953, p. 141.

85. See the commentary on these problems in the editorial "O kritike," *Teatr*, no. 4, 1954, pp. 37–48.

86. *Leninism: Selected Writings* (New York: International Publishers, 1942), p. 124.

87. *Teatr*, no. 8, 1956, pp. 49–50.

88. "Literaturnye zametki," *Novy mir*, no. 12, 1956, pp. 249–251.

89. "Poet i vremya," *Lit. gaz.*, July 3, 1956.

90. In 1959 an editor of a leading Moscow literary journal estimated, in conversation with the author, that during the preceding four years approximately one hundred persons had been excluded from the Writers' Union. In view of the stresses within the union during this period, the figure may be higher for these years than for earlier years.

91. *Novy mir*, no. 12, 1956, p. 248. A revealing account of revisions of literary works is available in Maurice Friedburg, "New Editions of Soviet Belles-Lettres," *American Slavic and East European Review*, XIV (February 1954), 72–88.

92. *Teatr*, no. 8, 1956, p. 50.
93. *Ibid.*
94. *Khod konya* (Moscow, Berlin: Gelicon, 1923), p. 17.
95. *Vtoroi syezd*, p. 145.

Chapter VII. Perspectives and Prospects

1. "Dorogu osilit idushchii," *Teatr*, no. 9, 1956, pp. 133–134.
2. *Literaturnaya gazeta*, November 17, 1959, p. 3.
3. "Rodine," *Novy mir*, no. 8, 1956, p. 26.
4. "To a Friend," trans. Babette Deutsch, *A Treasury of Russian Verse*, ed. Avrahm Yarmolinsky (New York: Macmillan, 1949), p. 221.

Index

RUSSIAN RESEARCH CENTER STUDIES

* Publications of the Harvard Project on the Soviet Social System.

† Published jointly with the Center for International Affairs, Harvard University.

‡ Out of print.